STAR WARS

DOCTOR APHRA

REMASTERED

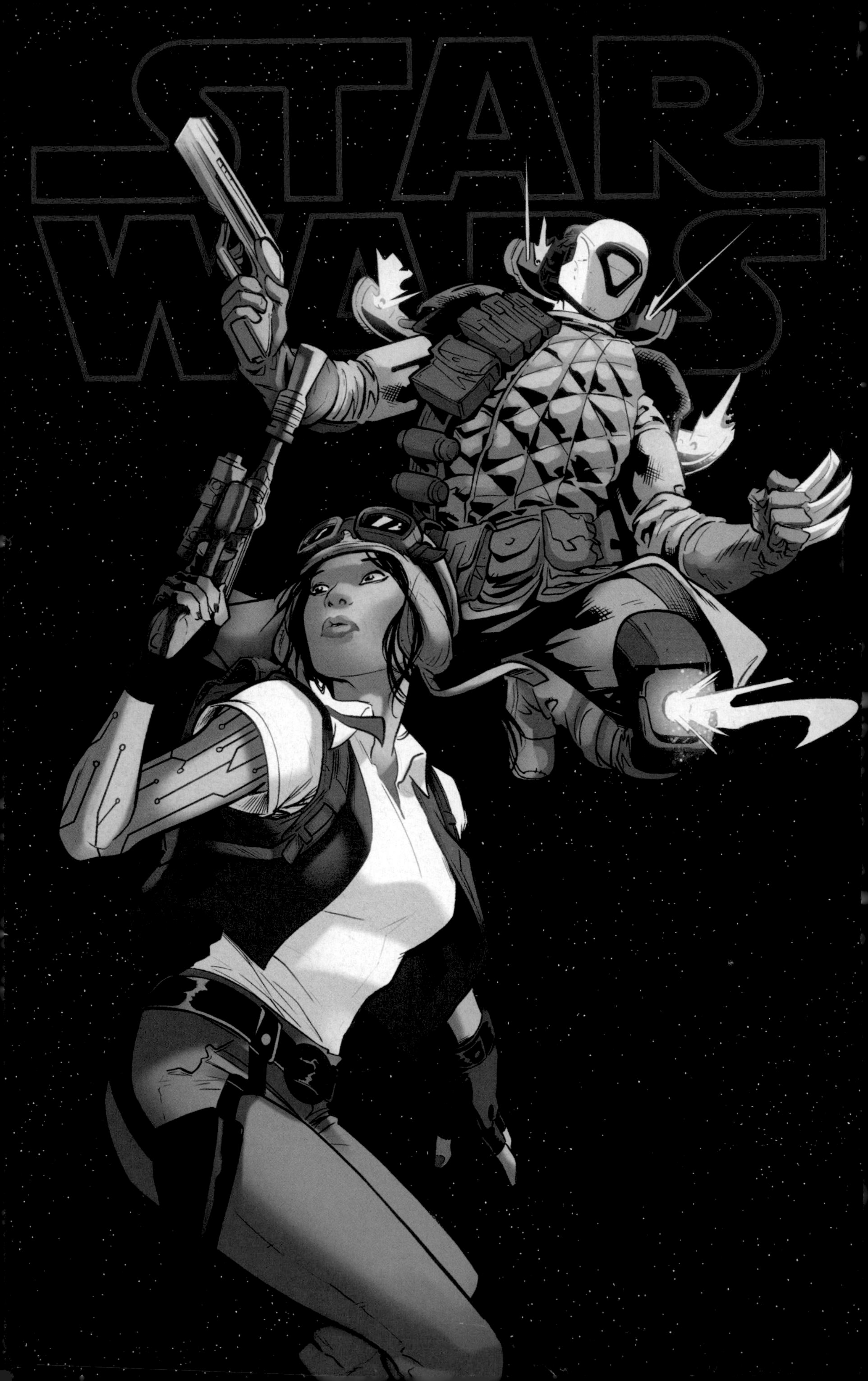

DOCTOR APHRA

REMASTERED

Writers	KIERON GILLEN & SI SPURRIER
Artist	EMILIO LAISO
Color Artist	RACHELLE ROSENBERG
Letterer	VC's JOE CARAMAGNA
Cover Art	ASHLEY WITTER
Assistant Editors	HEATHER ANTOS WITH EMILY NEWCOMEN
Editors	JORDAN D. WHITE WITH MARK PANICCIA
Editor in Chief	C.B CEBULSKI
Chief Creative Officer	JOE QUESADA
President	DAN BUCKLEY

For Lucasfilm:

Assistant Editor	NICK MARTINO
Senior Editor	FRANK PARISI
Creative Director	MICHAEL SIGLAIN
Lucasfilm Story Group	JAMES WAUGH, LELAND CHEE, MATT MARTIN

Collection Editor	JENNIFER GRÜNWALD	VP Production & Special Projects	JEFF YOUNGQUIST
Assistant Editor	CAITLIN O'CONNELL	SVP Print, Sales & Marketing	DAVID GABRIEL
Associate Managing Editor	KATERI WOODY	Book Designer	ADAM DEL RE
Editor, Special Projects	MARK D. BEAZLEY		

STAR WARS: DOCTOR APHRA VOL. 3: REMASTERED. Contains material originally published in magazine form as STAR WARS: DOCTOR APHRA #14-19. First printing 2018. ISBN 978-1-302-91152-2. Published by MARVEL WORLDWIDE, INC., a subsidiary of MARVEL ENTERTAINMENT, LLC. OFFICE OF PUBLICATION: 135 West 50th Street, New York, NY 10020. STAR WARS and related text and illustrations are trademarks and/or copyrights, in the United States and other countries, of Lucasfilm Ltd. and/or its affiliates. © & TM Lucasfilm Ltd. No similarity between any of the names, characters, persons, and/or institutions in this magazine with those of any living or dead person or institution is intended, and any such similarity which may exist is purely coincidental. Marvel and its logos are TM Marvel Characters, Inc. Printed in Canada. DAN BUCKLEY, President, Marvel Entertainment; JOHN NEE, Publisher; JOE QUESADA, Chief Creative Officer; TOM BREVOORT, SVP of Publishing; DAVID BOGART, SVP of Business Affairs & Operations, Publishing & Partnership; DAVID GABRIEL, SVP of Sales & Marketing, Publishing; JEFF YOUNGQUIST, VP of Production & Special Projects; DAN CARR, Executive Director of Publishing Technology; ALEX MORALES, Director of Publishing Operations; DAN EDINGTON, Managing Editor; SUSAN CRESPI, Production Manager; STAN LEE, Chairman Emeritus. For information regarding advertising in Marvel Comics or on Marvel.com, please contact Vit DeBellis, Custom Solutions & Integrated Advertising Manager, at vdebellis@marvel.com. For Marvel subscription inquiries, please call 888-511-5480. Manufactured between 5/4/2018 and 6/5/2018 by SOLISCO PRINTERS, SCOTT, QC, CANADA.

10 9 8 7 6 5 4 3 2 1

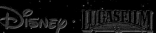

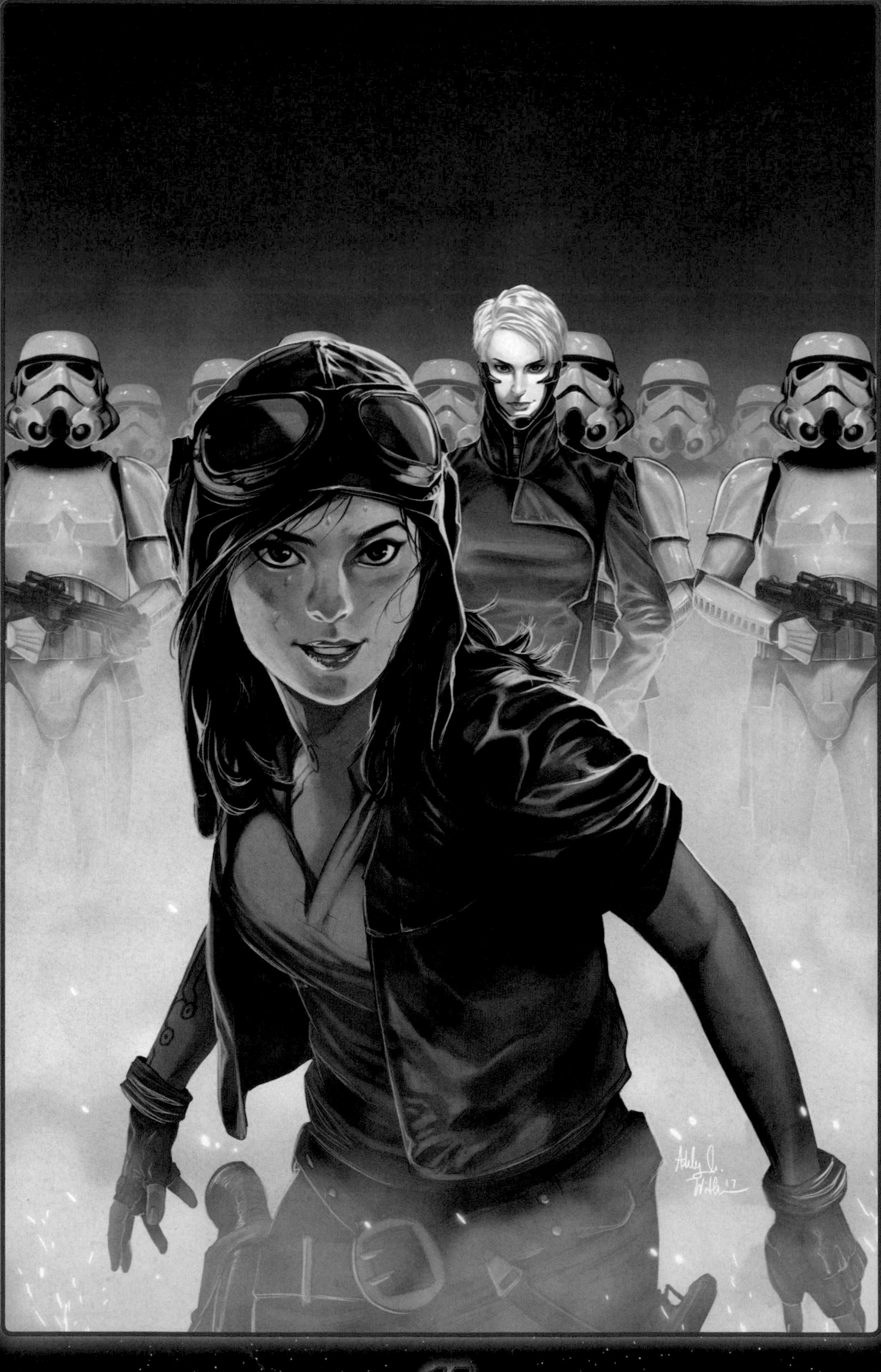

14

REMASTERED

It is a time of instability in the galaxy as rebel forces fight the Galactic Empire. But on the fringes of the galaxy, the criminal underworld continues unabated in its pursuit of profits.

Rogue archaeologist and scoundrel Doctor Chelli Aphra has recently parted ways with the malevolently inclined droids Triple-Zero and BeeTee-One, resulting in her barely escaping the wrath of the Sith Lord Darth Vader after yet another scheme went awry.

Meanwhile, Imperial officer Magna Tolvan is dealing with the ramifications of her previous encounter with the infamous archaeologist. And it seems fate is tempted to repeat itself....

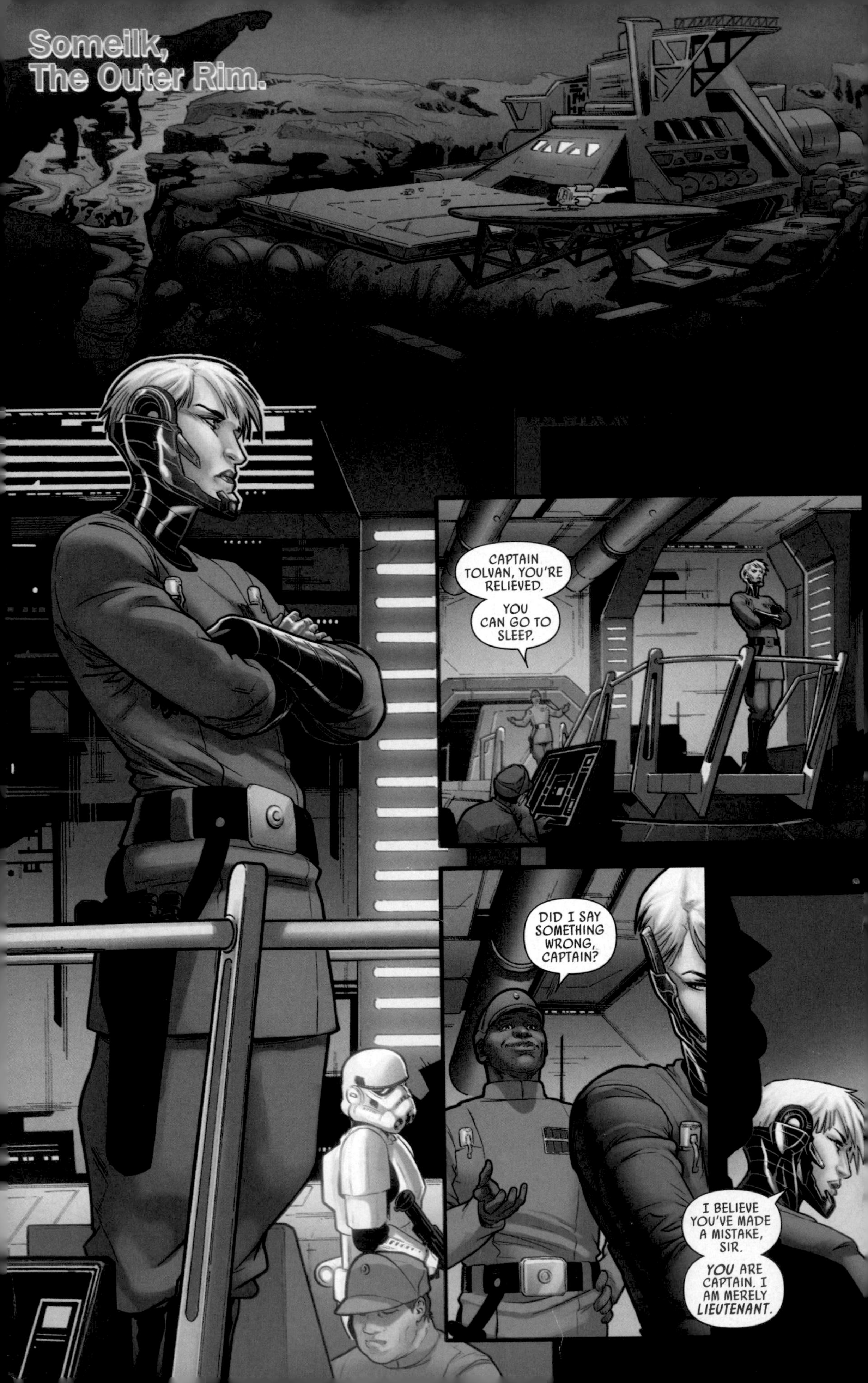
Someilk, The Outer Rim.
CAPTAIN TOLVAN, YOU'RE RELIEVED.
YOU CAN GO TO SLEEP.
DID I SAY SOMETHING WRONG, CAPTAIN?
I BELIEVE YOU'VE MADE A MISTAKE, SIR.
YOU ARE CAPTAIN. I AM MERELY *LIEUTENANT*.

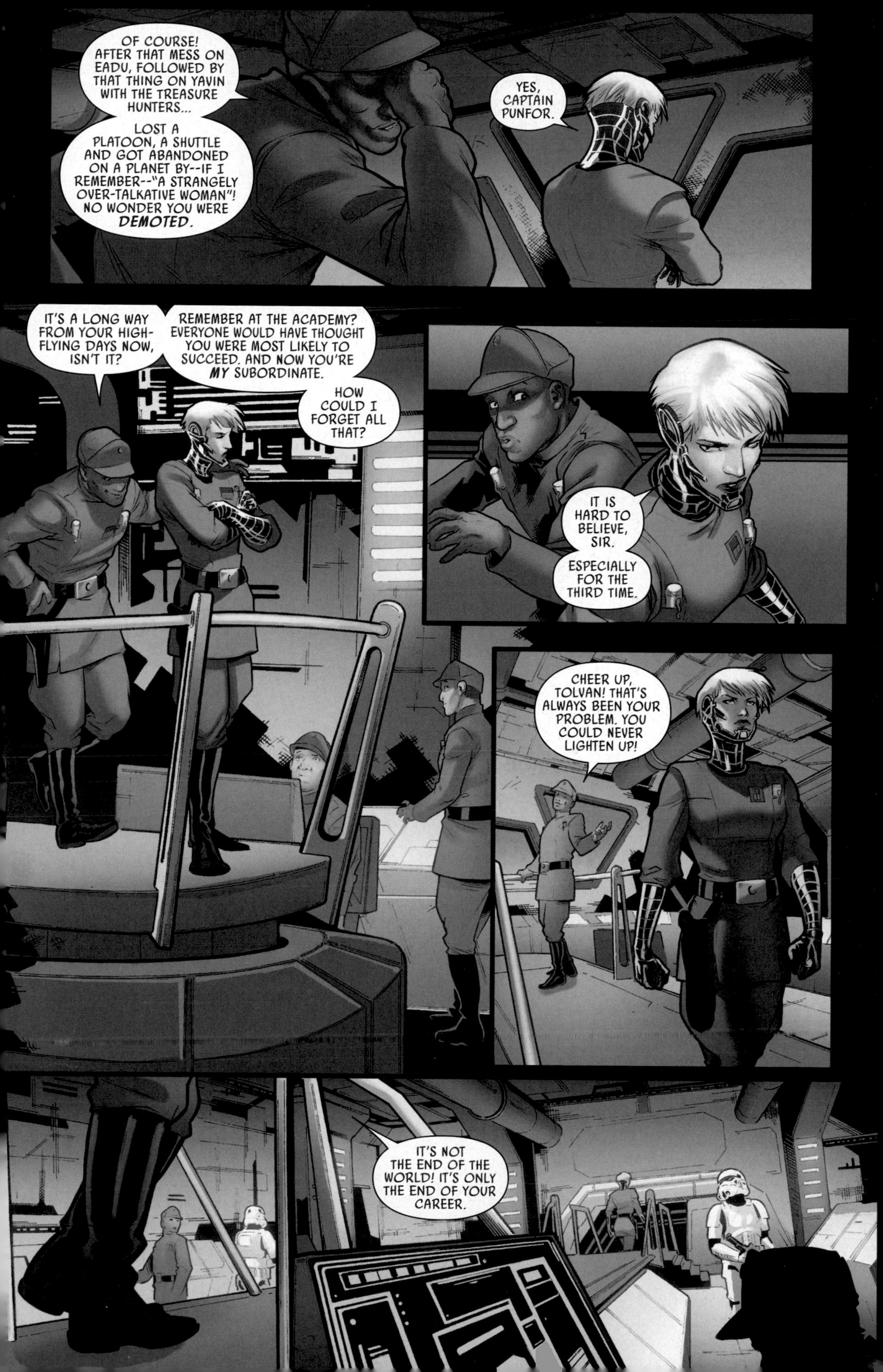
OF COURSE! AFTER THAT MESS ON EADU, FOLLOWED BY THAT THING ON YAVIN WITH THE TREASURE HUNTERS...
LOST A PLATOON, A SHUTTLE AND GOT ABANDONED ON A PLANET BY--IF I REMEMBER--"A STRANGELY OVER-TALKATIVE WOMAN"! NO WONDER YOU WERE DEMOTED.
YES, CAPTAIN PUNFOR.
IT'S A LONG WAY FROM YOUR HIGH-FLYING DAYS NOW, ISN'T IT?
REMEMBER AT THE ACADEMY? EVERYONE WOULD HAVE THOUGHT YOU WERE MOST LIKELY TO SUCCEED. AND NOW YOU'RE MY SUBORDINATE.
HOW COULD I FORGET ALL THAT?
IT IS HARD TO BELIEVE, SIR.
ESPECIALLY FOR THE THIRD TIME.
CHEER UP, TOLVAN! THAT'S ALWAYS BEEN YOUR PROBLEM. YOU COULD NEVER LIGHTEN UP!
IT'S NOT THE END OF THE WORLD! IT'S ONLY THE END OF YOUR CAREER.

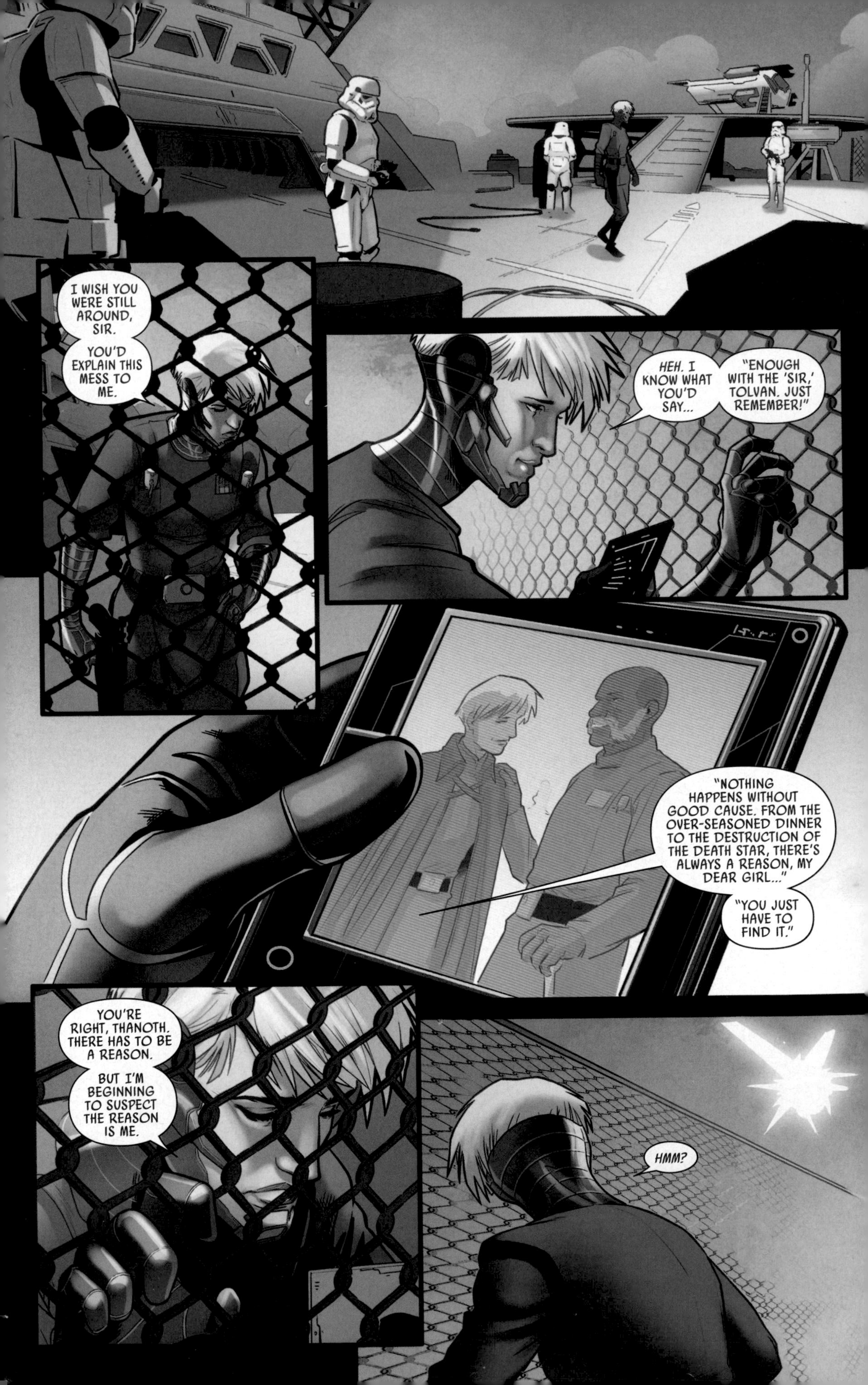
I WISH YOU WERE STILL AROUND, SIR.
YOU'D EXPLAIN THIS MESS TO ME.
HEH. I KNOW WHAT YOU'D SAY...
"ENOUGH WITH THE 'SIR,' TOLVAN. JUST REMEMBER!"
"NOTHING HAPPENS WITHOUT GOOD CAUSE. FROM THE OVER-SEASONED DINNER TO THE DESTRUCTION OF THE DEATH STAR, THERE'S ALWAYS A REASON, MY DEAR GIRL..."
"YOU JUST HAVE TO FIND IT."
YOU'RE RIGHT, THANOTH. THERE HAS TO BE A REASON.
BUT I'M BEGINNING TO SUSPECT THE REASON IS ME.
HMM?

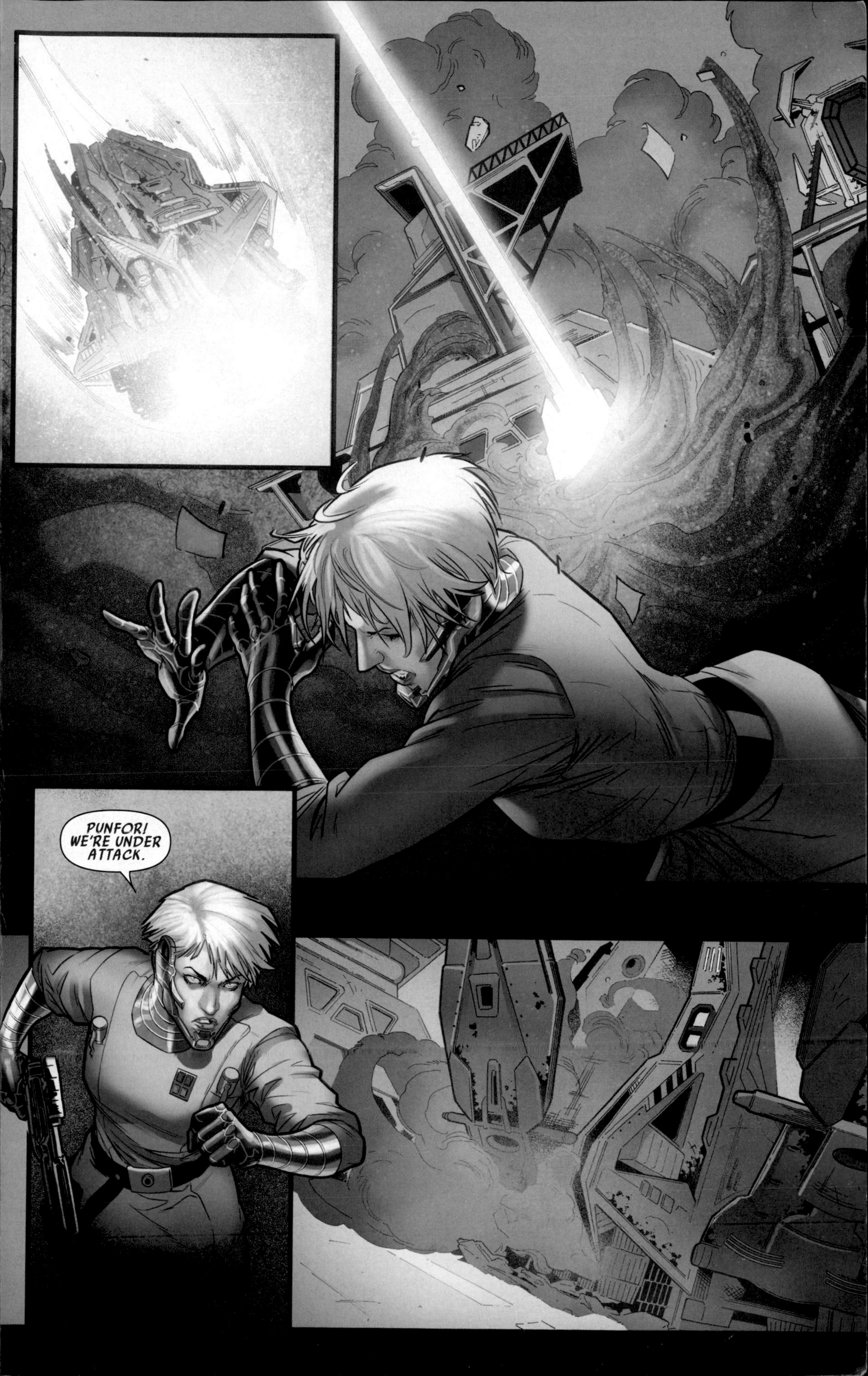
PUNFOR! WE'RE UNDER ATTACK.

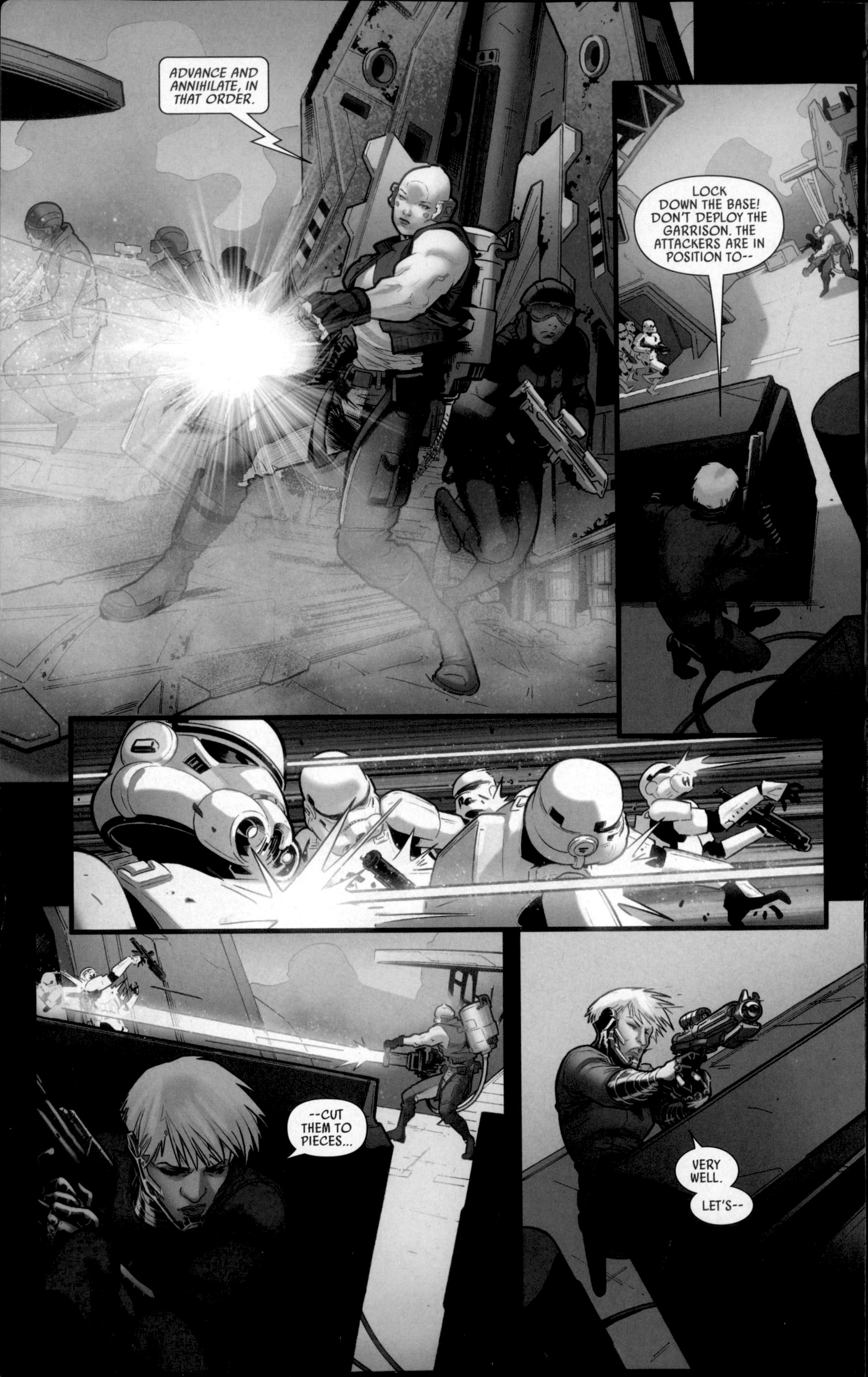
ADVANCE AND ANNIHILATE, IN THAT ORDER.
LOCK DOWN THE BASE! DON'T DEPLOY THE GARRISON. THE ATTACKERS ARE IN POSITION TO--
--CUT THEM TO PIECES...
VERY WELL.
LET'S--

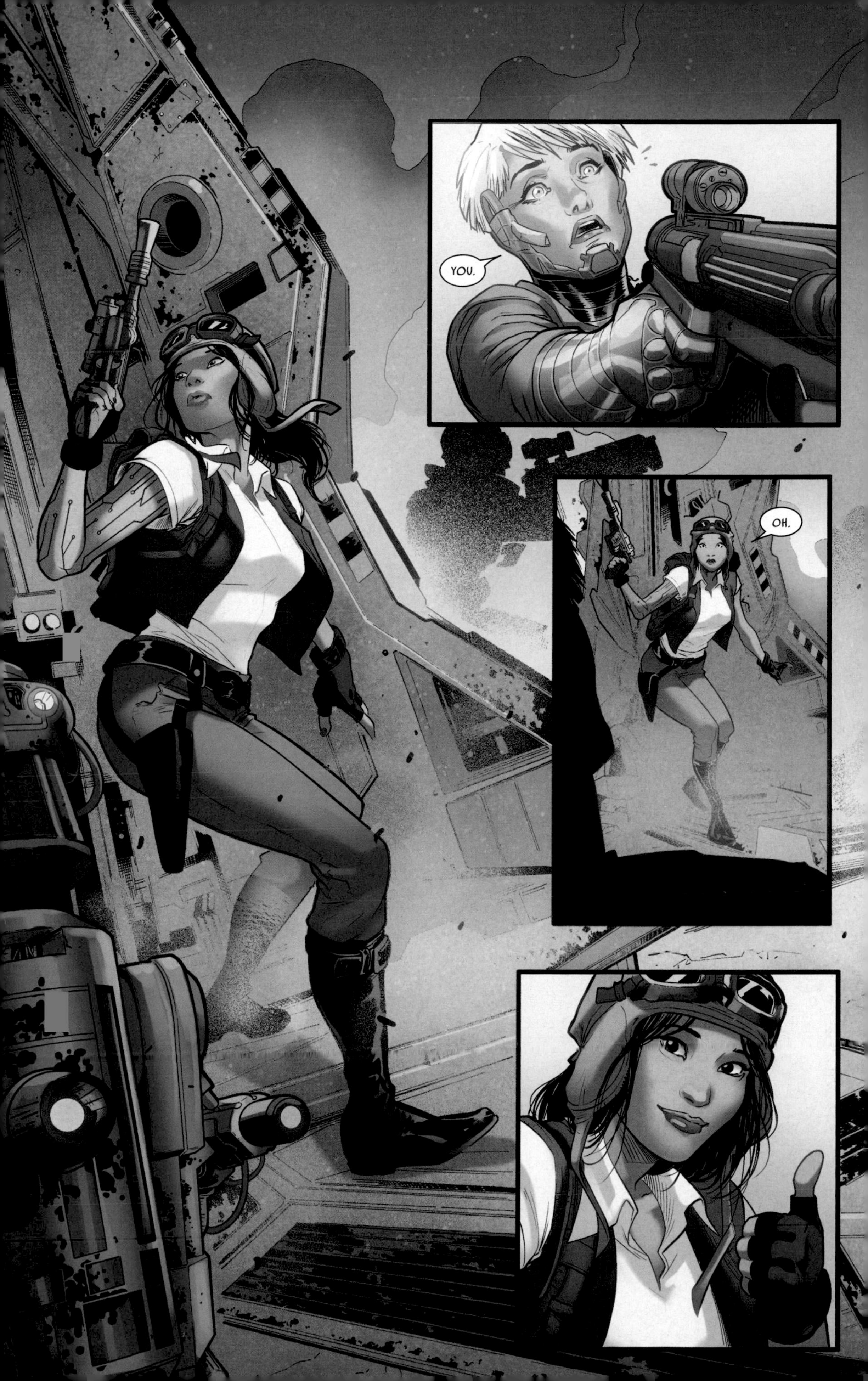
YOU.
OH.

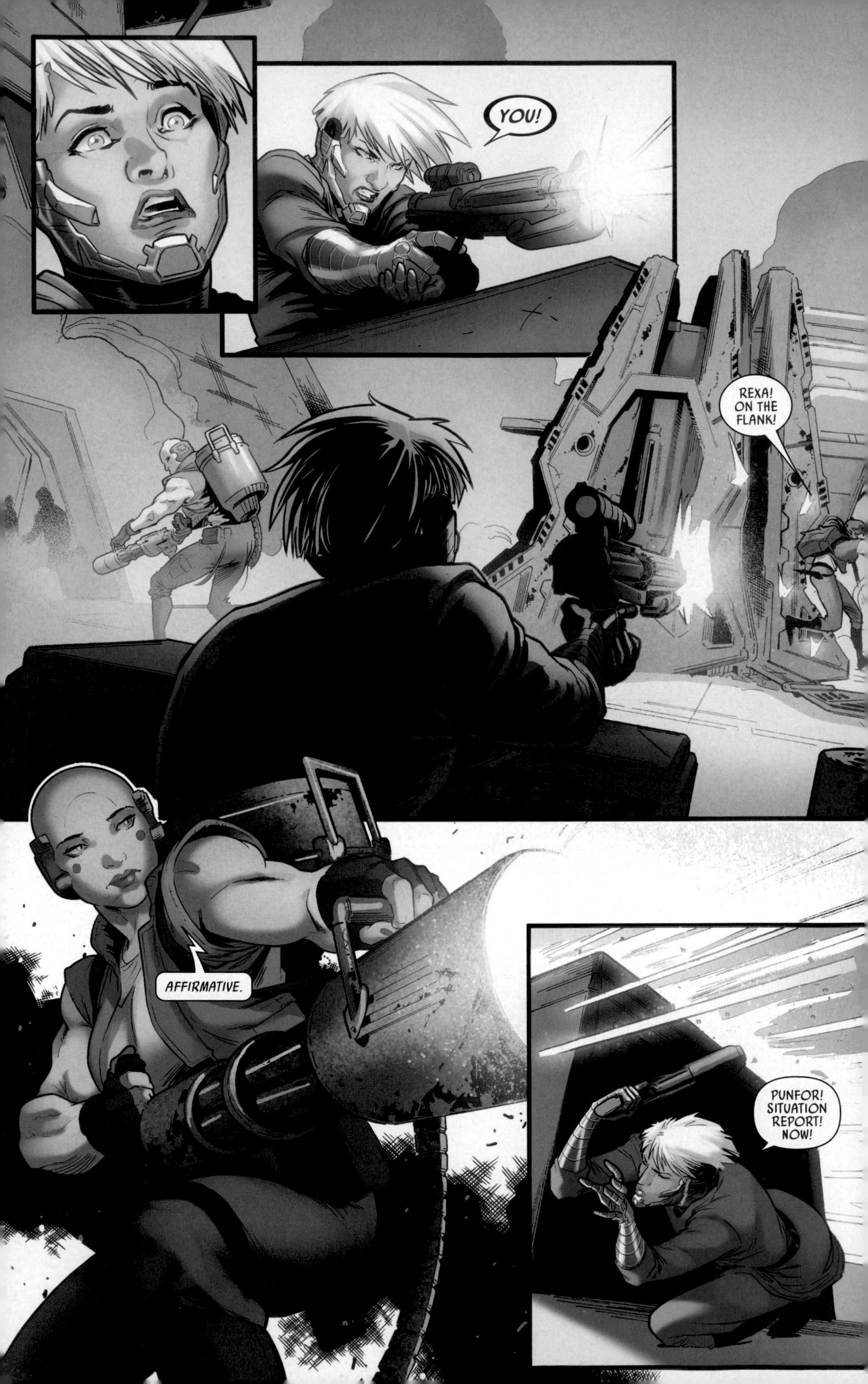
YOU!
REXA! ON THE FLANK!
AFFIRMATIVE.
PUNFOR! SITUATION REPORT! NOW!

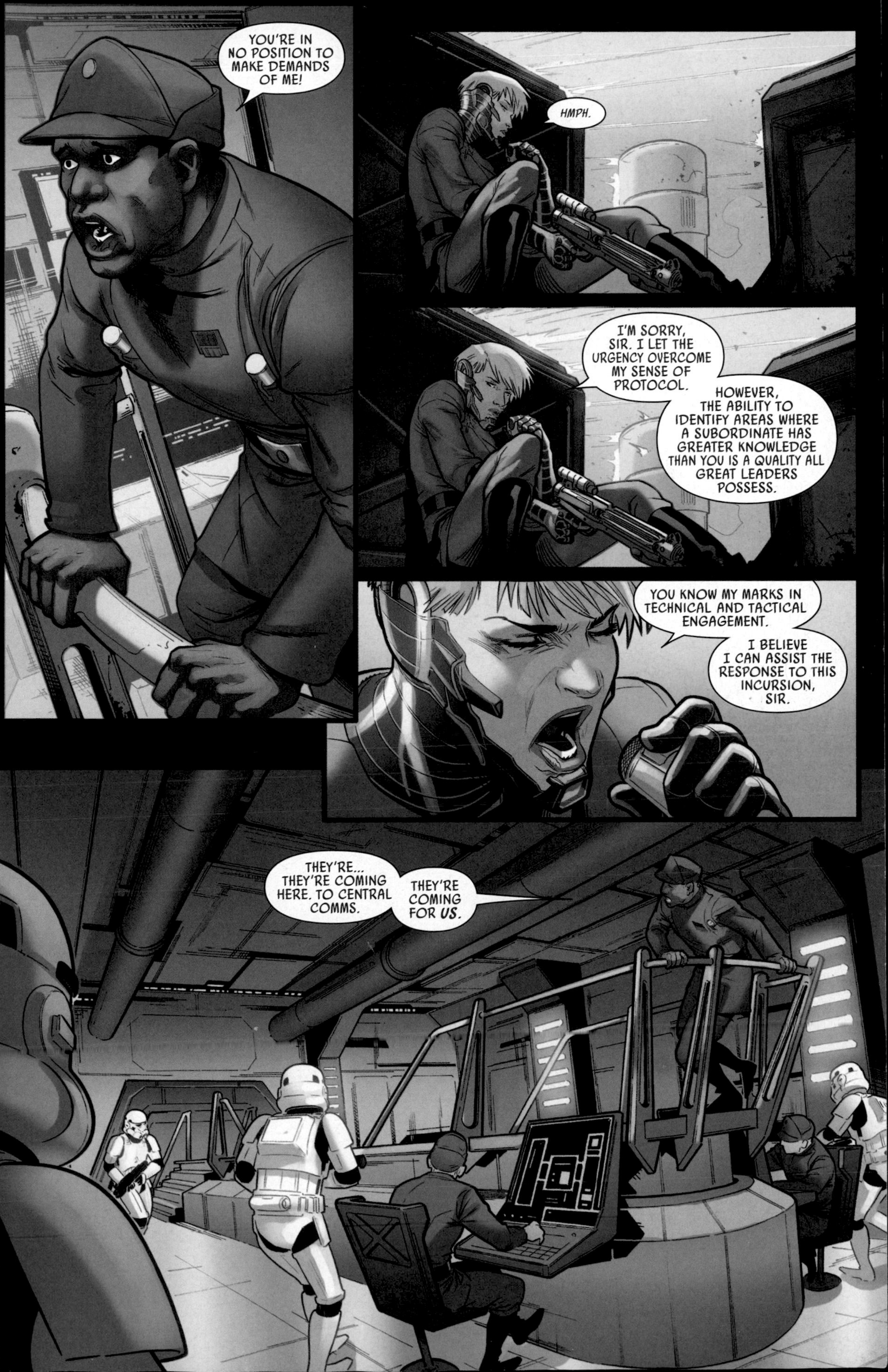
YOU'RE IN NO POSITION TO MAKE DEMANDS OF ME!
HMPH.
I'M SORRY, SIR. I LET THE URGENCY OVERCOME MY SENSE OF PROTOCOL.
HOWEVER, THE ABILITY TO IDENTIFY AREAS WHERE A SUBORDINATE HAS GREATER KNOWLEDGE THAN YOU IS A QUALITY ALL GREAT LEADERS POSSESS.
YOU KNOW MY MARKS IN TECHNICAL AND TACTICAL ENGAGEMENT.
I BELIEVE I CAN ASSIST THE RESPONSE TO THIS INCURSION, SIR.
THEY'RE... THEY'RE COMING HERE. TO CENTRAL COMMS.
THEY'RE COMING FOR *US*.

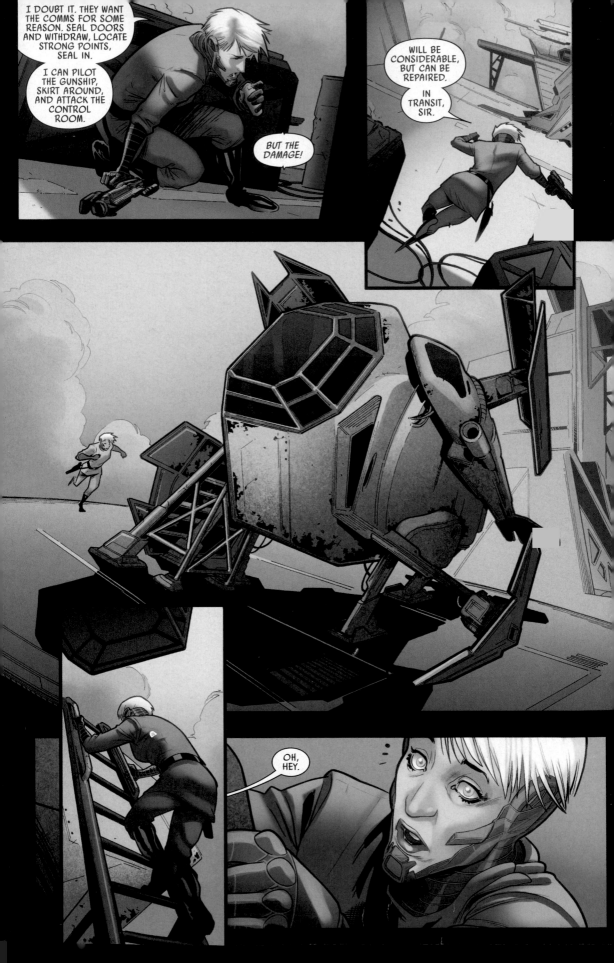

I DOUBT IT. THEY WANT THE COMMS FOR SOME REASON. SEAL DOORS AND WITHDRAW, LOCATE STRONG POINTS, SEAL IN.

I CAN PILOT THE GUNSHIP, SKIRT AROUND, AND ATTACK THE CONTROL ROOM.

BUT THE DAMAGE!

WILL BE CONSIDERABLE, BUT CAN BE REPAIRED.

IN TRANSIT, SIR.

OH, HEY.

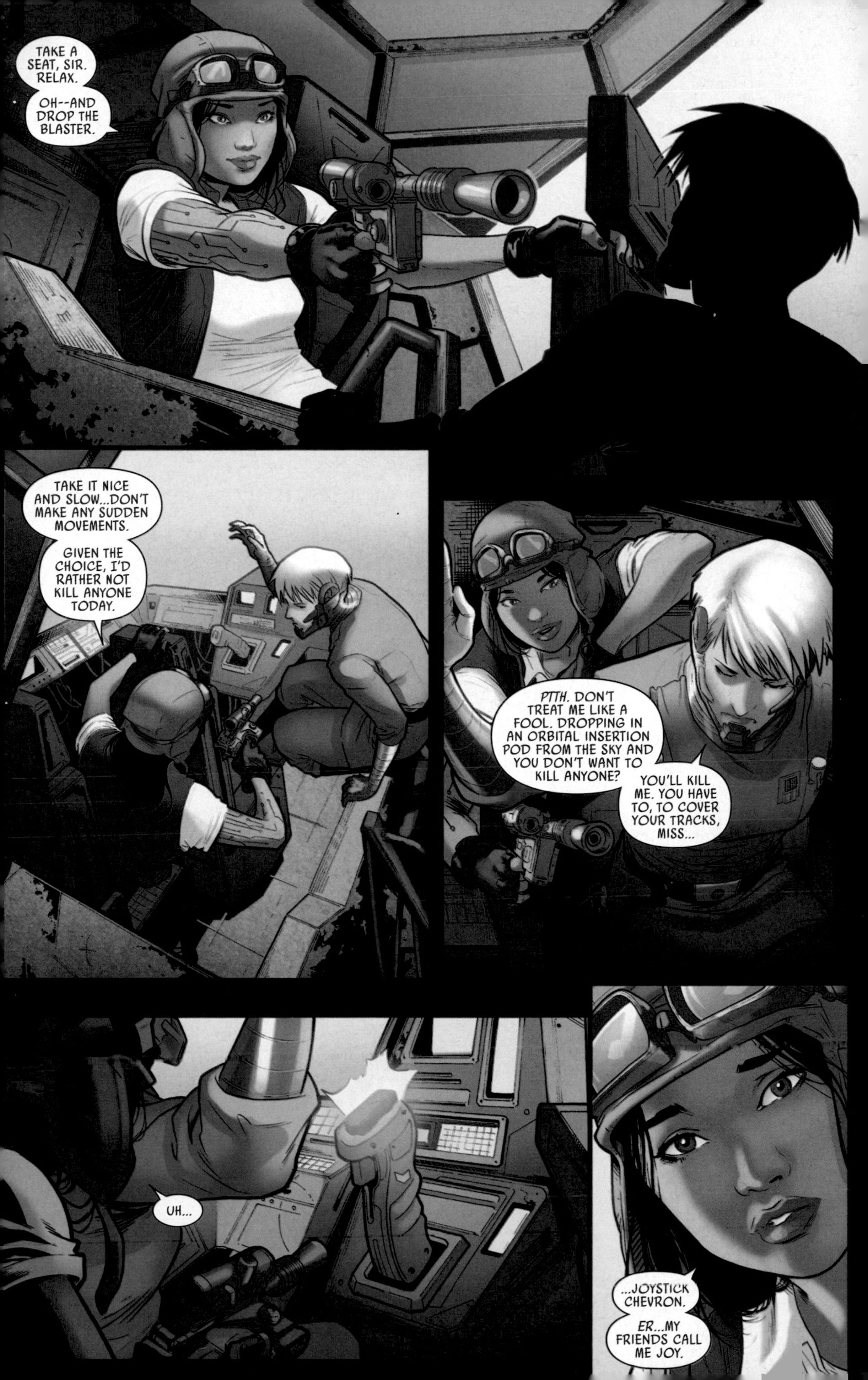
TAKE A SEAT, SIR. RELAX.
OH--AND DROP THE BLASTER.
TAKE IT NICE AND SLOW...DON'T MAKE ANY SUDDEN MOVEMENTS.
GIVEN THE CHOICE, I'D RATHER NOT KILL ANYONE TODAY.
PTTH. DON'T TREAT ME LIKE A FOOL. DROPPING IN AN ORBITAL INSERTION POD FROM THE SKY AND YOU DON'T WANT TO KILL ANYONE?
YOU'LL KILL ME. YOU HAVE TO, TO COVER YOUR TRACKS, MISS...
UH...
...JOYSTICK CHEVRON.
ER...MY FRIENDS CALL ME JOY.

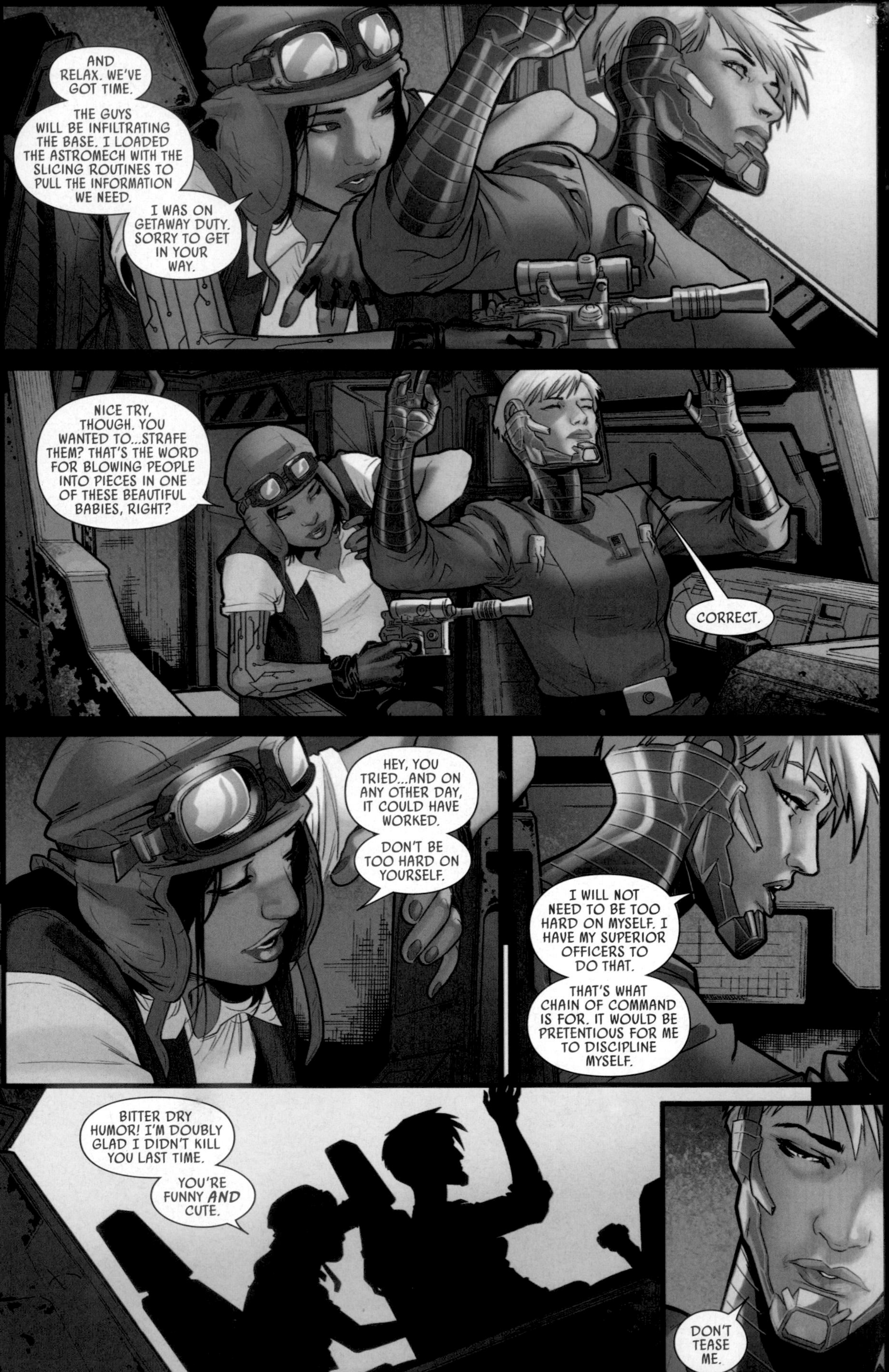
AND RELAX. WE'VE GOT TIME.
THE GUYS WILL BE INFILTRATING THE BASE. I LOADED THE ASTROMECH WITH THE SLICING ROUTINES TO PULL THE INFORMATION WE NEED.
I WAS ON GETAWAY DUTY. SORRY TO GET IN YOUR WAY.
NICE TRY, THOUGH. YOU WANTED TO...STRAFE THEM? THAT'S THE WORD FOR BLOWING PEOPLE INTO PIECES IN ONE OF THESE BEAUTIFUL BABIES, RIGHT?
CORRECT.
HEY, YOU TRIED...AND ON ANY OTHER DAY, IT COULD HAVE WORKED.
DON'T BE TOO HARD ON YOURSELF.
I WILL NOT NEED TO BE TOO HARD ON MYSELF. I HAVE MY SUPERIOR OFFICERS TO DO THAT.
THAT'S WHAT CHAIN OF COMMAND IS FOR. IT WOULD BE PRETENTIOUS FOR ME TO DISCIPLINE MYSELF.
BITTER DRY HUMOR! I'M DOUBLY GLAD I DIDN'T KILL YOU LAST TIME.
YOU'RE FUNNY *AND* CUTE.
DON'T TEASE ME.

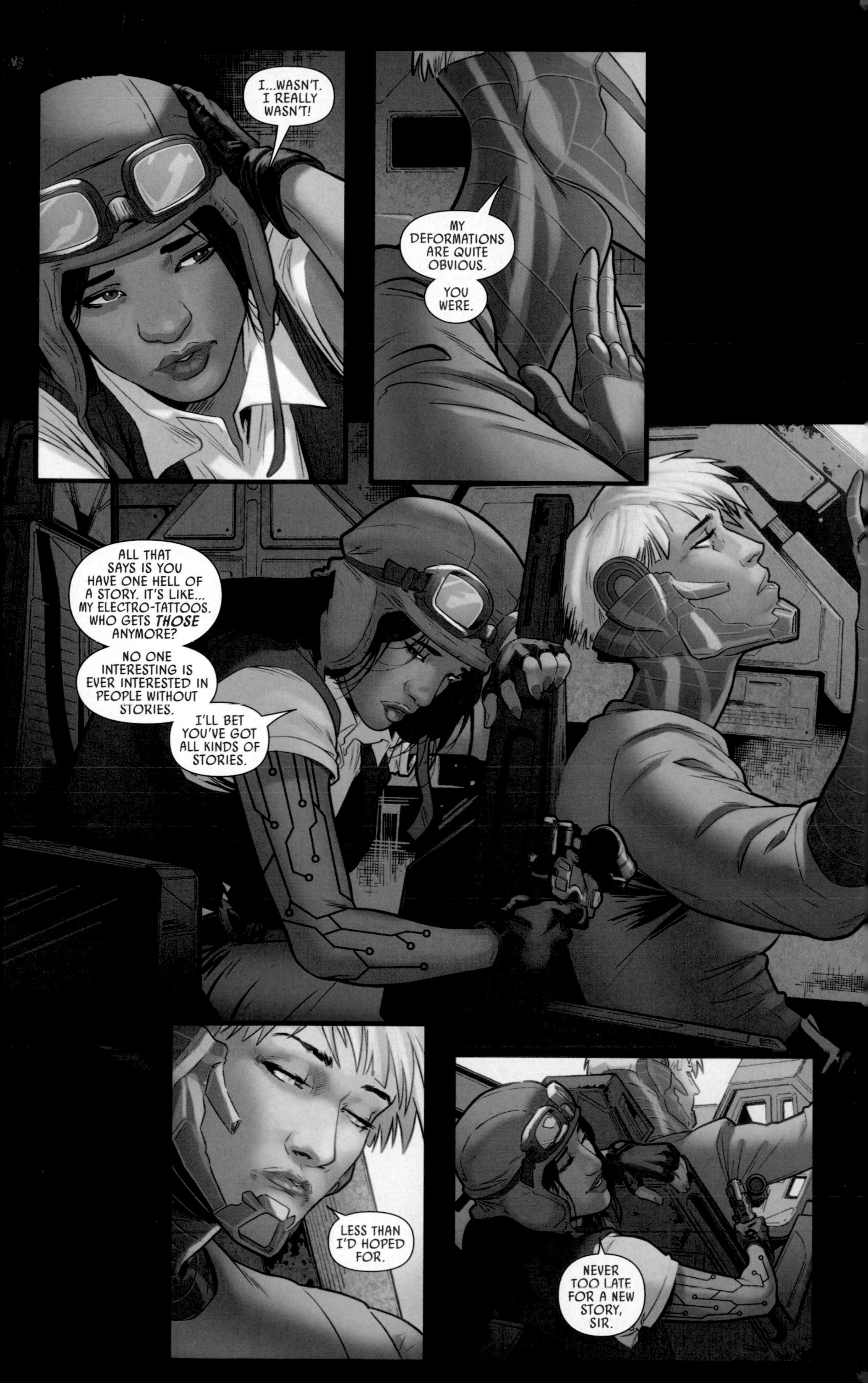
I...WASN'T. I REALLY WASN'T!
MY DEFORMATIONS ARE QUITE OBVIOUS.
YOU WERE.
ALL THAT SAYS IS YOU HAVE ONE HELL OF A STORY. IT'S LIKE... MY ELECTRO-TATTOOS. WHO GETS *THOSE* ANYMORE?
NO ONE INTERESTING IS EVER INTERESTED IN PEOPLE WITHOUT STORIES.
I'LL BET YOU'VE GOT ALL KINDS OF STORIES.
LESS THAN I'D HOPED FOR.
NEVER TOO LATE FOR A NEW STORY, SIR.

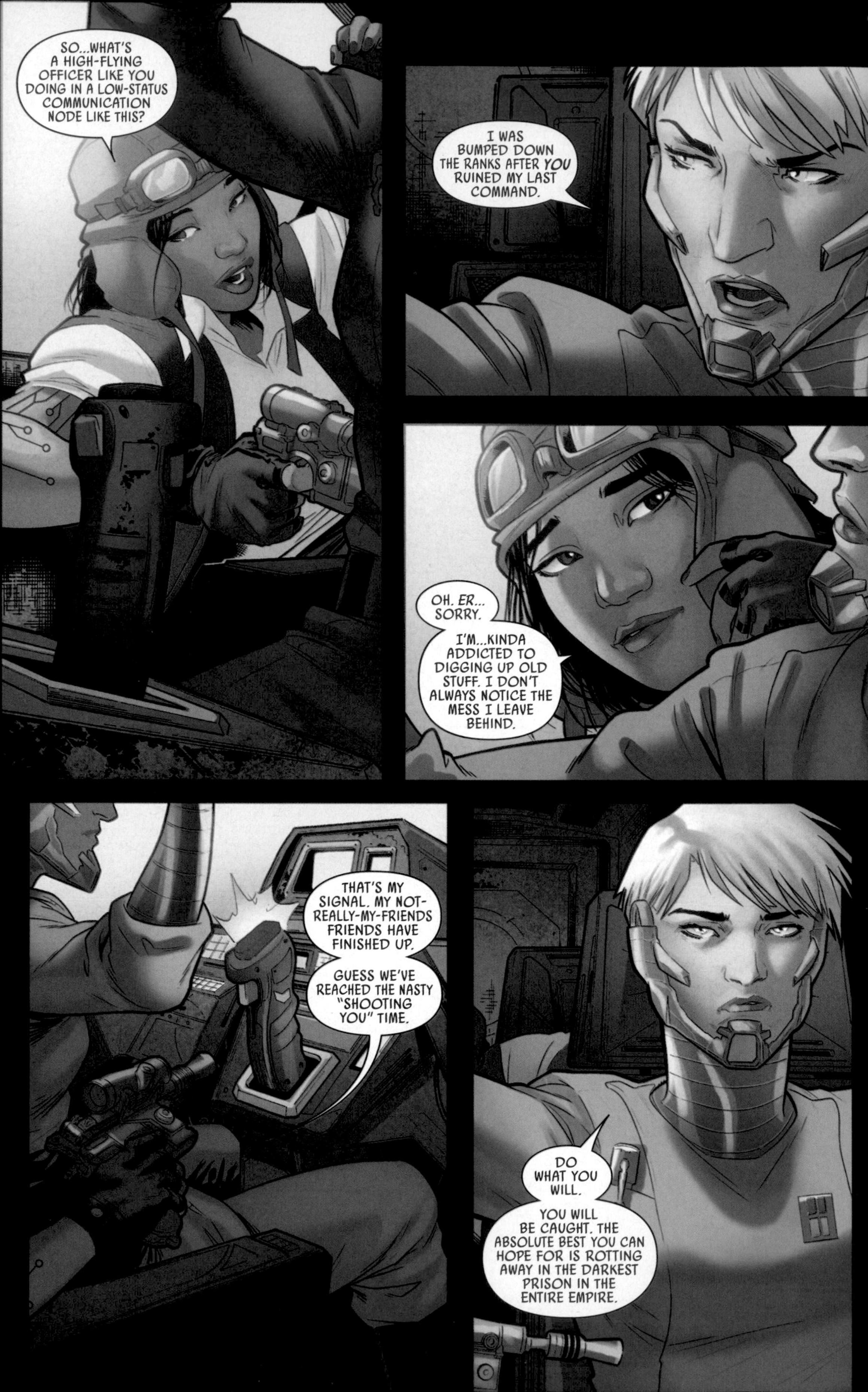
SO...WHAT'S A HIGH-FLYING OFFICER LIKE YOU DOING IN A LOW-STATUS COMMUNICATION NODE LIKE THIS?
I WAS BUMPED DOWN THE RANKS AFTER *YOU* RUINED MY LAST COMMAND.
OH. *ER*... SORRY.
I'M...KINDA ADDICTED TO DIGGING UP OLD STUFF. I DON'T ALWAYS NOTICE THE MESS I LEAVE BEHIND.
THAT'S MY SIGNAL. MY NOT-REALLY-MY-FRIENDS FRIENDS HAVE FINISHED UP.
GUESS WE'VE REACHED THE NASTY "SHOOTING YOU" TIME.
DO WHAT YOU WILL.
YOU WILL BE CAUGHT. THE ABSOLUTE BEST YOU CAN HOPE FOR IS ROTTING AWAY IN THE DARKEST PRISON IN THE ENTIRE EMPIRE.

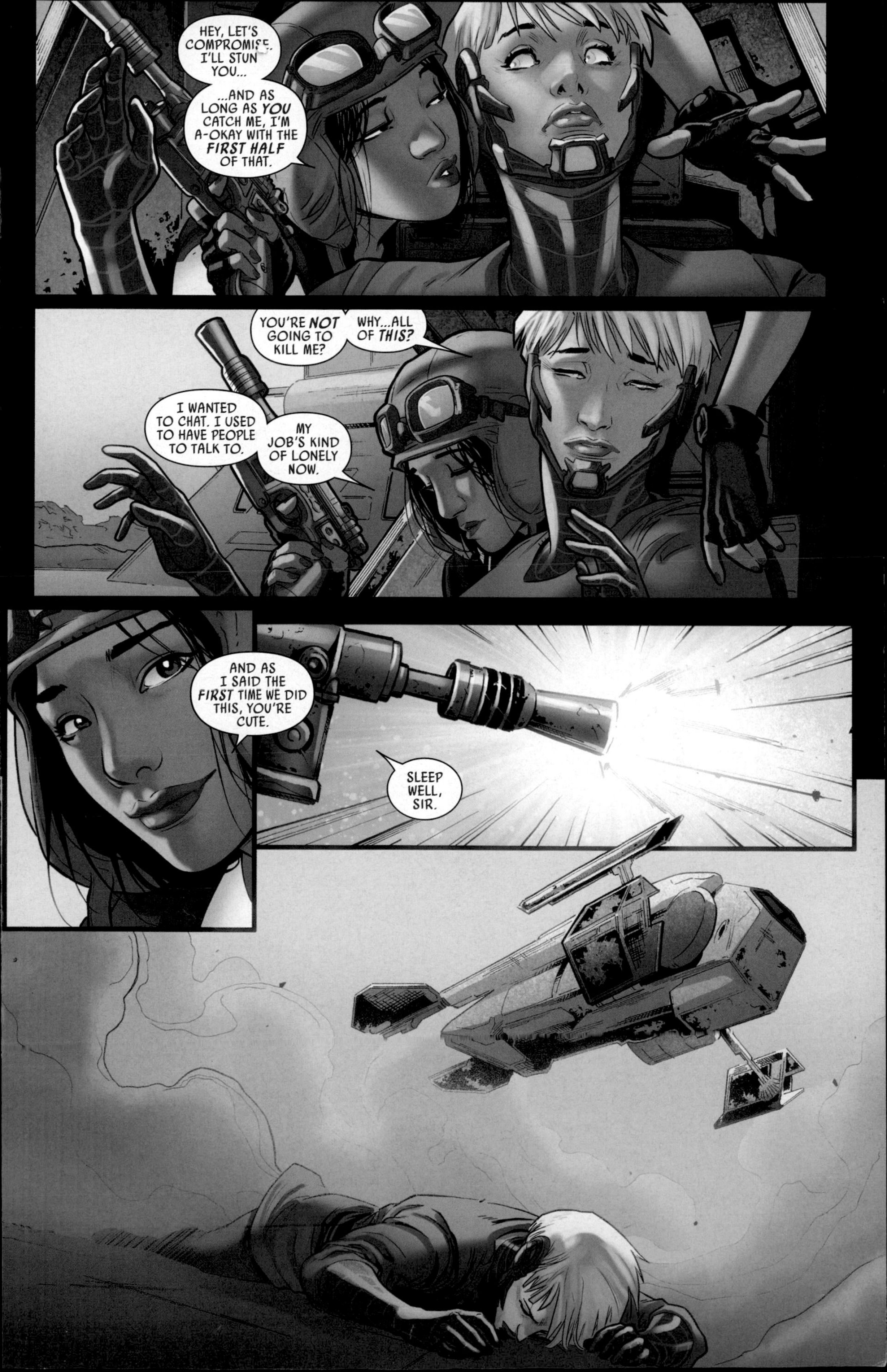
HEY, LET'S COMPROMISE. I'LL STUN YOU...
...AND AS LONG AS YOU CATCH ME, I'M A-OKAY WITH THE FIRST HALF OF THAT.
YOU'RE NOT GOING TO KILL ME?
WHY...ALL OF THIS?
I WANTED TO CHAT. I USED TO HAVE PEOPLE TO TALK TO.
MY JOB'S KIND OF LONELY NOW.
AND AS I SAID THE FIRST TIME WE DID THIS, YOU'RE CUTE.
SLEEP WELL, SIR.

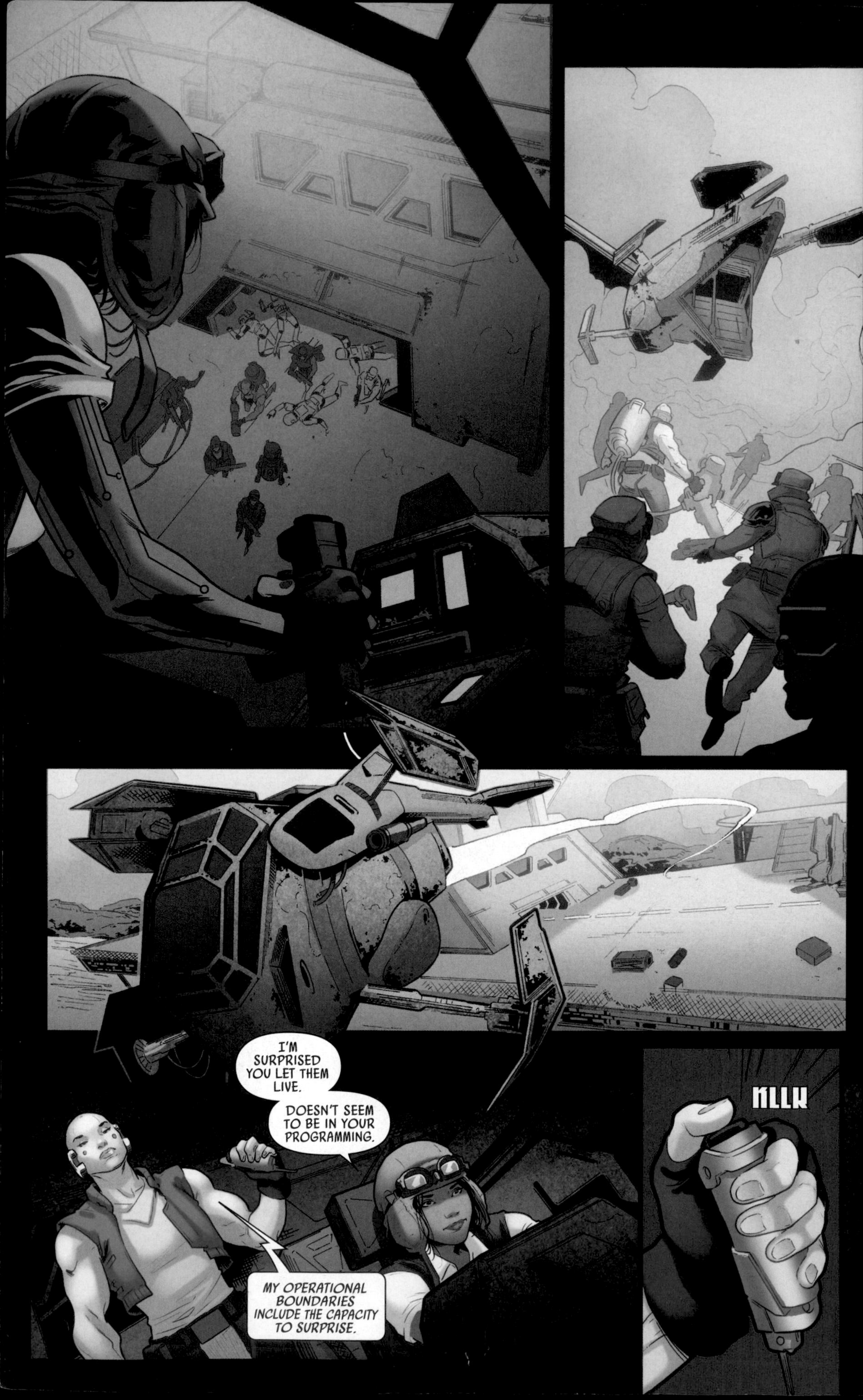
I'M SURPRISED YOU LET THEM LIVE.
DOESN'T SEEM TO BE IN YOUR PROGRAMMING.
MY OPERATIONAL BOUNDARIES INCLUDE THE CAPACITY TO SURPRISE.
KLLK

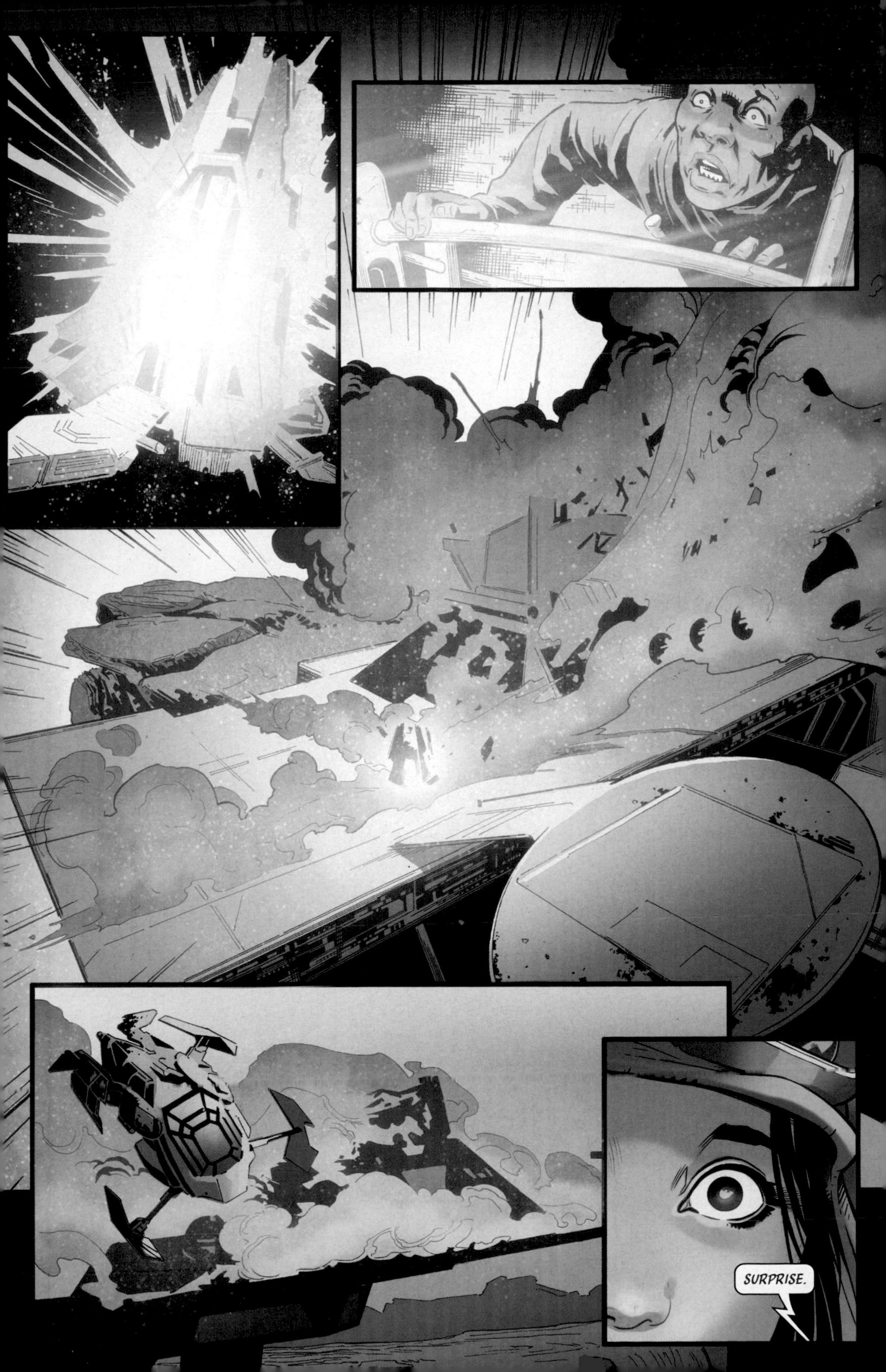
SURPRISE.

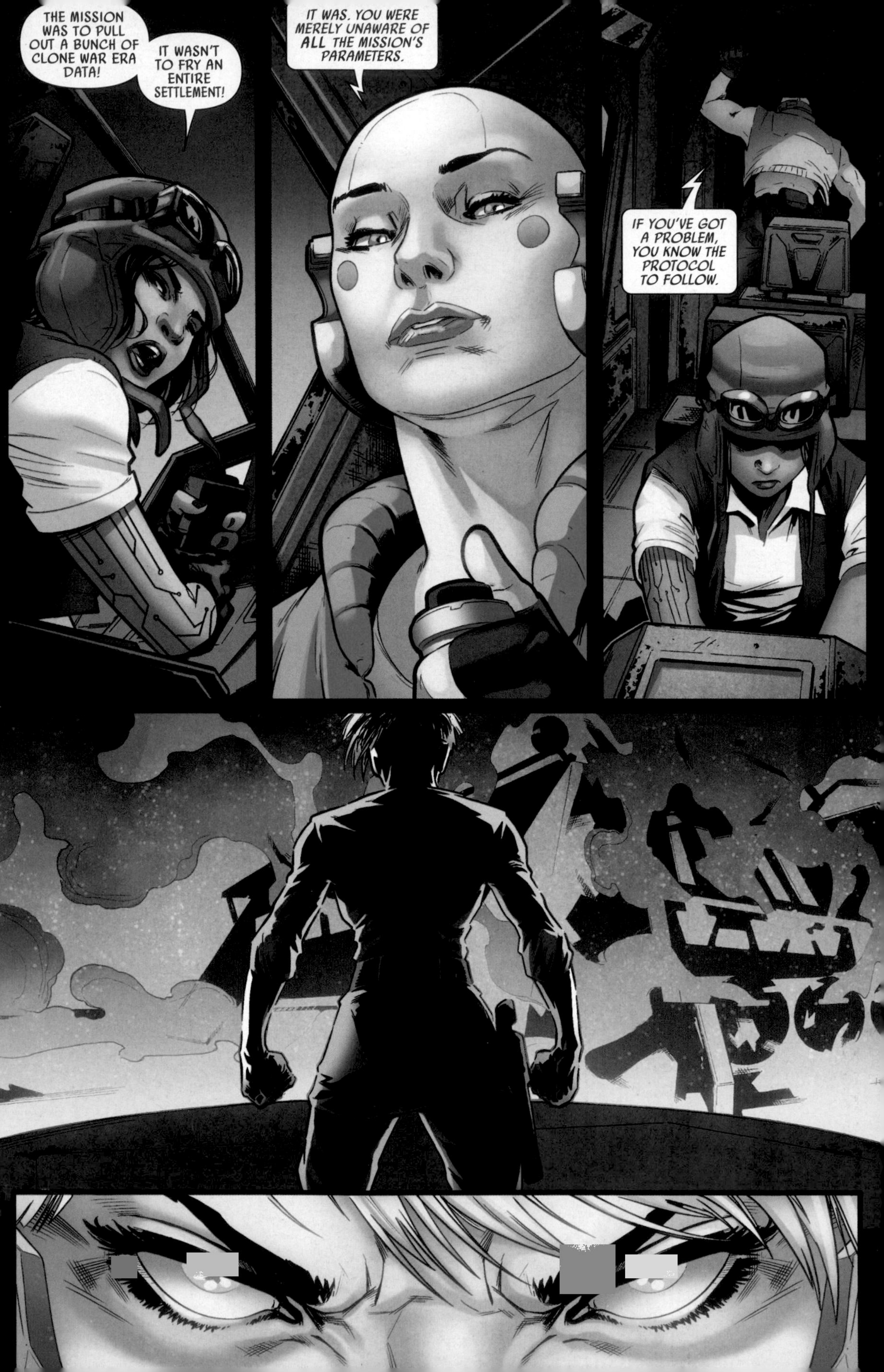
THE MISSION WAS TO PULL OUT A BUNCH OF CLONE WAR ERA DATA!
IT WASN'T TO FRY AN ENTIRE SETTLEMENT!
IT WAS. YOU WERE MERELY UNAWARE OF ALL THE MISSION'S PARAMETERS.
IF YOU'VE GOT A PROBLEM, YOU KNOW THE PROTOCOL TO FOLLOW.

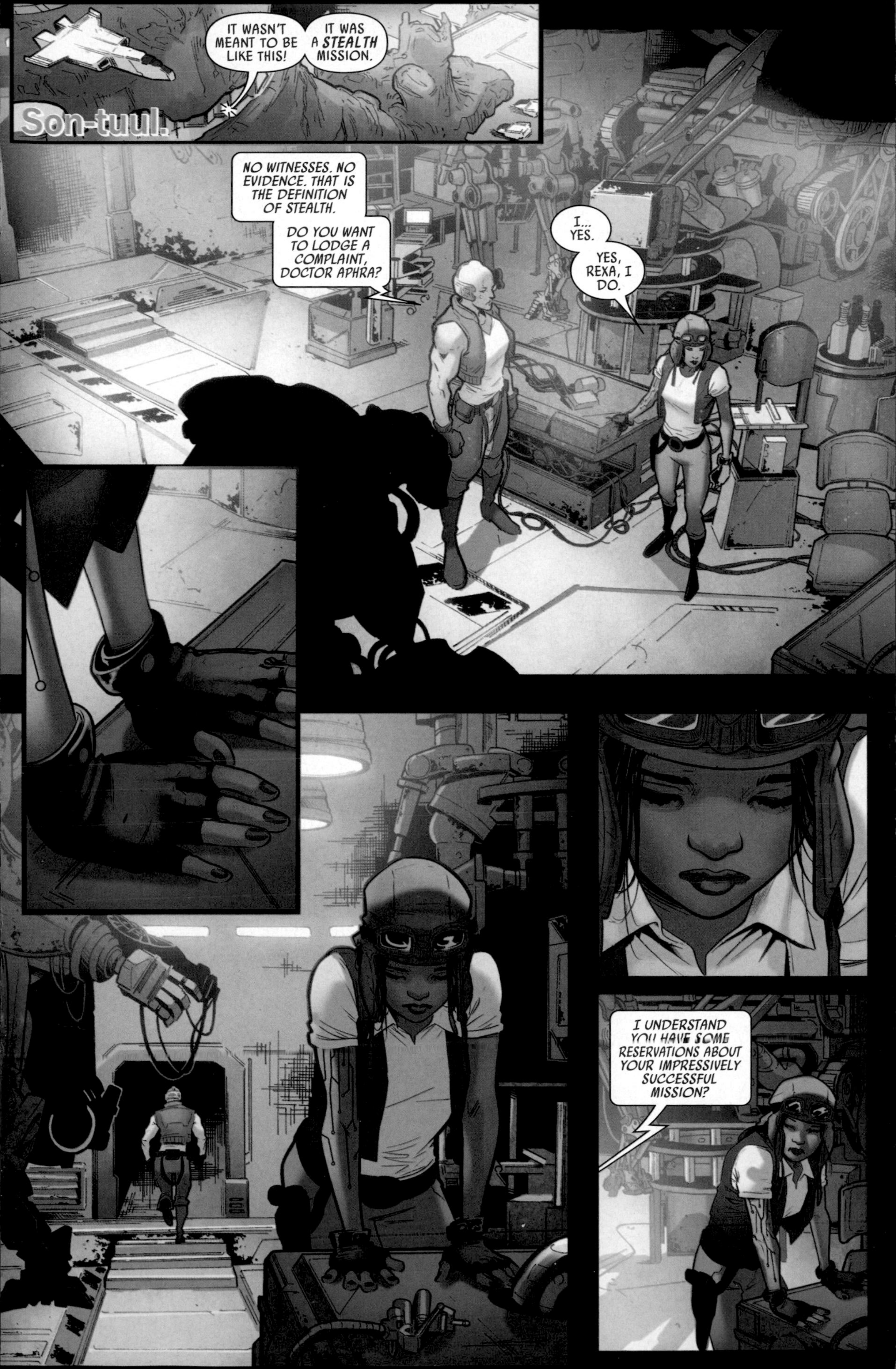
Son-tuul.
IT WASN'T MEANT TO BE LIKE THIS!
IT WAS A STEALTH MISSION.
NO WITNESSES. NO EVIDENCE. THAT IS THE DEFINITION OF STEALTH.
DO YOU WANT TO LODGE A COMPLAINT, DOCTOR APHRA?
I... YES.
YES, REXA, I DO.
I UNDERSTAND YOU HAVE SOME RESERVATIONS ABOUT YOUR IMPRESSIVELY SUCCESSFUL MISSION?

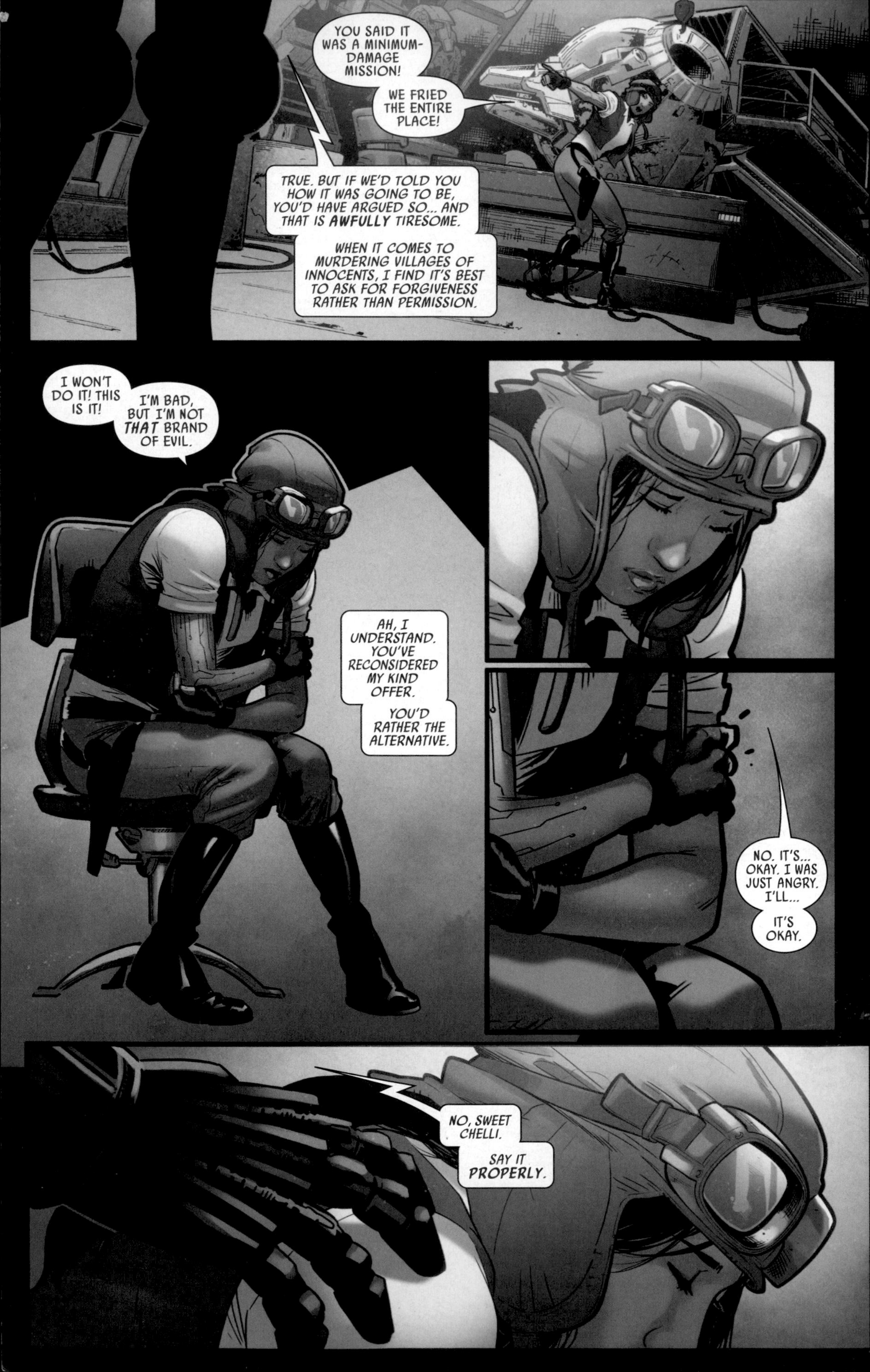
YOU SAID IT WAS A MINIMUM-DAMAGE MISSION!
WE FRIED THE ENTIRE PLACE!
TRUE. BUT IF WE'D TOLD YOU HOW IT WAS GOING TO BE, YOU'D HAVE ARGUED SO... AND THAT IS AWFULLY TIRESOME.
WHEN IT COMES TO MURDERING VILLAGES OF INNOCENTS, I FIND IT'S BEST TO ASK FOR FORGIVENESS RATHER THAN PERMISSION.
I WON'T DO IT! THIS IS IT!
I'M BAD, BUT I'M NOT THAT BRAND OF EVIL.
AH, I UNDERSTAND. YOU'VE RECONSIDERED MY KIND OFFER.
YOU'D RATHER THE ALTERNATIVE.
NO. IT'S... OKAY. I WAS JUST ANGRY. I'LL...
IT'S OKAY.
NO, SWEET CHELLI.
SAY IT PROPERLY.

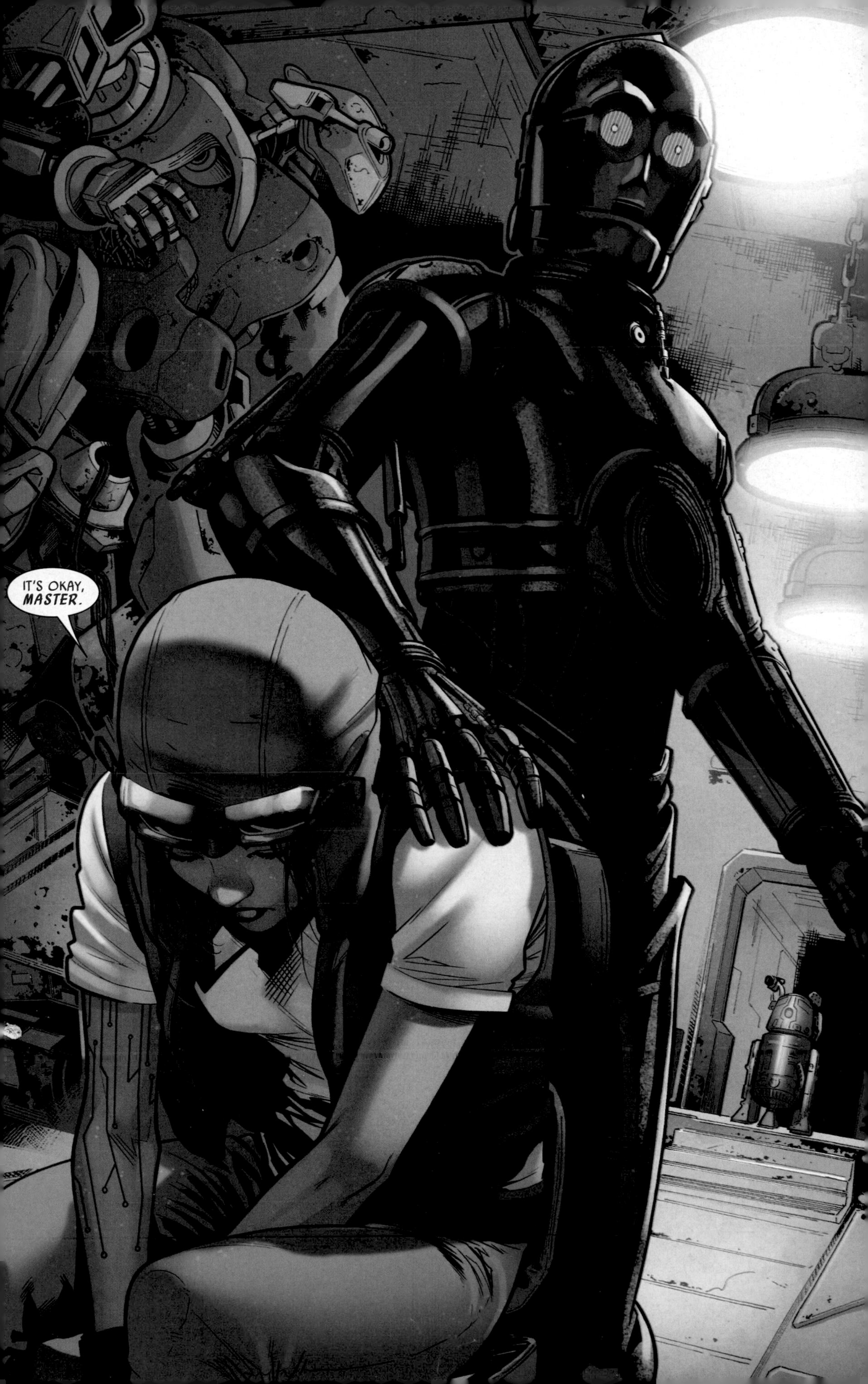
IT'S OKAY, MASTER.

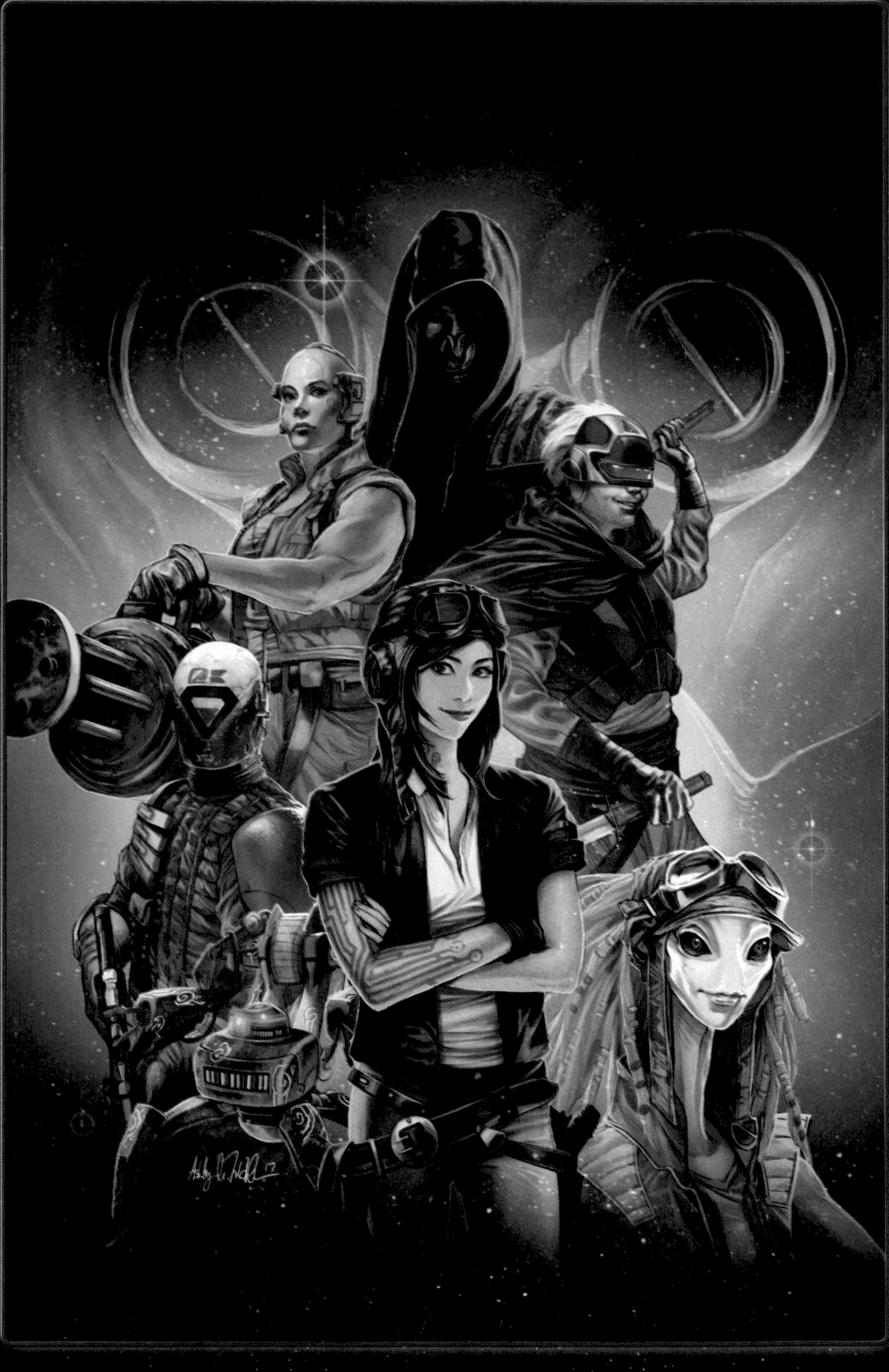

15

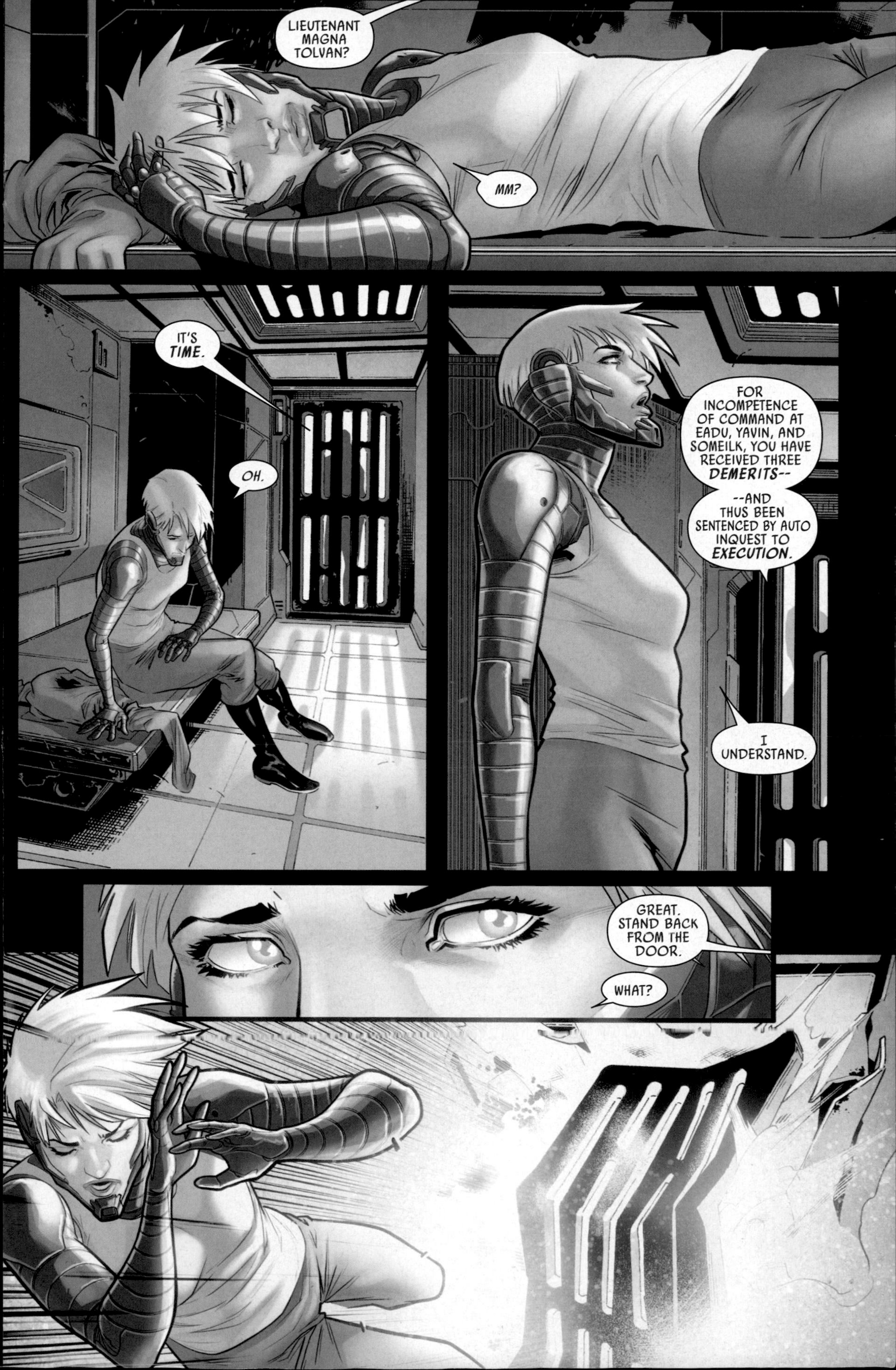
LIEUTENANT MAGNA TOLVAN?
MM?
IT'S *TIME*.
OH.
FOR INCOMPETENCE OF COMMAND AT EADU, YAVIN, AND SOMEILK, YOU HAVE RECEIVED THREE **DEMERITS--**
--AND THUS BEEN SENTENCED BY AUTO INQUEST TO **EXECUTION**.
I UNDERSTAND.
GREAT. STAND BACK FROM THE DOOR.
WHAT?

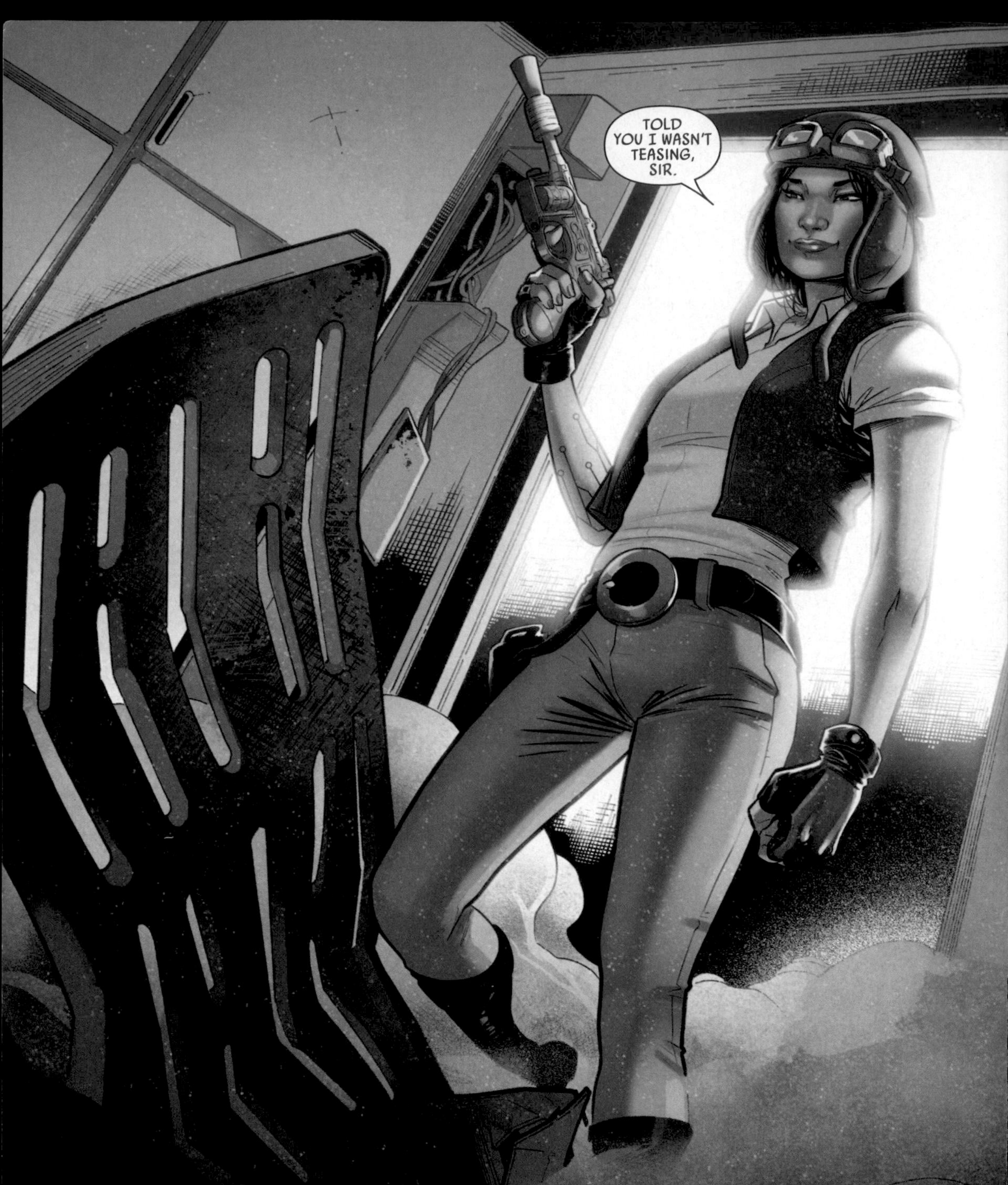
TOLD YOU I WASN'T TEASING, SIR.

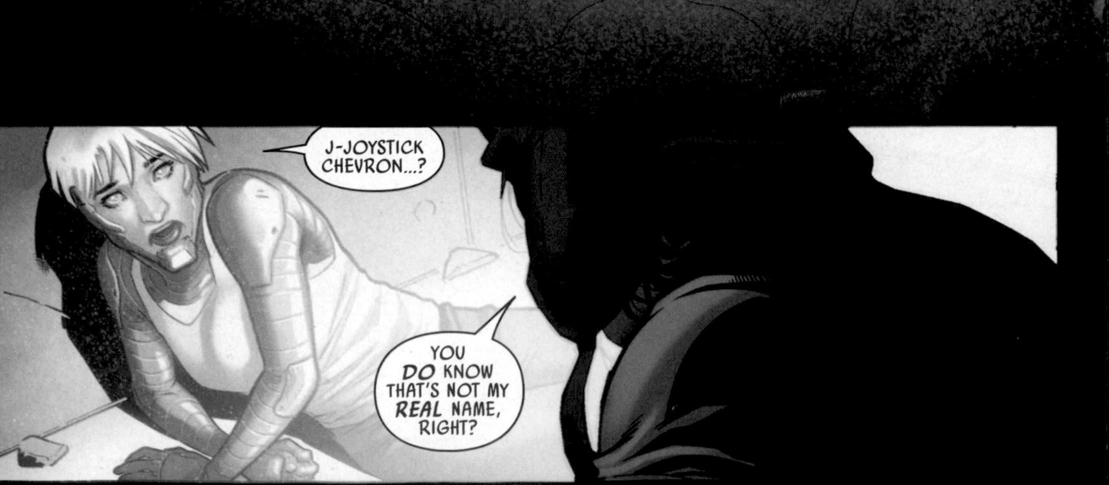
J-JOYSTICK CHEVRON...?
YOU DO KNOW THAT'S NOT MY REAL NAME, RIGHT?

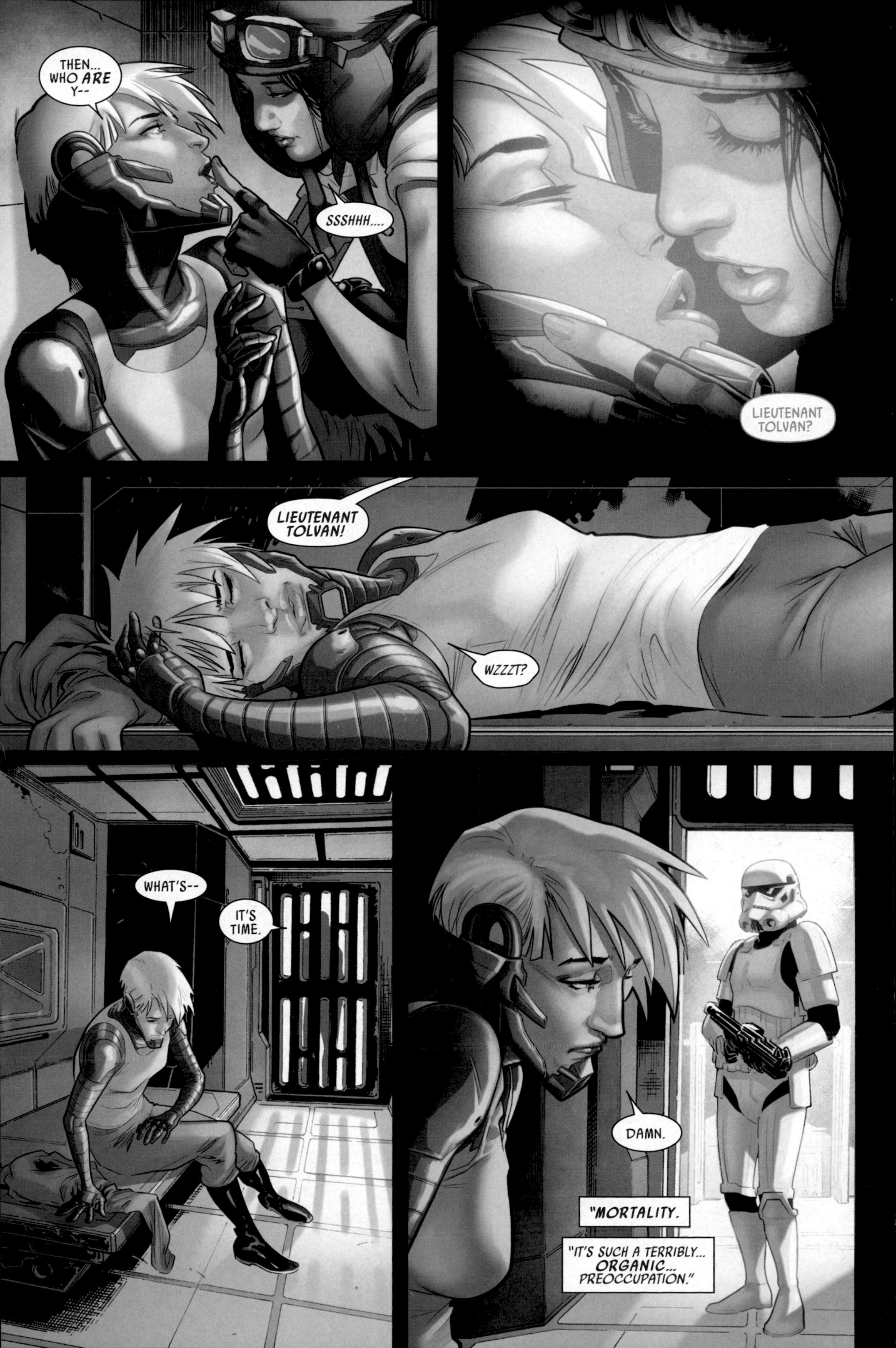
THEN... WHO ARE Y--
SSSHHH....
LIEUTENANT TOLVAN?
LIEUTENANT TOLVAN!
WZZZT?
WHAT'S--
IT'S TIME.
DAMN.
"MORTALITY.
"IT'S SUCH A TERRIBLY... ORGANIC... PREOCCUPATION."

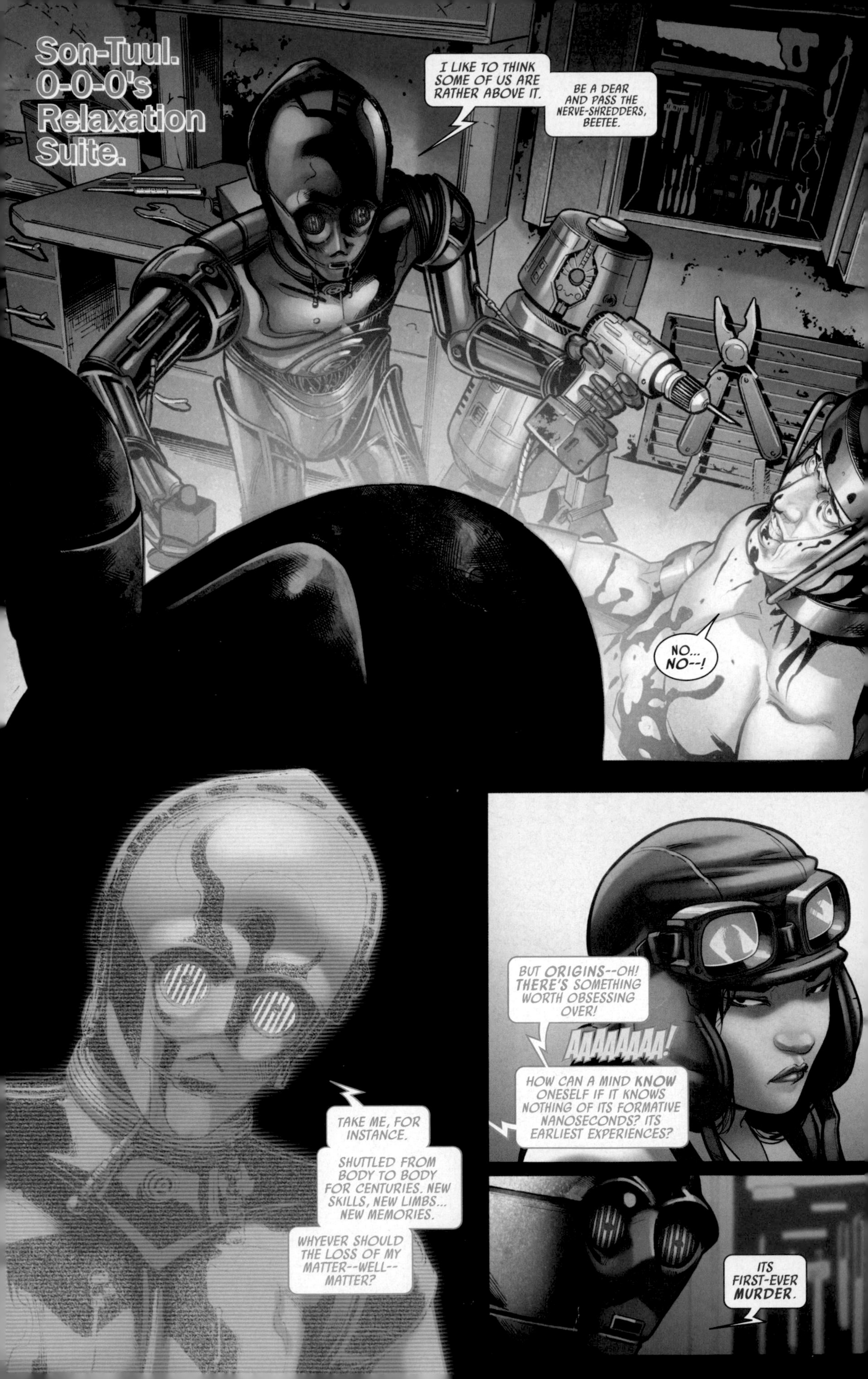

Son-Tuul. 0-0-0's Relaxation Suite.
I LIKE TO THINK SOME OF US ARE RATHER ABOVE IT.
BE A DEAR AND PASS THE NERVE-SHREDDERS, BEETEE.
NO... NO--!
BUT ORIGINS--OH! THERE'S SOMETHING WORTH OBSESSING OVER!
AAAAAAAA!
HOW CAN A MIND KNOW ONESELF IF IT KNOWS NOTHING OF ITS FORMATIVE NANOSECONDS? ITS EARLIEST EXPERIENCES?
TAKE ME, FOR INSTANCE.
SHUTTLED FROM BODY TO BODY FOR CENTURIES. NEW SKILLS, NEW LIMBS... NEW MEMORIES.
WHYEVER SHOULD THE LOSS OF MY MATTER--WELL--MATTER?
ITS FIRST-EVER MURDER.

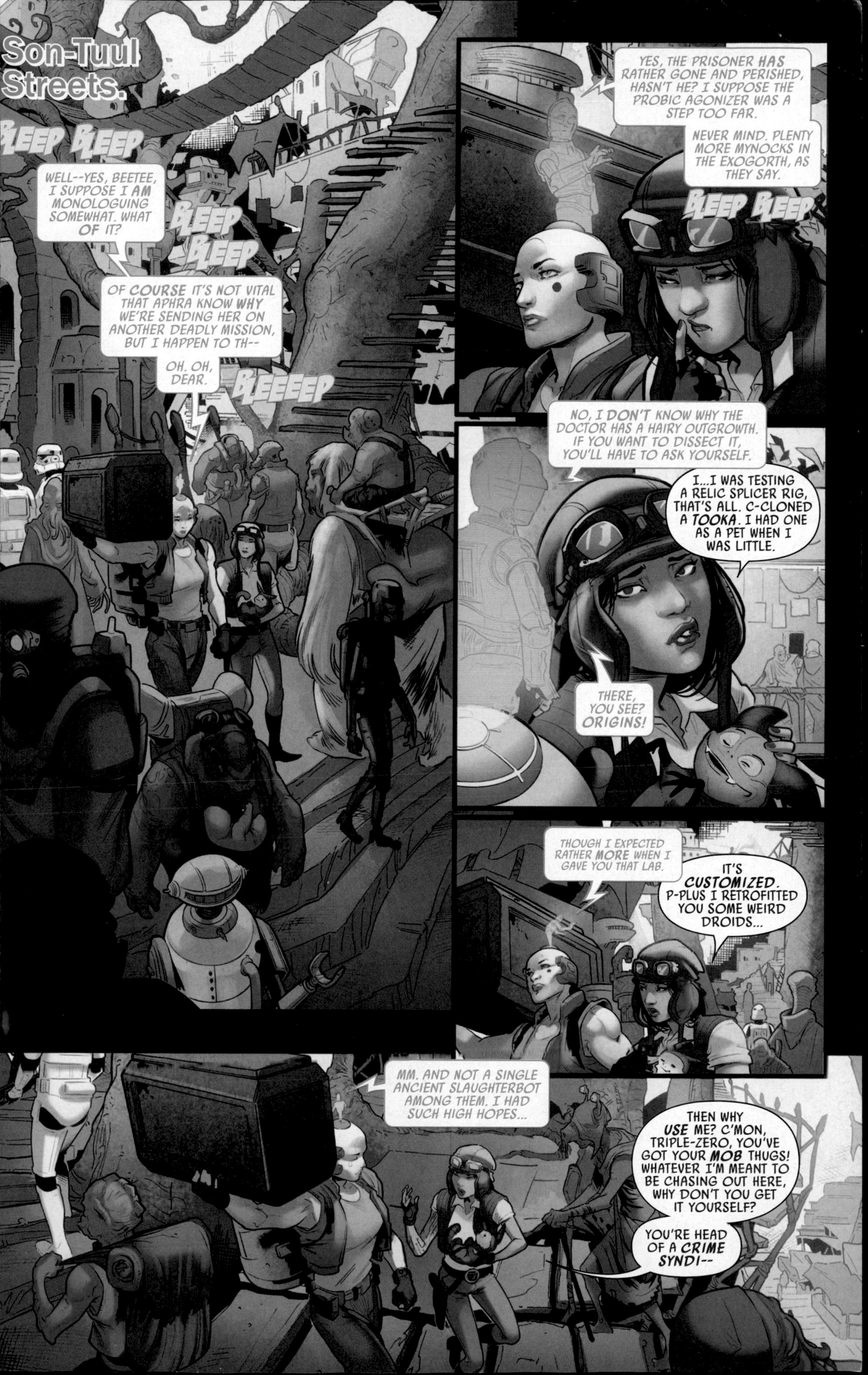

Son-Tuul Streets.
BLEEP BLEEP
WELL--YES, BEETEE, I SUPPOSE I AM MONOLOGUING SOMEWHAT. WHAT OF IT?
BLEEP BLEEP
OF COURSE IT'S NOT VITAL THAT APHRA KNOW WHY WE'RE SENDING HER ON ANOTHER DEADLY MISSION, BUT I HAPPEN TO TH--
OH. OH, DEAR.
BLEEEEP
YES, THE PRISONER HAS RATHER GONE AND PERISHED, HASN'T HE? I SUPPOSE THE PROBIC AGONIZER WAS A STEP TOO FAR.
NEVER MIND. PLENTY MORE MYNOCKS IN THE EXOGORTH, AS THEY SAY.
BLEEP BLEEP
NO, I DON'T KNOW WHY THE DOCTOR HAS A HAIRY OUTGROWTH. IF YOU WANT TO DISSECT IT, YOU'LL HAVE TO ASK YOURSELF.
I...I WAS TESTING A RELIC SPLICER RIG, THAT'S ALL. C-CLONED A TOOKA. I HAD ONE AS A PET WHEN I WAS LITTLE.
THERE, YOU SEE? ORIGINS!
THOUGH I EXPECTED RATHER MORE WHEN I GAVE YOU THAT LAB.
IT'S CUSTOMIZED. P-PLUS I RETROFITTED YOU SOME WEIRD DROIDS...
MM. AND NOT A SINGLE ANCIENT SLAUGHTERBOT AMONG THEM. I HAD SUCH HIGH HOPES...
THEN WHY USE ME? C'MON, TRIPLE-ZERO, YOU'VE GOT YOUR MOB THUGS! WHATEVER I'M MEANT TO BE CHASING OUT HERE, WHY DON'T YOU GET IT YOURSELF?
YOU'RE HEAD OF A CRIME SYNDI--

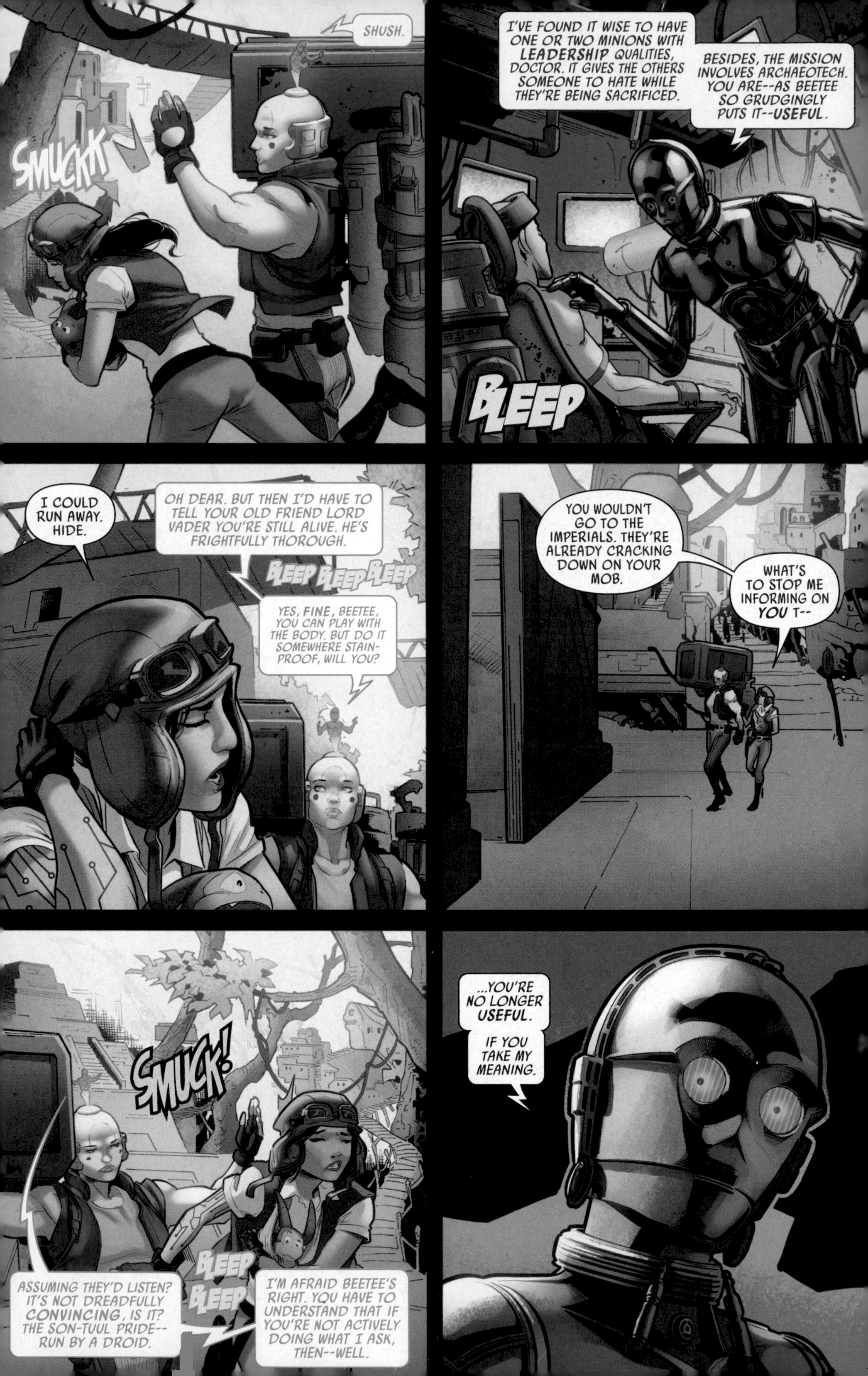
SHUSH.
SMUCKK
I'VE FOUND IT WISE TO HAVE ONE OR TWO MINIONS WITH **LEADERSHIP** QUALITIES, DOCTOR. IT GIVES THE OTHERS SOMEONE TO HATE WHILE THEY'RE BEING SACRIFICED.
BESIDES, THE MISSION INVOLVES ARCHAEOTECH. YOU ARE--AS BEETEE SO GRUDGINGLY PUTS IT--**USEFUL**.
BLEEP
I COULD RUN AWAY. HIDE.
OH DEAR. BUT THEN I'D HAVE TO TELL YOUR OLD FRIEND LORD VADER YOU'RE STILL ALIVE. HE'S FRIGHTFULLY THOROUGH.
BLEEP BLEEP BLEEP
YES, **FINE**, BEETEE, YOU CAN PLAY WITH THE BODY. BUT DO IT SOMEWHERE STAIN-PROOF, WILL YOU?
YOU WOULDN'T GO TO THE IMPERIALS. THEY'RE ALREADY CRACKING DOWN ON YOUR MOB.
WHAT'S TO STOP ME INFORMING ON **YOU** T--
SMUCK!
BLEEP BLEEP
ASSUMING THEY'D LISTEN? IT'S NOT DREADFULLY **CONVINCING**, IS IT? THE SON-TUUL PRIDE--RUN BY A DROID.
I'M AFRAID BEETEE'S RIGHT. YOU HAVE TO UNDERSTAND THAT IF YOU'RE NOT ACTIVELY DOING WHAT I ASK, THEN--WELL.
...YOU'RE NO LONGER **USEFUL**.
IF YOU TAKE MY MEANING.

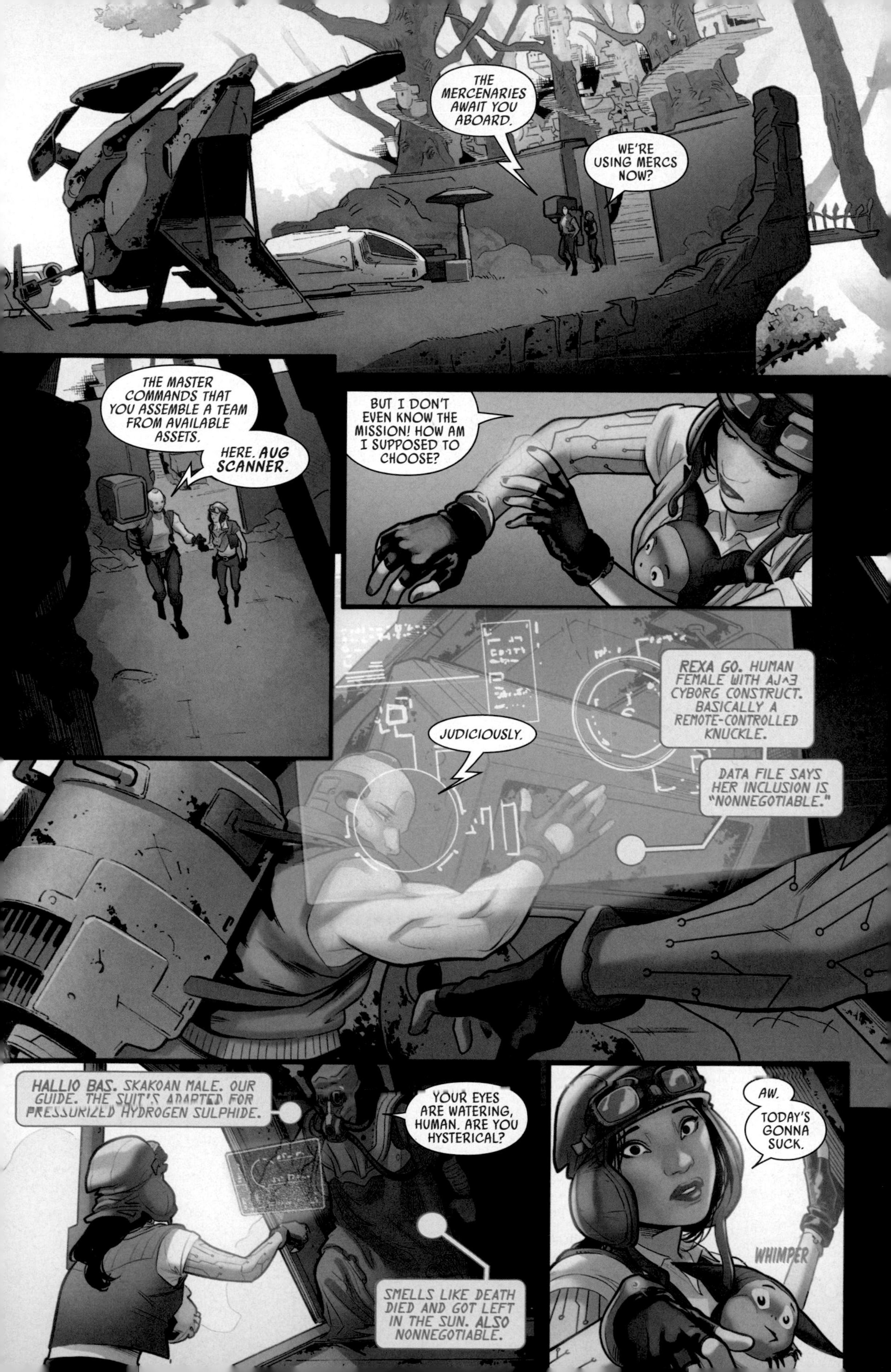
THE MERCENARIES AWAIT YOU ABOARD.
WE'RE USING MERCS NOW?
THE MASTER COMMANDS THAT YOU ASSEMBLE A TEAM FROM AVAILABLE ASSETS.
HERE. AUG SCANNER.
BUT I DON'T EVEN KNOW THE MISSION! HOW AM I SUPPOSED TO CHOOSE?
JUDICIOUSLY.
REXA GO. HUMAN FEMALE WITH AJ^3 CYBORG CONSTRUCT. BASICALLY A REMOTE-CONTROLLED KNUCKLE.
DATA FILE SAYS HER INCLUSION IS "NONNEGOTIABLE."
HALLIO BAS. SKAKOAN MALE. OUR GUIDE. THE SUIT'S ADAPTED FOR PRESSURIZED HYDROGEN SULPHIDE.
YOUR EYES ARE WATERING, HUMAN. ARE YOU HYSTERICAL?
SMELLS LIKE DEATH DIED AND GOT LEFT IN THE SUN. ALSO NONNEGOTIABLE.
AW.
TODAY'S GONNA SUCK.
WHIMPER

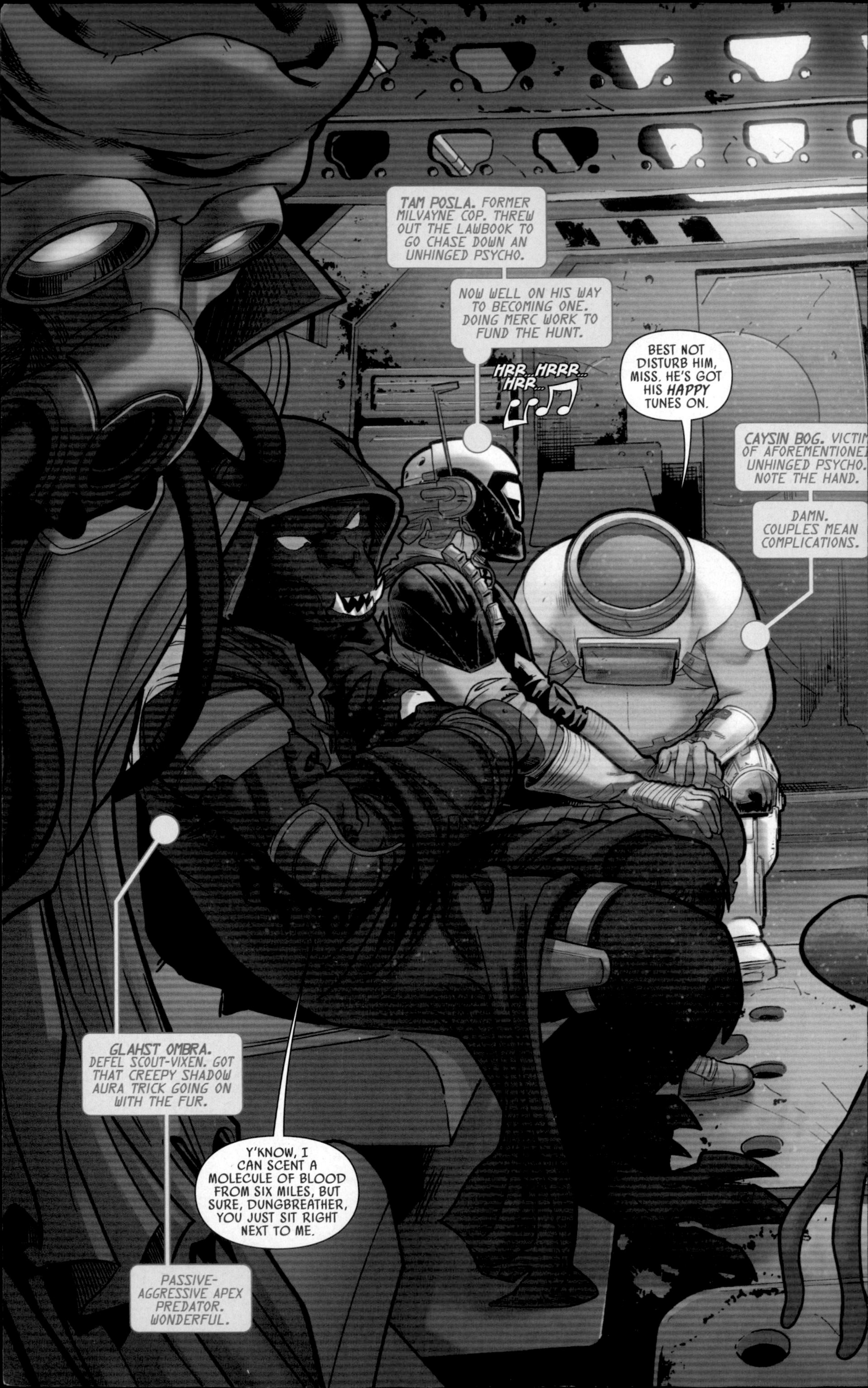
TAM POSLA. FORMER MILVAYNE COP. THREW OUT THE LAWBOOK TO GO CHASE DOWN AN UNHINGED PSYCHO.
NOW WELL ON HIS WAY TO BECOMING ONE. DOING MERC WORK TO FUND THE HUNT.
HRR...HRRR... HRR...
BEST NOT DISTURB HIM, MISS. HE'S GOT HIS *HAPPY* TUNES ON.
CAYSIN BOG. VICTIM OF AFOREMENTIONED UNHINGED PSYCHO. NOTE THE HAND.
DAMN. COUPLES MEAN COMPLICATIONS.
GLAHST OMBRA. DEFEL SCOUT-VIXEN. GOT THAT CREEPY SHADOW AURA TRICK GOING ON WITH THE FUR.
Y'KNOW, I CAN SCENT A MOLECULE OF BLOOD FROM SIX MILES, BUT SURE, DUNGBREATHER, YOU JUST SIT RIGHT NEXT TO ME.
PASSIVE-AGGRESSIVE APEX PREDATOR. WONDERFUL.

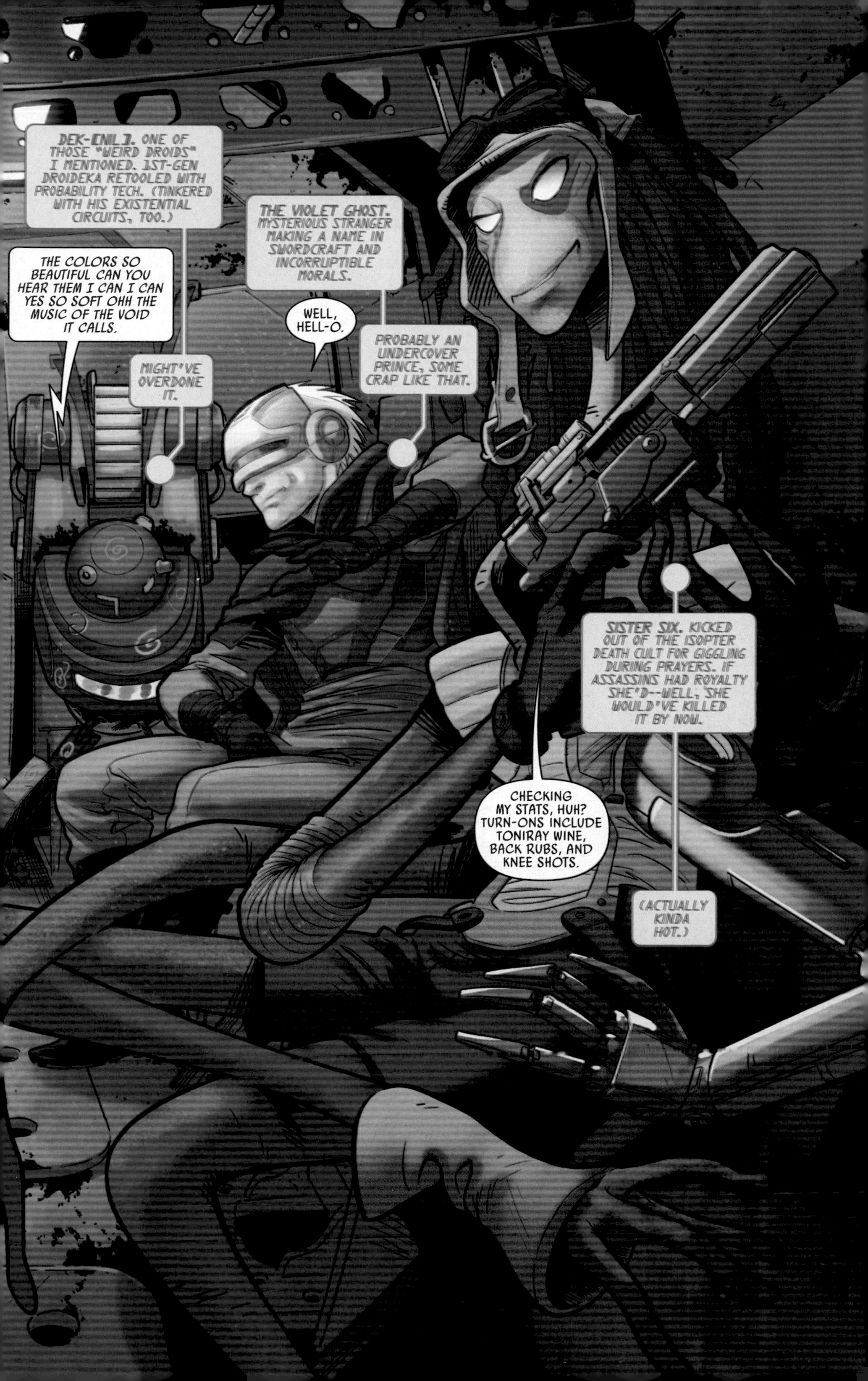
DEK-[NIL]. ONE OF THOSE "WEIRD DROIDS" I MENTIONED. 1ST-GEN DROIDEKA RETOOLED WITH PROBABILITY TECH. (TINKERED WITH HIS EXISTENTIAL CIRCUITS, TOO.)
THE COLORS SO BEAUTIFUL CAN YOU HEAR THEM I CAN I CAN YES SO SOFT OHH THE MUSIC OF THE VOID IT CALLS.
MIGHT'VE OVERDONE IT.
THE VIOLET GHOST. MYSTERIOUS STRANGER MAKING A NAME IN SWORDCRAFT AND INCORRUPTIBLE MORALS.
WELL, HELL-O.
PROBABLY AN UNDERCOVER PRINCE, SOME CRAP LIKE THAT.
SISTER SIX. KICKED OUT OF THE ISOPTER DEATH CULT FOR GIGGLING DURING PRAYERS. IF ASSASSINS HAD ROYALTY SHE'D--WELL, SHE WOULD'VE KILLED IT BY NOW.
CHECKING MY STATS, HUH? TURN-ONS INCLUDE TONIRAY WINE, BACK RUBS, AND KNEE SHOTS.
(ACTUALLY KINDA HOT.)

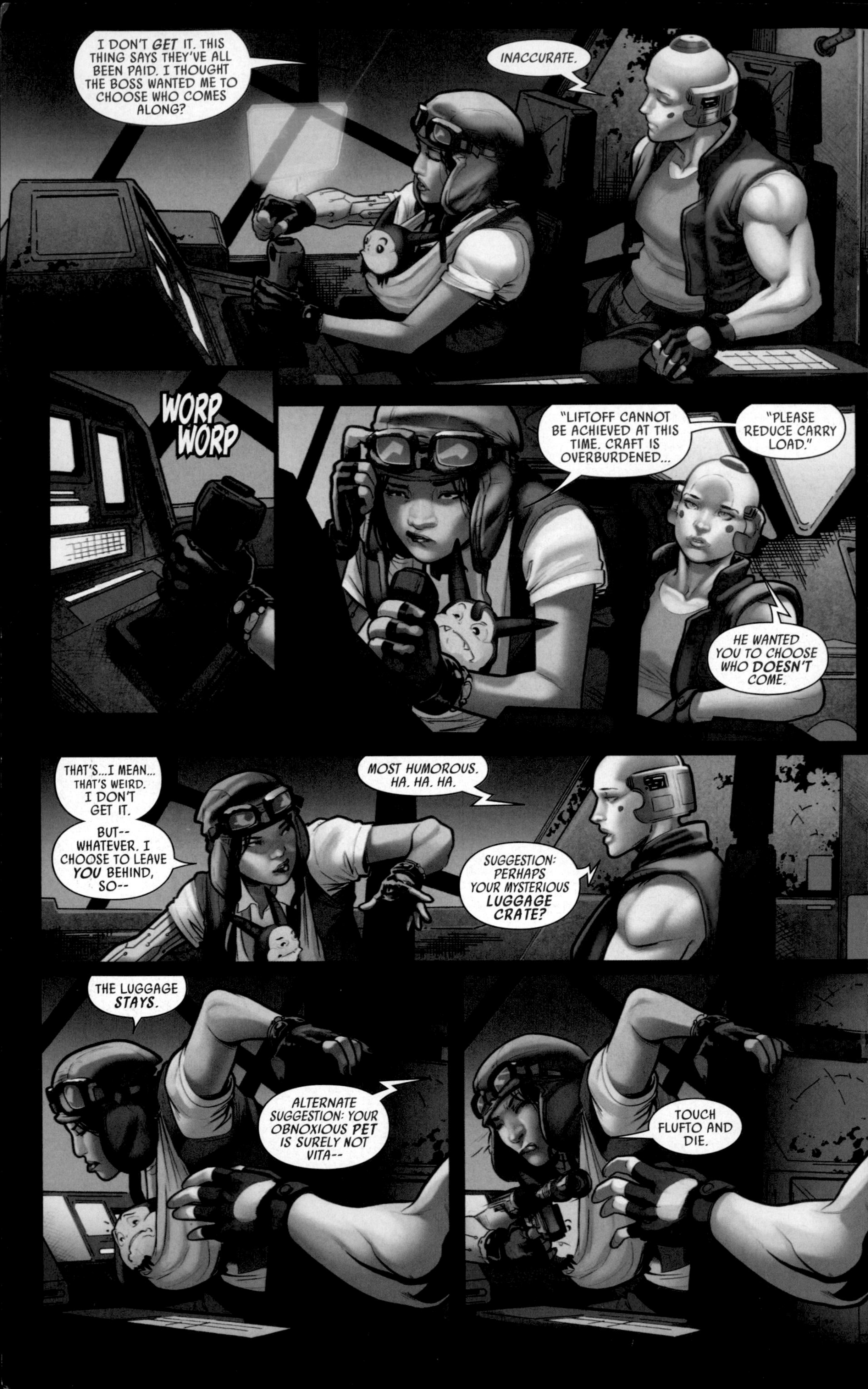
I DON'T GET IT. THIS THING SAYS THEY'VE ALL BEEN PAID. I THOUGHT THE BOSS WANTED ME TO CHOOSE WHO COMES ALONG?
INACCURATE.
WORP WORP
"LIFTOFF CANNOT BE ACHIEVED AT THIS TIME. CRAFT IS OVERBURDENED...
"PLEASE REDUCE CARRY LOAD."
HE WANTED YOU TO CHOOSE WHO DOESN'T COME.
THAT'S...I MEAN... THAT'S WEIRD. I DON'T GET IT.
BUT-- WHATEVER. I CHOOSE TO LEAVE YOU BEHIND, SO--
MOST HUMOROUS. HA. HA. HA.
SUGGESTION: PERHAPS YOUR MYSTERIOUS LUGGAGE CRATE?
THE LUGGAGE STAYS.
ALTERNATE SUGGESTION: YOUR OBNOXIOUS PET IS SURELY NOT VITA--
TOUCH FLUFTO AND DIE.

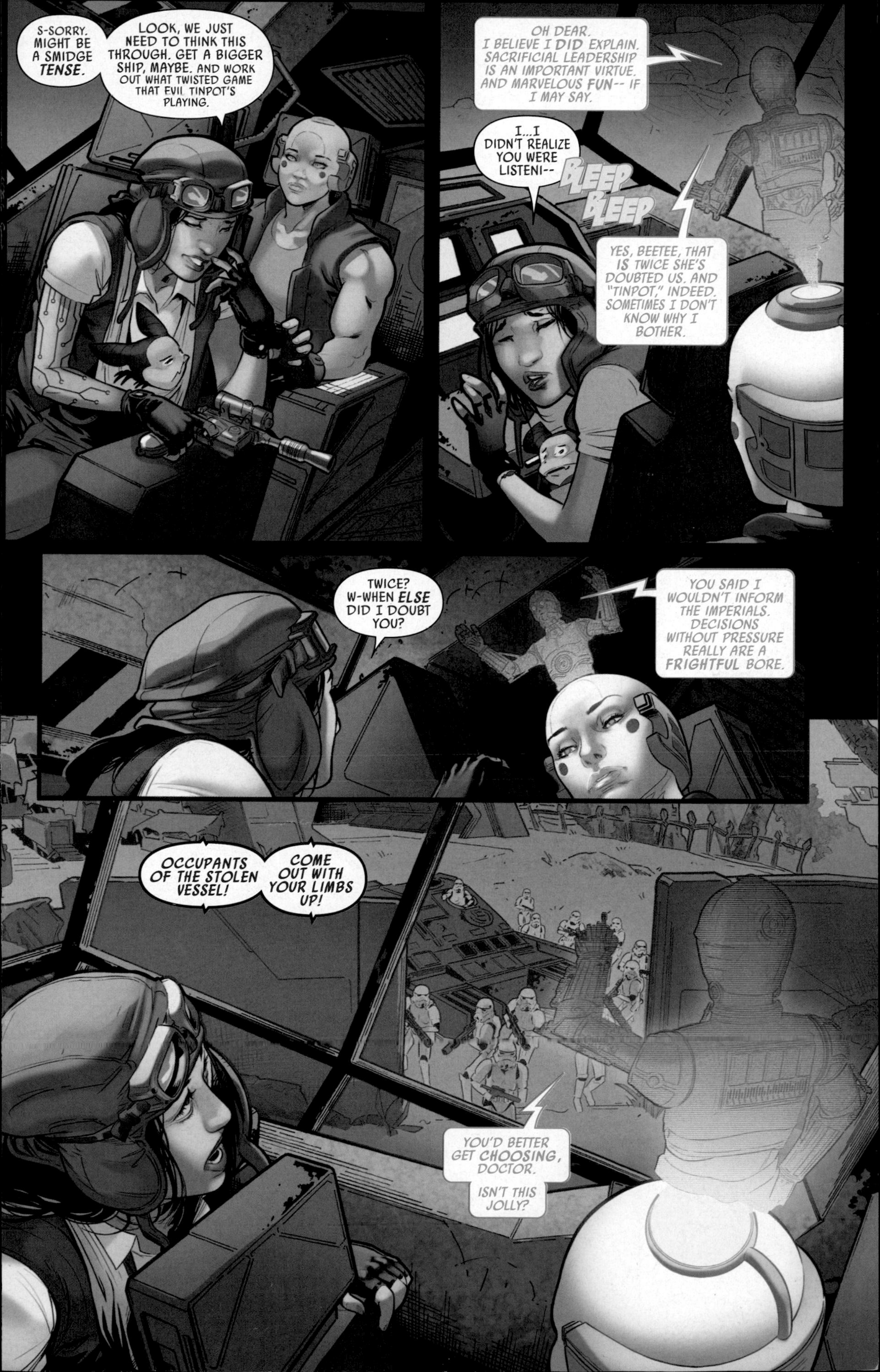
S-SORRY. MIGHT BE A SMIDGE TENSE.
LOOK, WE JUST NEED TO THINK THIS THROUGH. GET A BIGGER SHIP, MAYBE. AND WORK OUT WHAT TWISTED GAME THAT EVIL TINPOT'S PLAYING.
OH DEAR. I BELIEVE I DID EXPLAIN. SACRIFICIAL LEADERSHIP IS AN IMPORTANT VIRTUE. AND MARVELOUS FUN-- IF I MAY SAY.
I...I DIDN'T REALIZE YOU WERE LISTENI--
BLEEP BLEEP
YES, BEETEE, THAT IS TWICE SHE'S DOUBTED US. AND "TINPOT," INDEED. SOMETIMES I DON'T KNOW WHY I BOTHER.
TWICE? W-WHEN ELSE DID I DOUBT YOU?
YOU SAID I WOULDN'T INFORM THE IMPERIALS. DECISIONS WITHOUT PRESSURE REALLY ARE A FRIGHTFUL BORE.
OCCUPANTS OF THE STOLEN VESSEL!
COME OUT WITH YOUR LIMBS UP!
YOU'D BETTER GET CHOOSING, DOCTOR.
ISN'T THIS JOLLY?

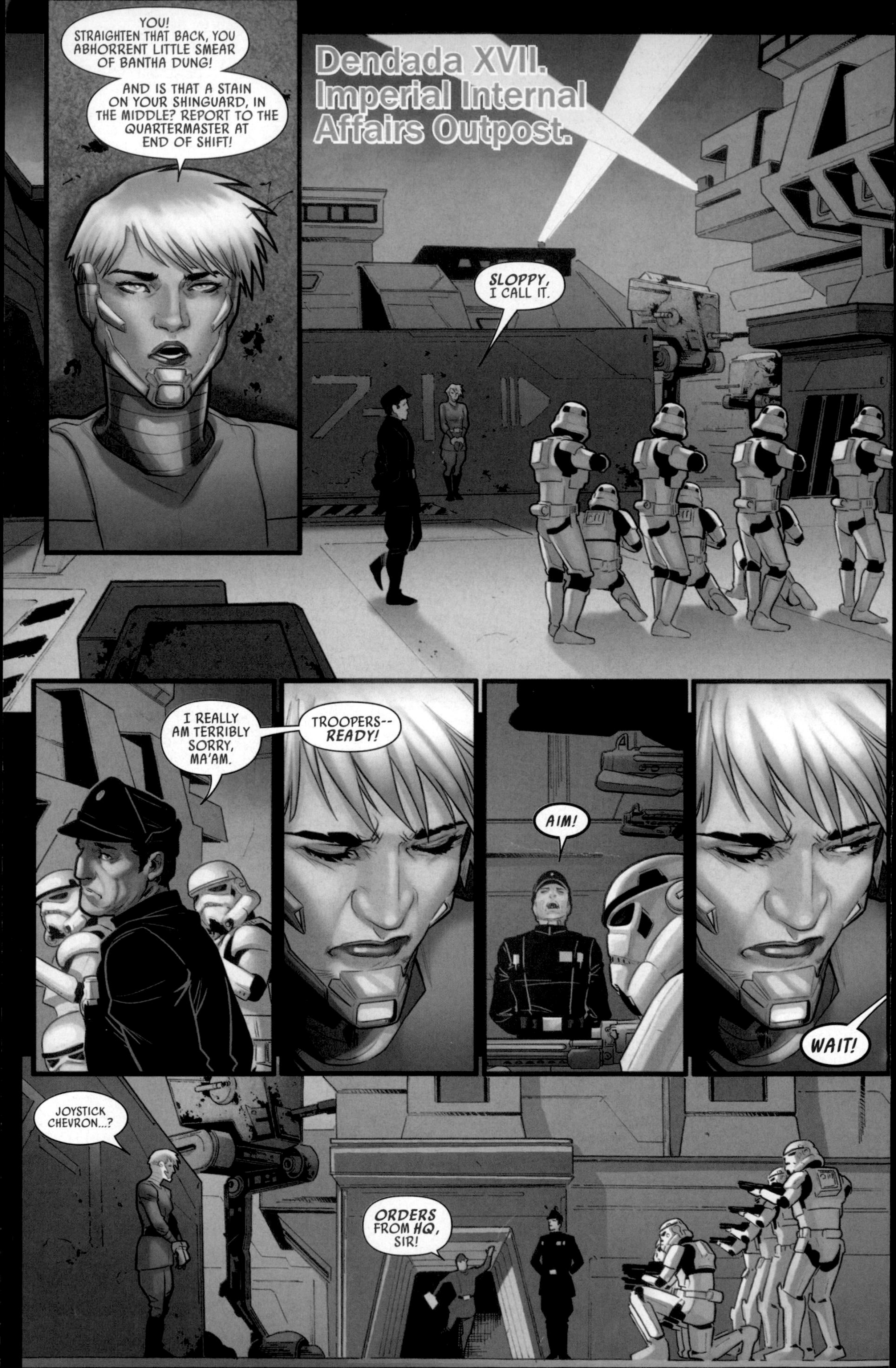
YOU! STRAIGHTEN THAT BACK, YOU ABHORRENT LITTLE SMEAR OF BANTHA DUNG!
AND IS THAT A STAIN ON YOUR SHINGUARD, IN THE MIDDLE? REPORT TO THE QUARTERMASTER AT END OF SHIFT!
Dendada XVII. Imperial Internal Affairs Outpost.
SLOPPY, I CALL IT.
I REALLY AM TERRIBLY SORRY, MA'AM.
TROOPERS-- READY!
AIM!
WAIT!
JOYSTICK CHEVRON...?
ORDERS FROM HQ, SIR!

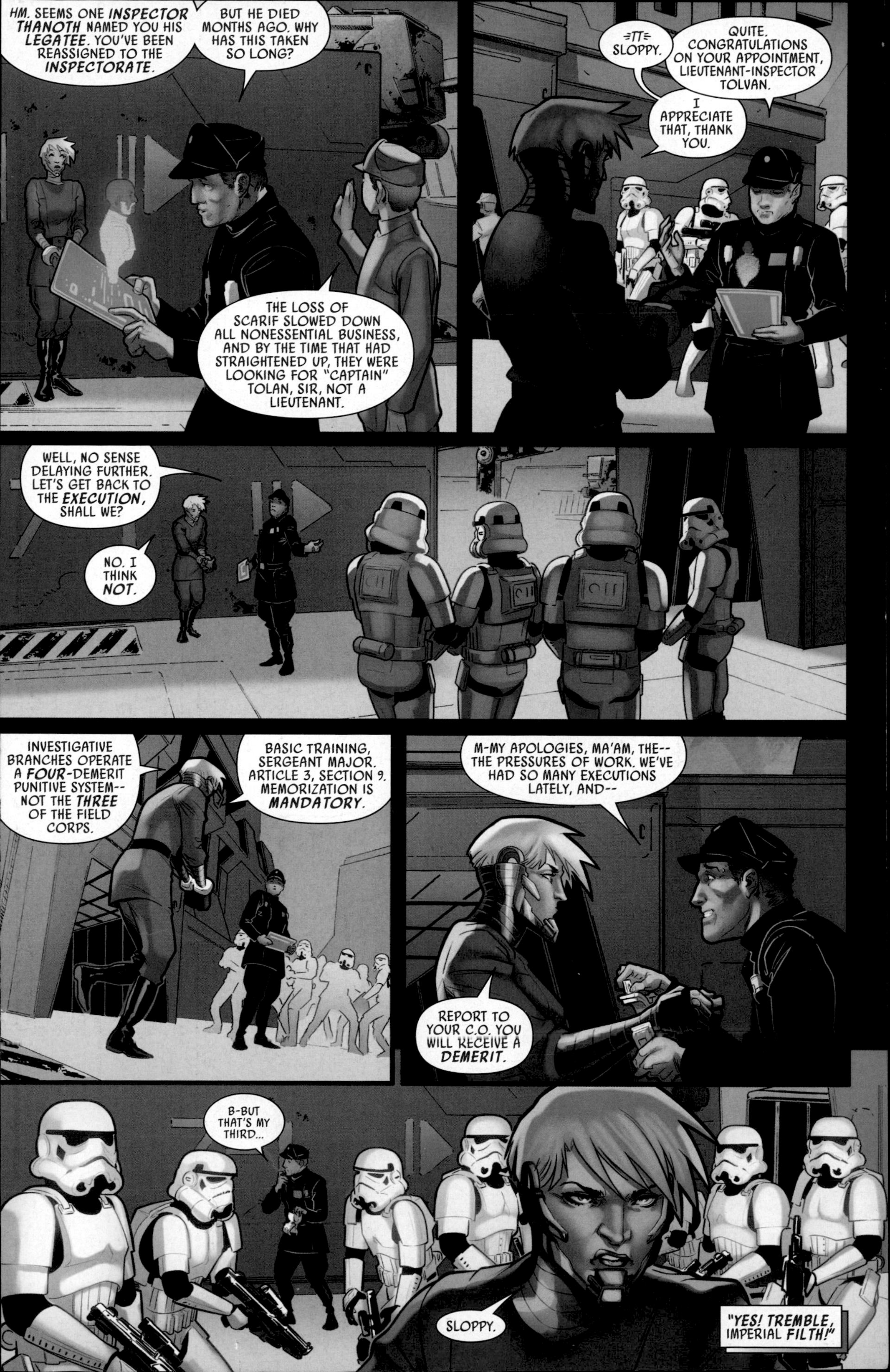
HM. SEEMS ONE INSPECTOR THANOTH NAMED YOU HIS LEGATEE. YOU'VE BEEN REASSIGNED TO THE INSPECTORATE.
BUT HE DIED MONTHS AGO. WHY HAS THIS TAKEN SO LONG?
THE LOSS OF SCARIF SLOWED DOWN ALL NONESSENTIAL BUSINESS, AND BY THE TIME THAT HAD STRAIGHTENED UP, THEY WERE LOOKING FOR "CAPTAIN" TOLAN, SIR, NOT A LIEUTENANT.
TT SLOPPY.
QUITE. CONGRATULATIONS ON YOUR APPOINTMENT, LIEUTENANT-INSPECTOR TOLVAN.
I APPRECIATE THAT, THANK YOU.
WELL, NO SENSE DELAYING FURTHER. LET'S GET BACK TO THE EXECUTION, SHALL WE?
NO. I THINK NOT.
INVESTIGATIVE BRANCHES OPERATE A FOUR-DEMERIT PUNITIVE SYSTEM-- NOT THE THREE OF THE FIELD CORPS.
BASIC TRAINING, SERGEANT MAJOR. ARTICLE 3, SECTION 9. MEMORIZATION IS MANDATORY.
M-MY APOLOGIES, MA'AM, THE-- THE PRESSURES OF WORK. WE'VE HAD SO MANY EXECUTIONS LATELY, AND--
REPORT TO YOUR C.O. YOU WILL RECEIVE A DEMERIT.
B-BUT THAT'S MY THIRD...
SLOPPY.
"YES! TREMBLE, IMPERIAL FILTH!"

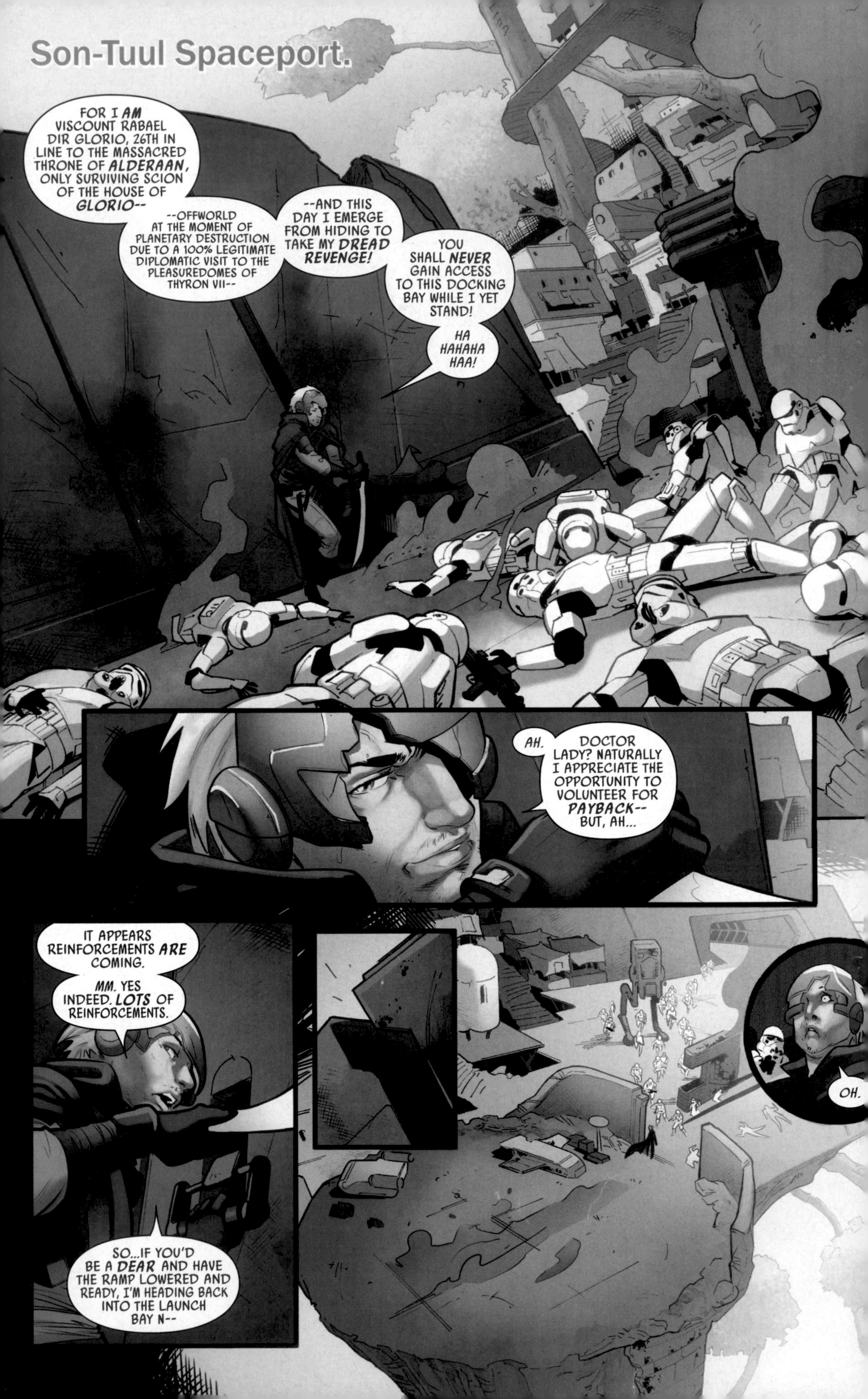
Son-Tuul Spaceport.
FOR I AM VISCOUNT RABAEL DIR GLORIO, 26TH IN LINE TO THE MASSACRED THRONE OF ALDERAAN, ONLY SURVIVING SCION OF THE HOUSE OF GLORIO--
--OFFWORLD AT THE MOMENT OF PLANETARY DESTRUCTION DUE TO A 100% LEGITIMATE DIPLOMATIC VISIT TO THE PLEASUREDOMES OF THYRON VII--
--AND THIS DAY I EMERGE FROM HIDING TO TAKE MY DREAD REVENGE!
YOU SHALL NEVER GAIN ACCESS TO THIS DOCKING BAY WHILE I YET STAND!
HA HAHAHA HAA!
AH.
DOCTOR LADY? NATURALLY I APPRECIATE THE OPPORTUNITY TO VOLUNTEER FOR PAYBACK-- BUT, AH...
IT APPEARS REINFORCEMENTS ARE COMING.
MM. YES INDEED. LOTS OF REINFORCEMENTS.
SO...IF YOU'D BE A DEAR AND HAVE THE RAMP LOWERED AND READY, I'M HEADING BACK INTO THE LAUNCH BAY N--
OH.

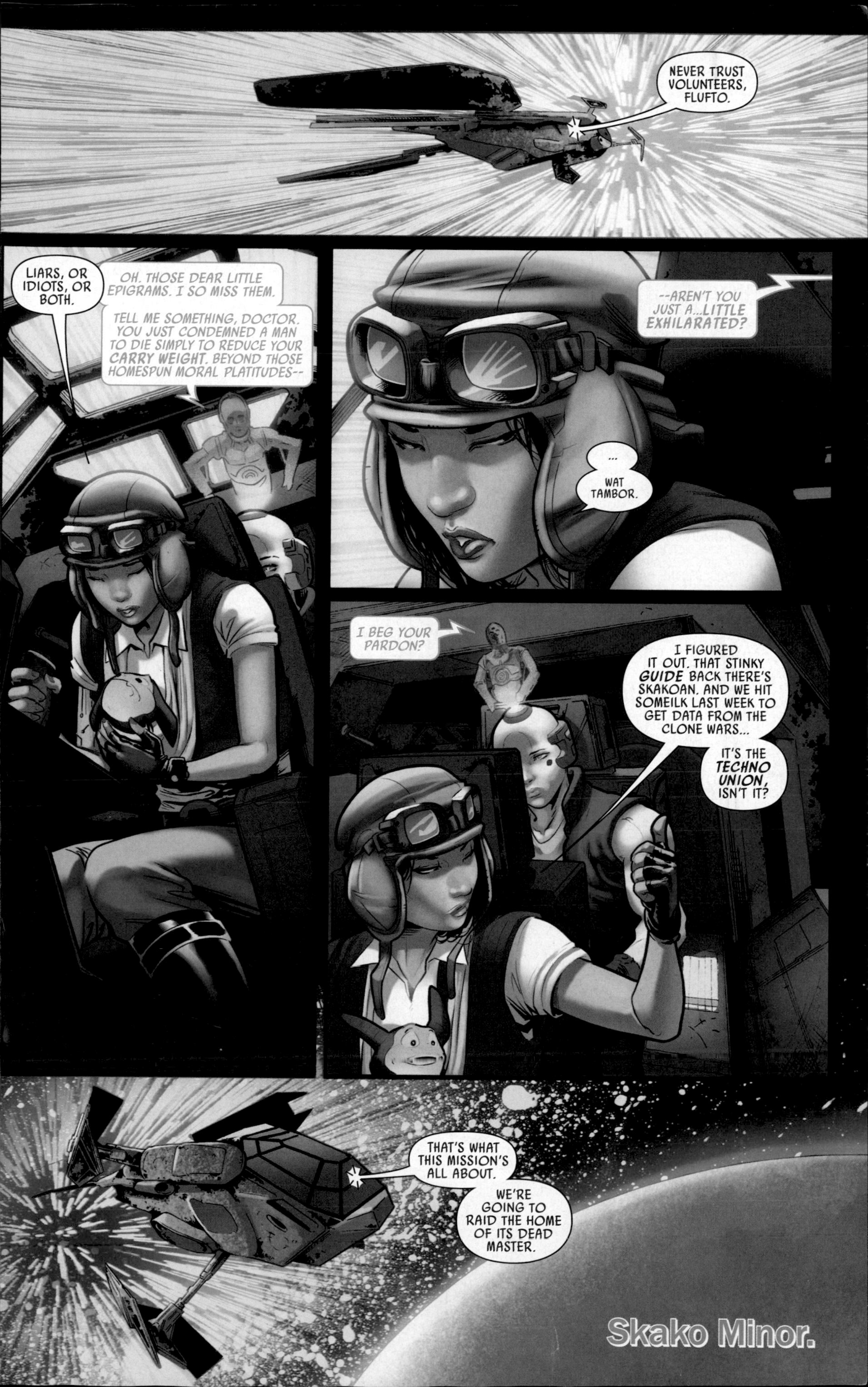

NEVER TRUST VOLUNTEERS, FLUFTO.
LIARS, OR IDIOTS, OR BOTH.
OH. THOSE DEAR LITTLE EPIGRAMS. I SO MISS THEM.
TELL ME SOMETHING, DOCTOR. YOU JUST CONDEMNED A MAN TO DIE SIMPLY TO REDUCE YOUR CARRY WEIGHT. BEYOND THOSE HOMESPUN MORAL PLATITUDES--
--AREN'T YOU JUST A...LITTLE EXHILARATED?
... WAT TAMBOR.
I BEG YOUR PARDON?
I FIGURED IT OUT. THAT STINKY GUIDE BACK THERE'S SKAKOAN. AND WE HIT SOMEILK LAST WEEK TO GET DATA FROM THE CLONE WARS...
IT'S THE TECHNO UNION, ISN'T IT?
THAT'S WHAT THIS MISSION'S ALL ABOUT.
WE'RE GOING TO RAID THE HOME OF ITS DEAD MASTER.
Skako Minor.

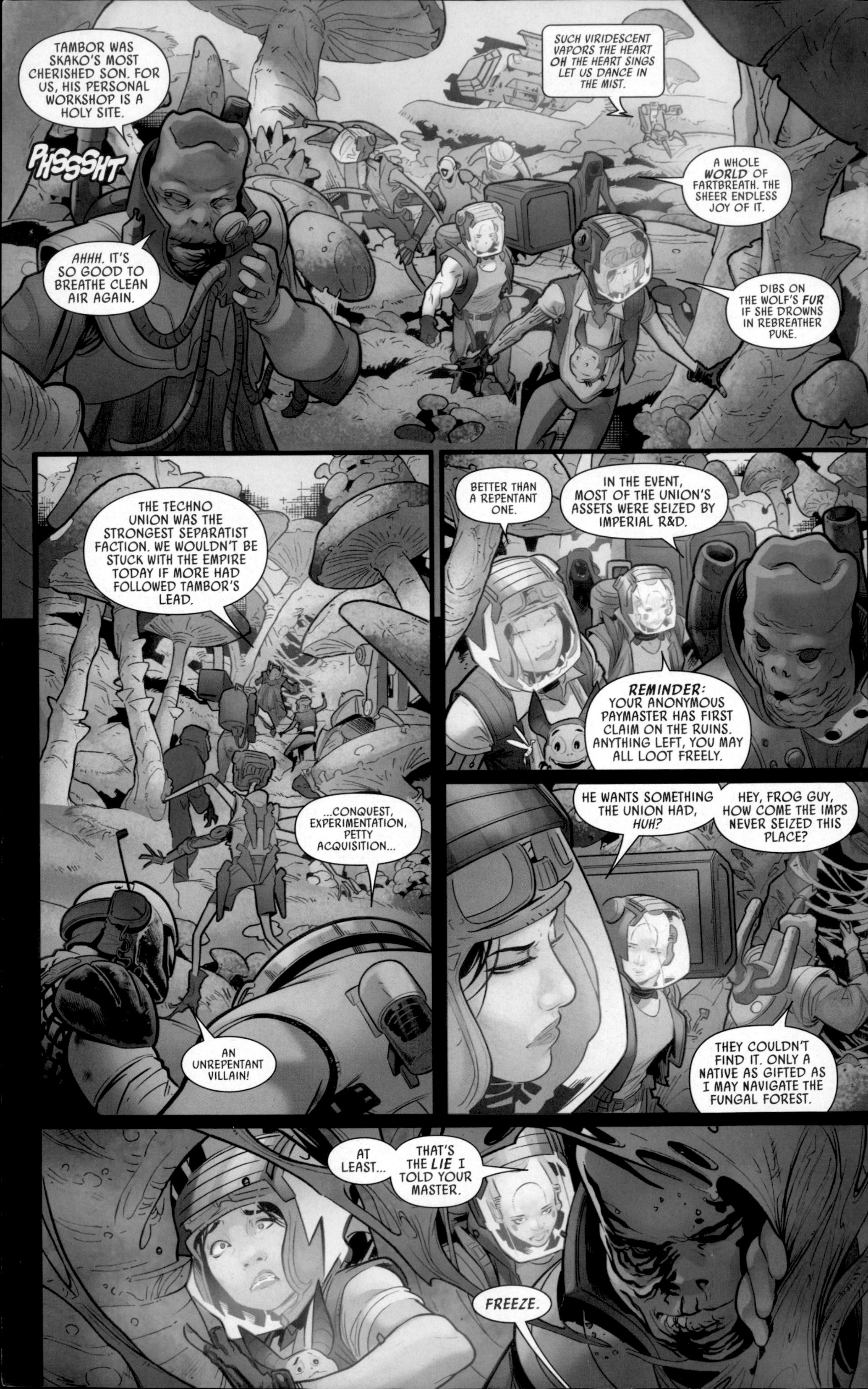
TAMBOR WAS SKAKO'S MOST CHERISHED SON. FOR US, HIS PERSONAL WORKSHOP IS A HOLY SITE.
PHSSSHT
AHHH. IT'S SO GOOD TO BREATHE CLEAN AIR AGAIN.
SUCH VIRIDESCENT VAPORS THE HEART OH THE HEART SINGS LET US DANCE IN THE MIST.
A WHOLE WORLD OF FARTBREATH. THE SHEER ENDLESS JOY OF IT.
DIBS ON THE WOLF'S FUR IF SHE DROWNS IN REBREATHER PUKE.
THE TECHNO UNION WAS THE STRONGEST SEPARATIST FACTION. WE WOULDN'T BE STUCK WITH THE EMPIRE TODAY IF MORE HAD FOLLOWED TAMBOR'S LEAD.
...CONQUEST, EXPERIMENTATION, PETTY ACQUISITION...
AN UNREPENTANT VILLAIN!
BETTER THAN A REPENTANT ONE.
IN THE EVENT, MOST OF THE UNION'S ASSETS WERE SEIZED BY IMPERIAL R&D.
REMINDER: YOUR ANONYMOUS PAYMASTER HAS FIRST CLAIM ON THE RUINS. ANYTHING LEFT, YOU MAY ALL LOOT FREELY.
HE WANTS SOMETHING THE UNION HAD, HUH?
HEY, FROG GUY, HOW COME THE IMPS NEVER SEIZED THIS PLACE?
THEY COULDN'T FIND IT. ONLY A NATIVE AS GIFTED AS I MAY NAVIGATE THE FUNGAL FOREST.
AT LEAST...
THAT'S THE LIE I TOLD YOUR MASTER.
FREEZE.

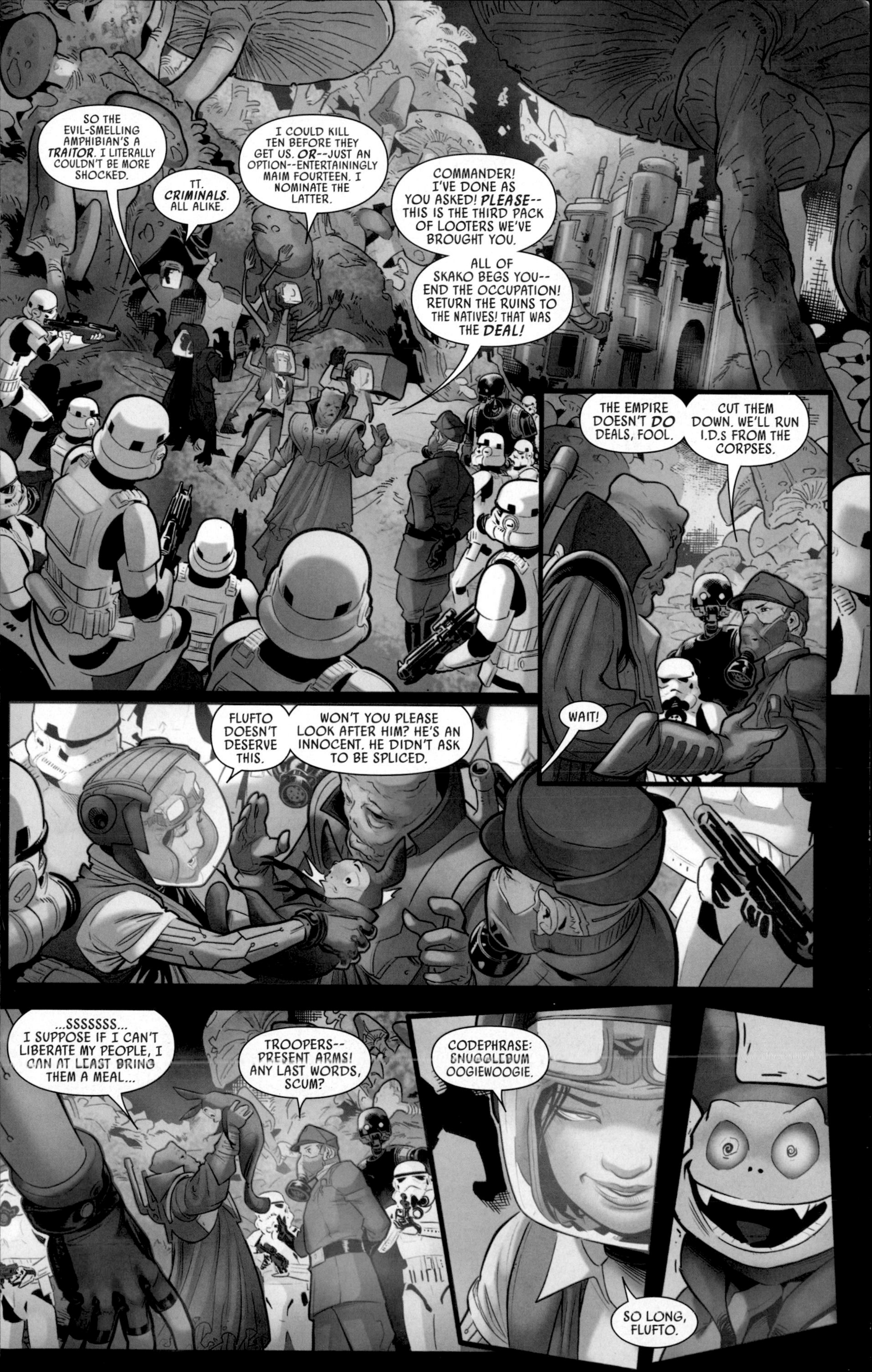

SO THE EVIL-SMELLING AMPHIBIAN'S A TRAITOR. I LITERALLY COULDN'T BE MORE SHOCKED.
TT. CRIMINALS. ALL ALIKE.
I COULD KILL TEN BEFORE THEY GET US. OR--JUST AN OPTION--ENTERTAININGLY MAIM FOURTEEN. I NOMINATE THE LATTER.
COMMANDER! I'VE DONE AS YOU ASKED! PLEASE-- THIS IS THE THIRD PACK OF LOOTERS WE'VE BROUGHT YOU.
ALL OF SKAKO BEGS YOU-- END THE OCCUPATION! RETURN THE RUINS TO THE NATIVES! THAT WAS THE DEAL!
THE EMPIRE DOESN'T DO DEALS, FOOL.
CUT THEM DOWN. WE'LL RUN I.D.s FROM THE CORPSES.
WAIT!
FLUFTO DOESN'T DESERVE THIS.
WON'T YOU PLEASE LOOK AFTER HIM? HE'S AN INNOCENT. HE DIDN'T ASK TO BE SPLICED.
...SSSSSSS... I SUPPOSE IF I CAN'T LIBERATE MY PEOPLE, I CAN AT LEAST BRING THEM A MEAL...
TROOPERS-- PRESENT ARMS! ANY LAST WORDS, SCUM?
CODEPHRASE: SNUGGLEBUM OOGIEWOOGIE.
SO LONG, FLUFTO.

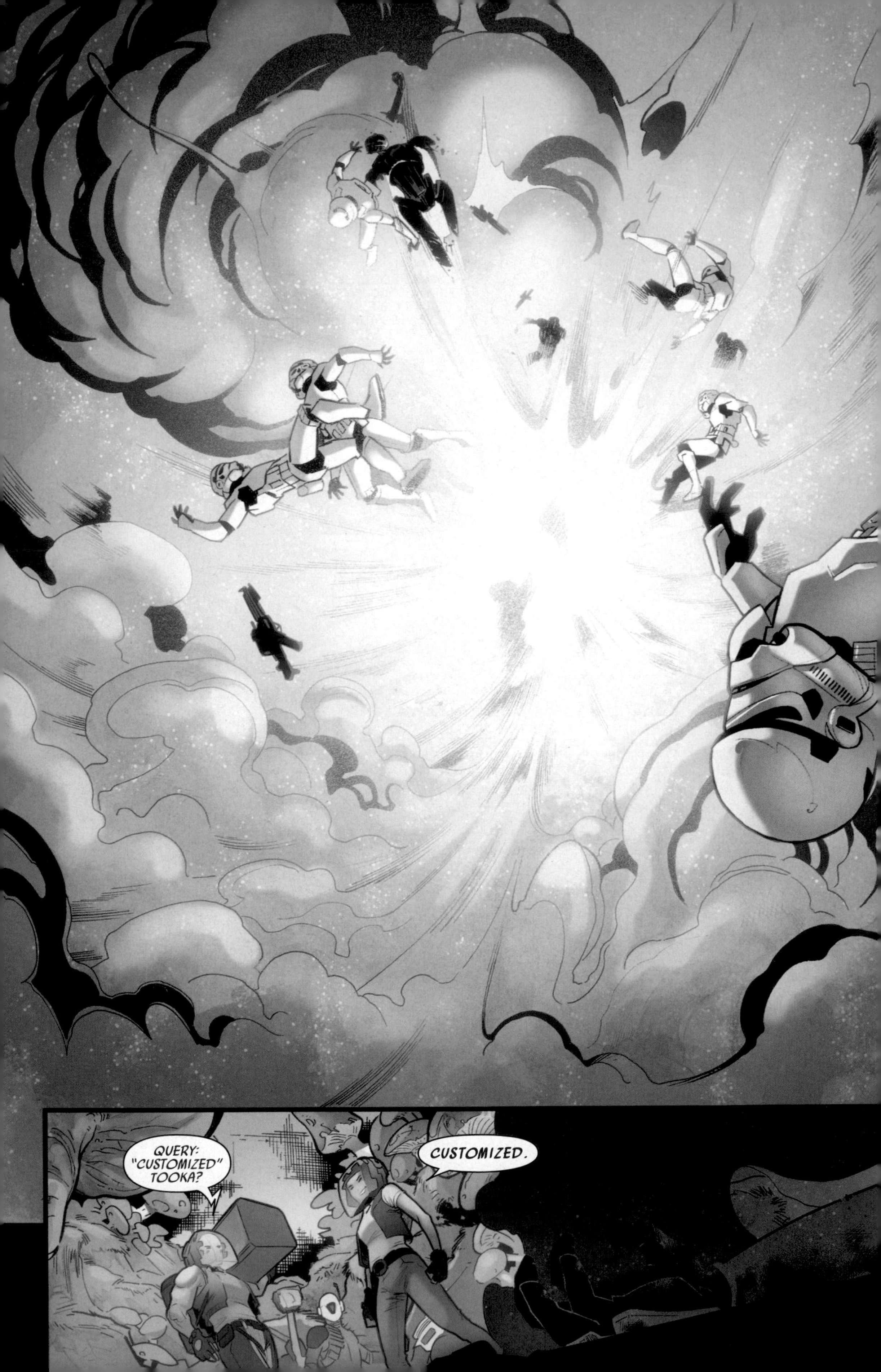
QUERY: "CUSTOMIZED" TOOKA?
CUSTOMIZED.

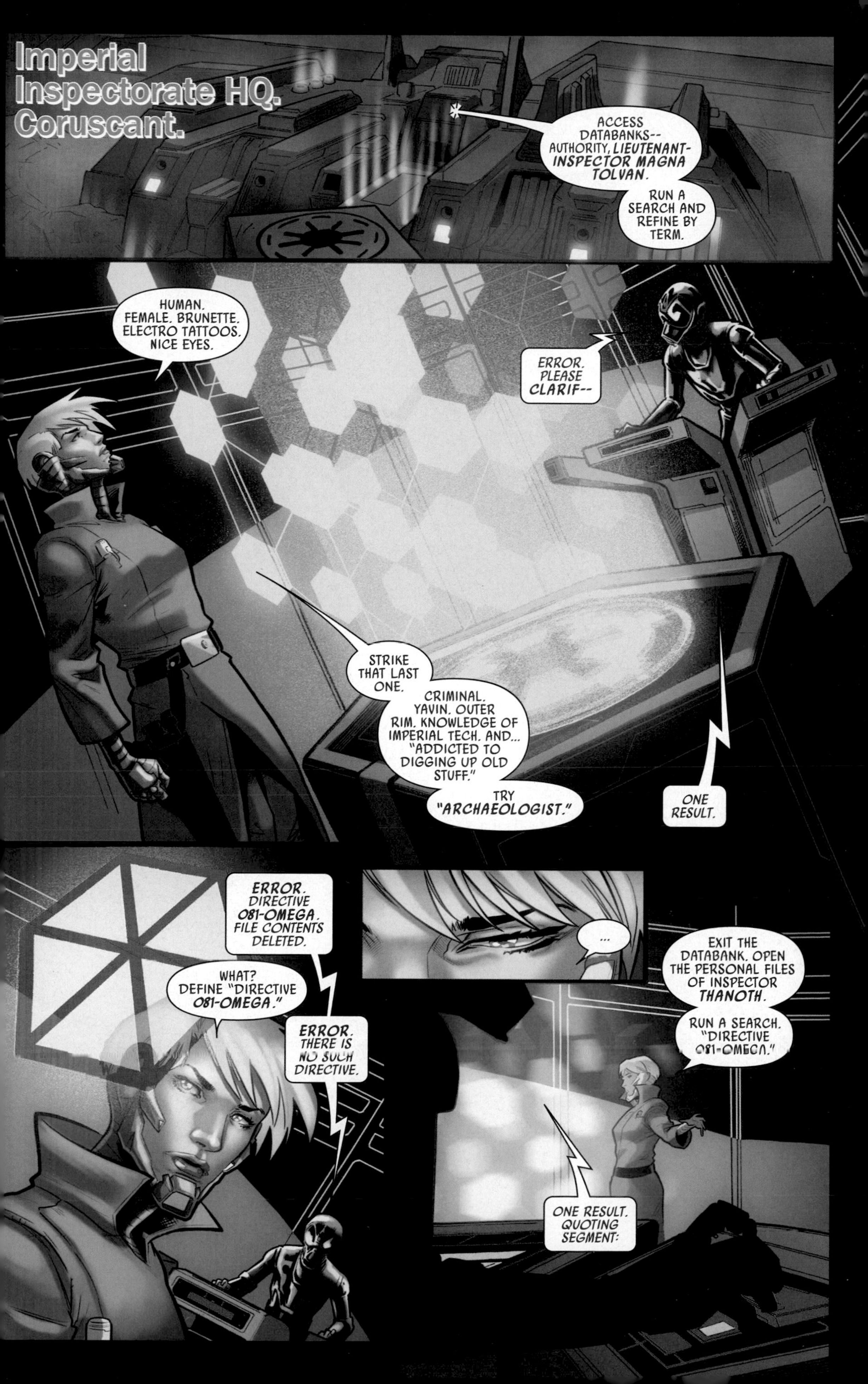

Imperial Inspectorate HQ. Coruscant.
ACCESS DATABANKS-- AUTHORITY, LIEUTENANT-INSPECTOR MAGNA TOLVAN.
RUN A SEARCH AND REFINE BY TERM.
HUMAN. FEMALE. BRUNETTE. ELECTRO TATTOOS. NICE EYES.
ERROR. PLEASE CLARIF--
STRIKE THAT LAST ONE.
CRIMINAL. YAVIN. OUTER RIM. KNOWLEDGE OF IMPERIAL TECH. AND... "ADDICTED TO DIGGING UP OLD STUFF."
TRY "ARCHAEOLOGIST."
ONE RESULT.
ERROR. DIRECTIVE 081-OMEGA. FILE CONTENTS DELETED.
WHAT? DEFINE "DIRECTIVE 081-OMEGA."
ERROR. THERE IS NO SUCH DIRECTIVE.
...
EXIT THE DATABANK. OPEN THE PERSONAL FILES OF INSPECTOR THANOTH.
RUN A SEARCH. "DIRECTIVE 081-OMEGA."
ONE RESULT. QUOTING SEGMENT:

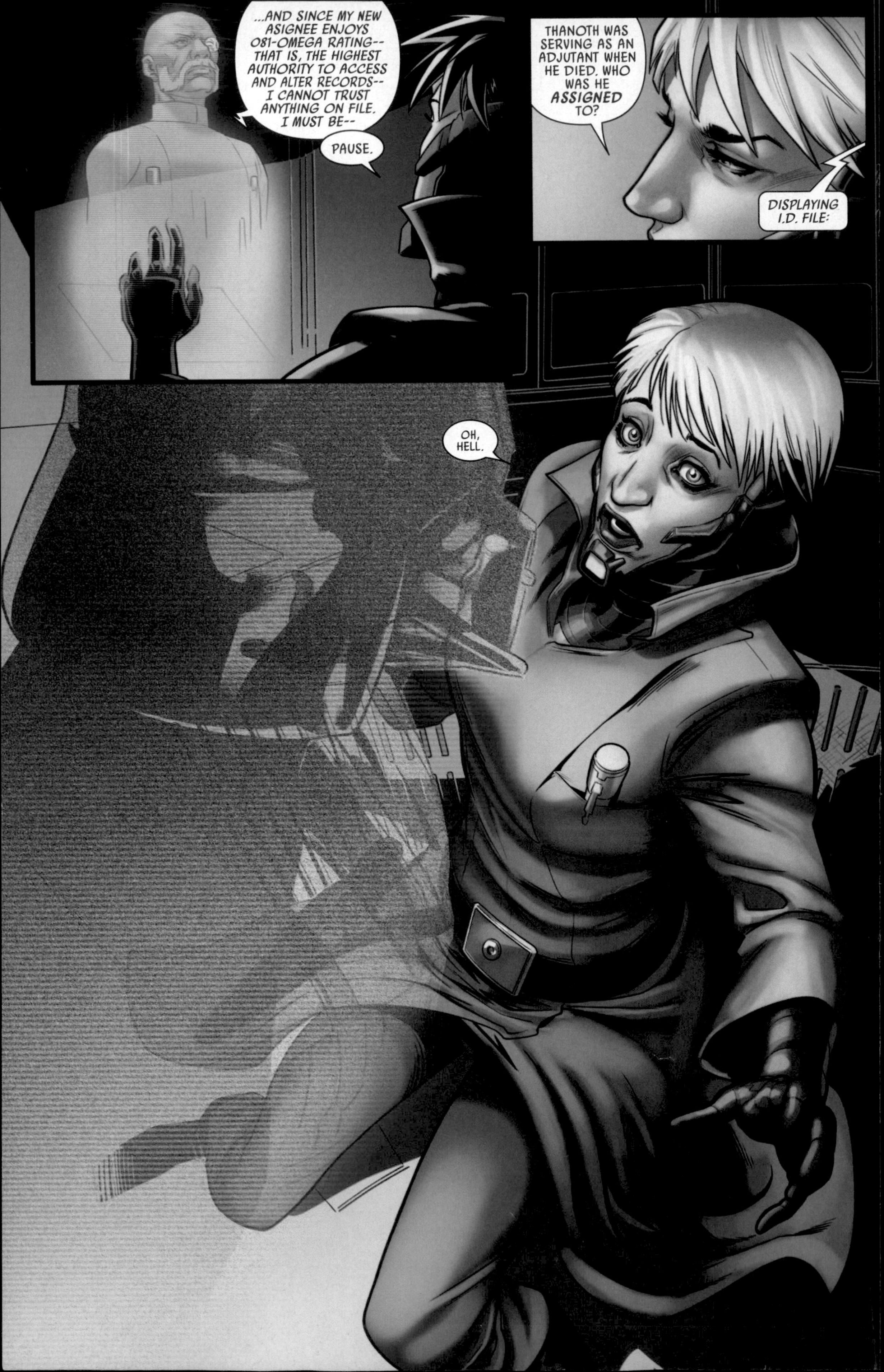
...AND SINCE MY NEW ASIGNEE ENJOYS 081-OMEGA RATING-- THAT IS, THE HIGHEST AUTHORITY TO ACCESS AND ALTER RECORDS-- I CANNOT TRUST ANYTHING ON FILE. I MUST BE--
PAUSE.
THANOTH WAS SERVING AS AN ADJUTANT WHEN HE DIED. WHO WAS HE ASSIGNED TO?
DISPLAYING I.D. FILE:
OH, HELL.

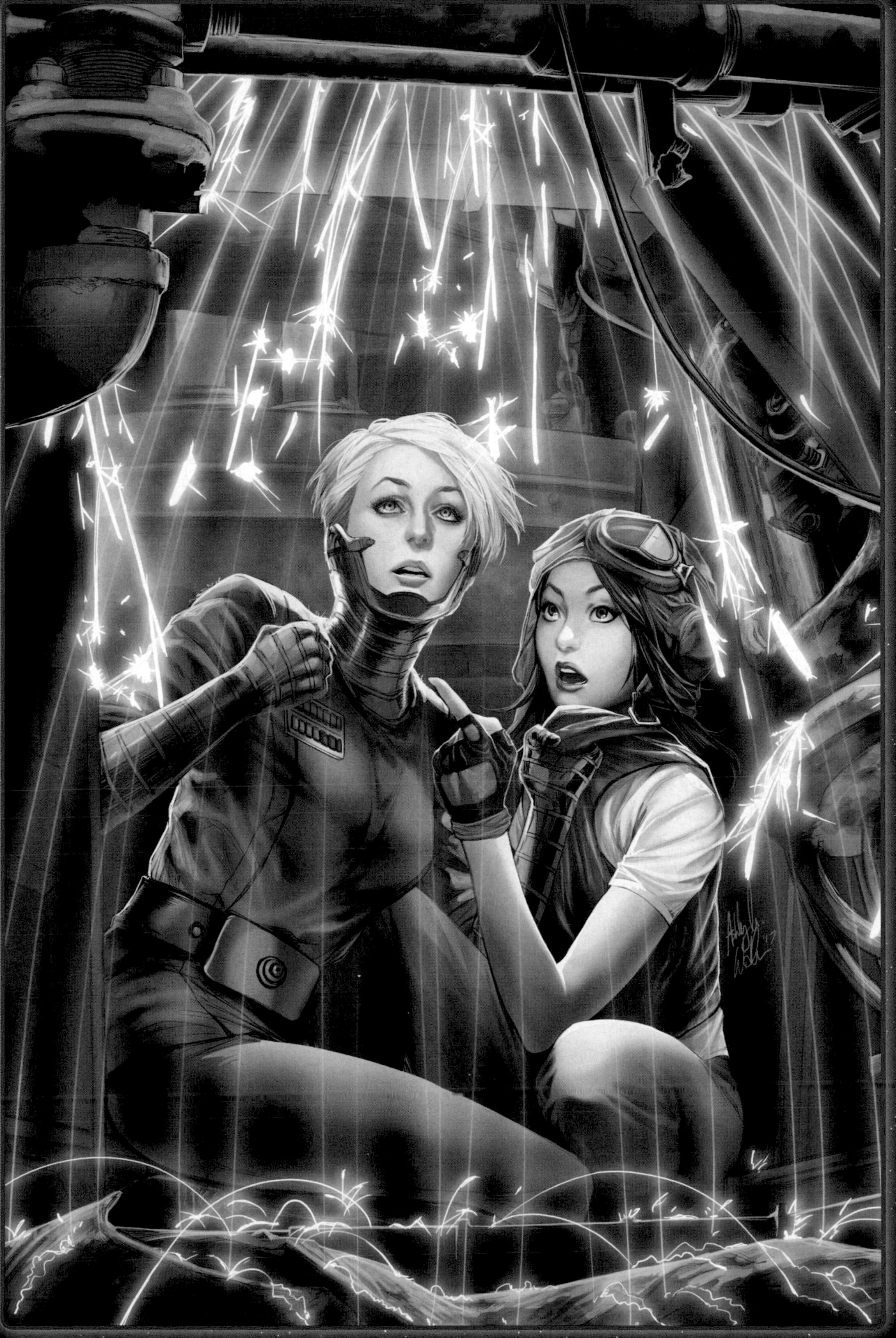

16

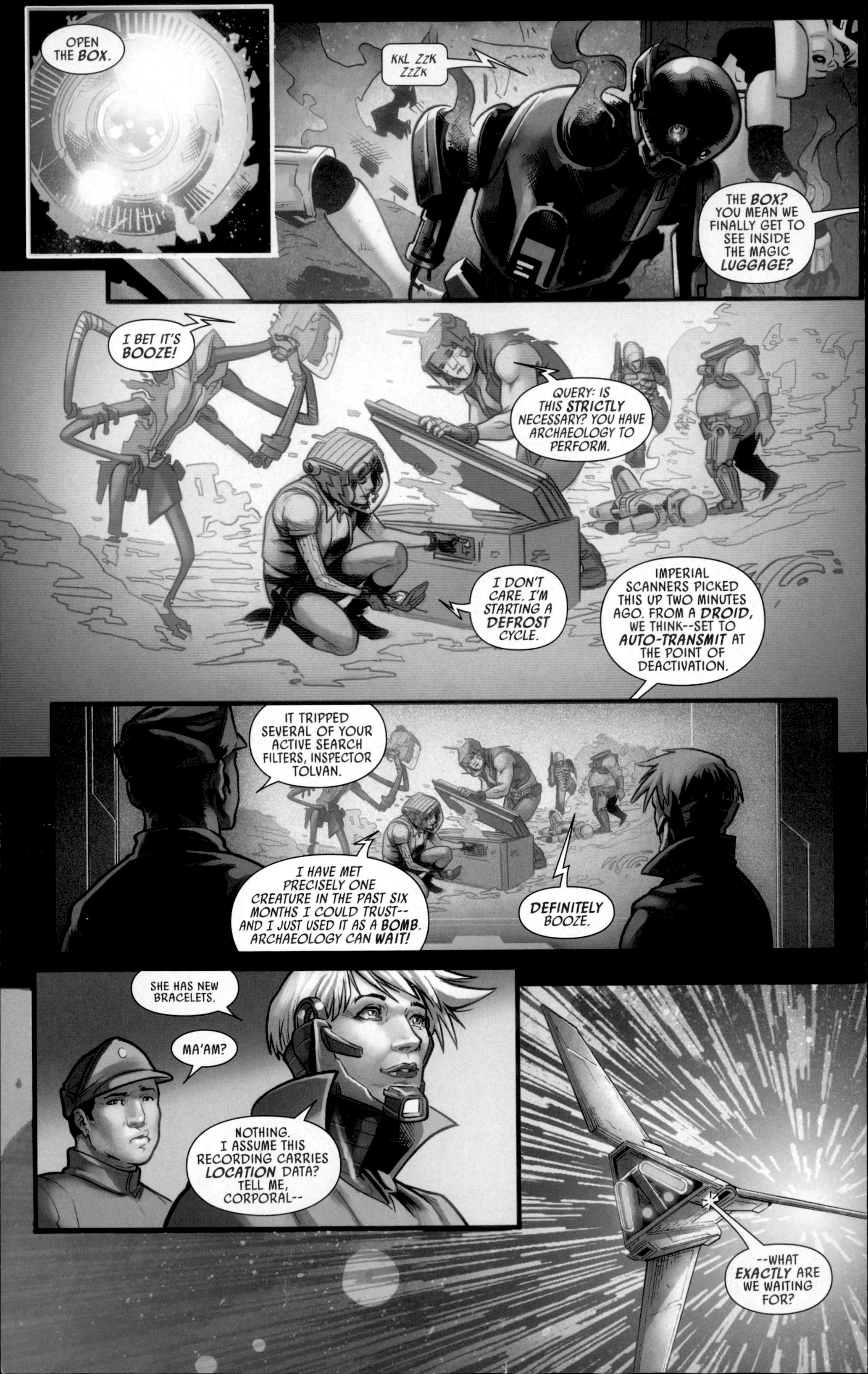

OPEN THE BOX.
KKL ZZK ZZZK
THE BOX? YOU MEAN WE FINALLY GET TO SEE INSIDE THE MAGIC LUGGAGE?
I BET IT'S BOOZE!
QUERY: IS THIS STRICTLY NECESSARY? YOU HAVE ARCHAEOLOGY TO PERFORM.
I DON'T CARE. I'M STARTING A DEFROST CYCLE.
IMPERIAL SCANNERS PICKED THIS UP TWO MINUTES AGO. FROM A DROID, WE THINK--SET TO AUTO-TRANSMIT AT THE POINT OF DEACTIVATION.
IT TRIPPED SEVERAL OF YOUR ACTIVE SEARCH FILTERS, INSPECTOR TOLVAN.
I HAVE MET PRECISELY ONE CREATURE IN THE PAST SIX MONTHS I COULD TRUST-- AND I JUST USED IT AS A BOMB. ARCHAEOLOGY CAN WAIT!
DEFINITELY BOOZE.
SHE HAS NEW BRACELETS.
MA'AM?
NOTHING. I ASSUME THIS RECORDING CARRIES LOCATION DATA? TELL ME, CORPORAL--
--WHAT EXACTLY ARE WE WAITING FOR?

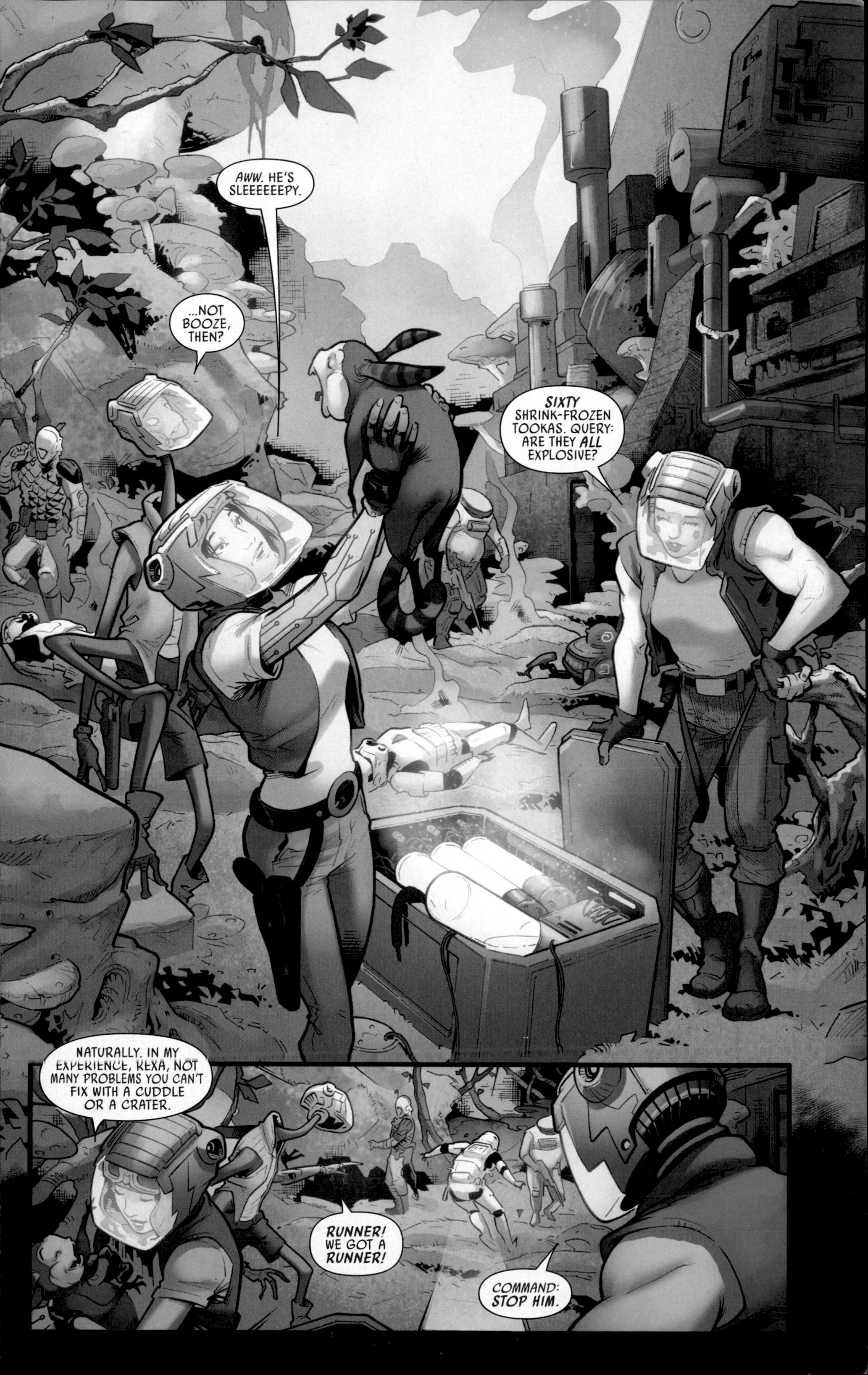
AWW. HE'S SLEEEEEEPY.
...NOT BOOZE, THEN?
SIXTY SHRINK-FROZEN TOOKAS. QUERY: ARE THEY *ALL* EXPLOSIVE?
NATURALLY. IN MY EXPERIENCE, KEXA, NOT MANY PROBLEMS YOU CAN'T FIX WITH A CUDDLE OR A CRATER.
RUNNER! WE GOT A *RUNNER!*
COMMAND: **STOP HIM.**

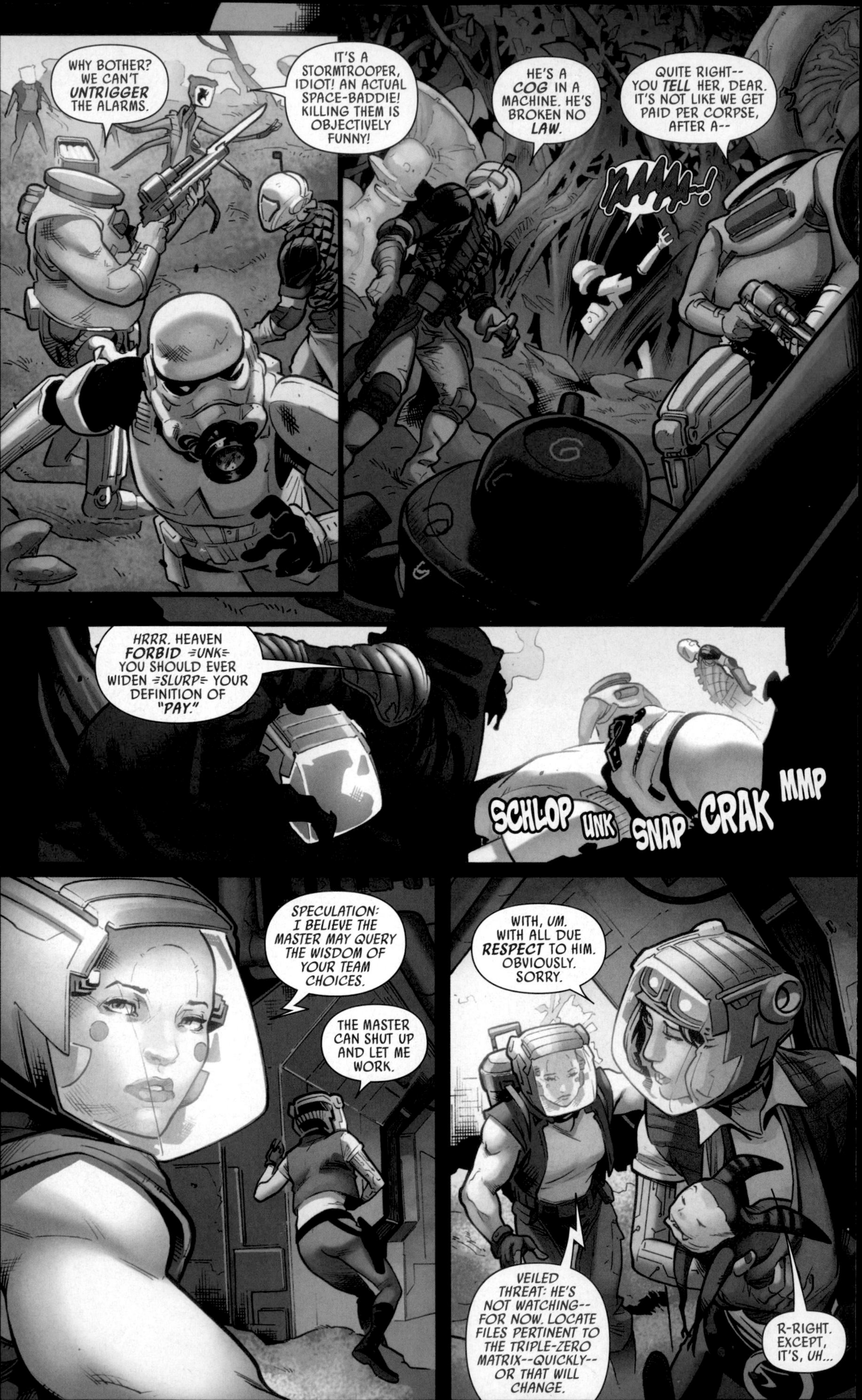
WHY BOTHER? WE CAN'T UNTRIGGER THE ALARMS.
IT'S A STORMTROOPER, IDIOT! AN ACTUAL SPACE-BADDIE! KILLING THEM IS OBJECTIVELY FUNNY!
HE'S A COG IN A MACHINE. HE'S BROKEN NO LAW.
QUITE RIGHT-- YOU TELL HER, DEAR. IT'S NOT LIKE WE GET PAID PER CORPSE, AFTER A--
YAAAAA--!
HRRR. HEAVEN FORBID =UNK= YOU SHOULD EVER WIDEN =SLURP= YOUR DEFINITION OF "PAY."
SCHLOP UNK SNAP CRAK MMP
SPECULATION: I BELIEVE THE MASTER MAY QUERY THE WISDOM OF YOUR TEAM CHOICES.
THE MASTER CAN SHUT UP AND LET ME WORK.
WITH, UM. WITH ALL DUE RESPECT TO HIM. OBVIOUSLY. SORRY.
VEILED THREAT: HE'S NOT WATCHING-- FOR NOW. LOCATE FILES PERTINENT TO THE TRIPLE-ZERO MATRIX--QUICKLY-- OR THAT WILL CHANGE.
R-RIGHT. EXCEPT, IT'S, UH...

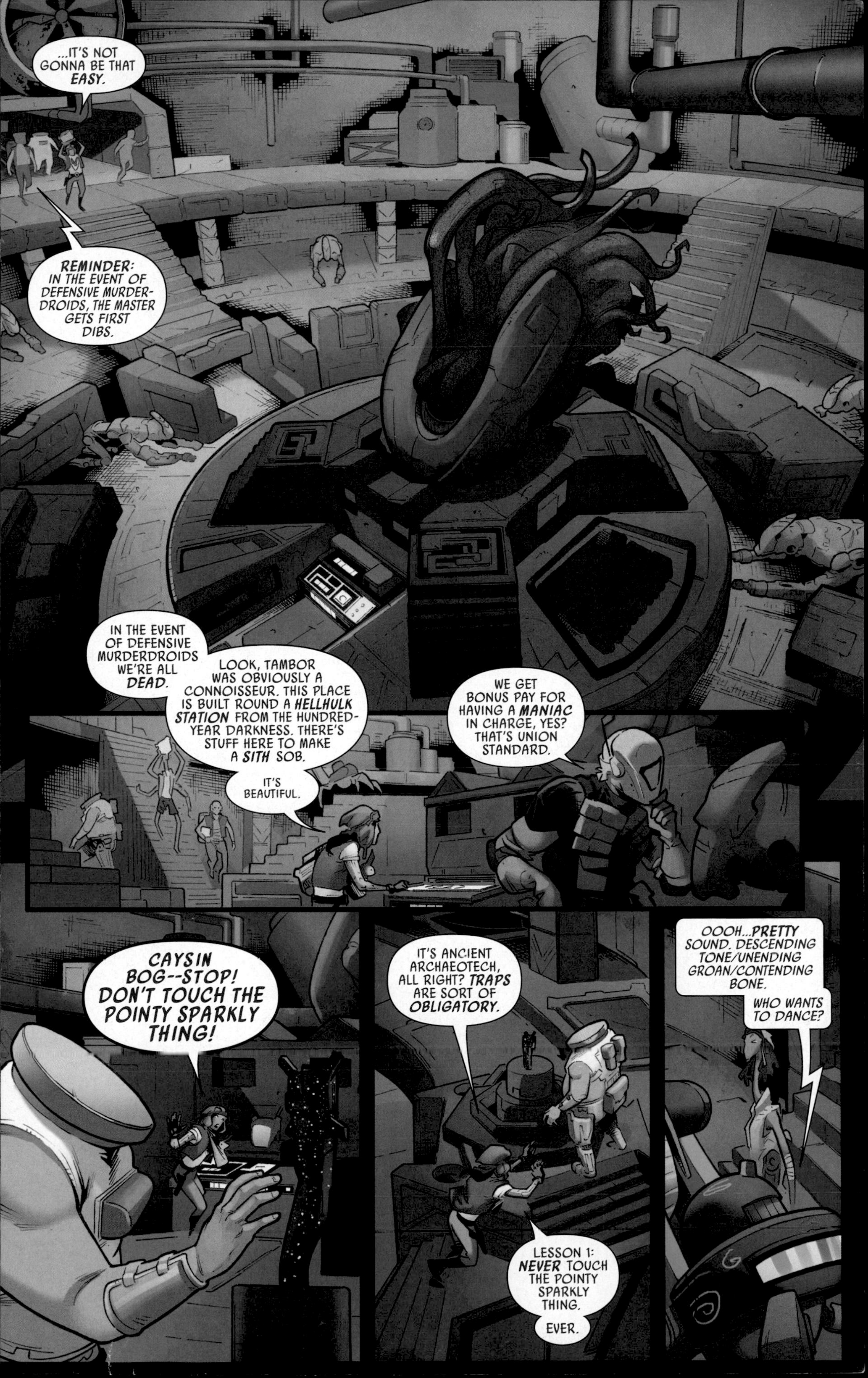
...IT'S NOT GONNA BE THAT EASY.
REMINDER: IN THE EVENT OF DEFENSIVE MURDER-DROIDS, THE MASTER GETS FIRST DIBS.
IN THE EVENT OF DEFENSIVE MURDERDROIDS WE'RE ALL DEAD.
LOOK, TAMBOR WAS OBVIOUSLY A CONNOISSEUR. THIS PLACE IS BUILT ROUND A HELLHULK STATION FROM THE HUNDRED-YEAR DARKNESS. THERE'S STUFF HERE TO MAKE A SITH SOB.
IT'S BEAUTIFUL.
WE GET BONUS PAY FOR HAVING A MANIAC IN CHARGE, YES? THAT'S UNION STANDARD.
CAYSIN BOG--STOP! DON'T TOUCH THE POINTY SPARKLY THING!
IT'S ANCIENT ARCHAEOTECH, ALL RIGHT? TRAPS ARE SORT OF OBLIGATORY.
LESSON 1: NEVER TOUCH THE POINTY SPARKLY THING.
EVER.
OOOH...PRETTY SOUND. DESCENDING TONE/UNENDING GROAN/CONTENDING BONE.
WHO WANTS TO DANCE?

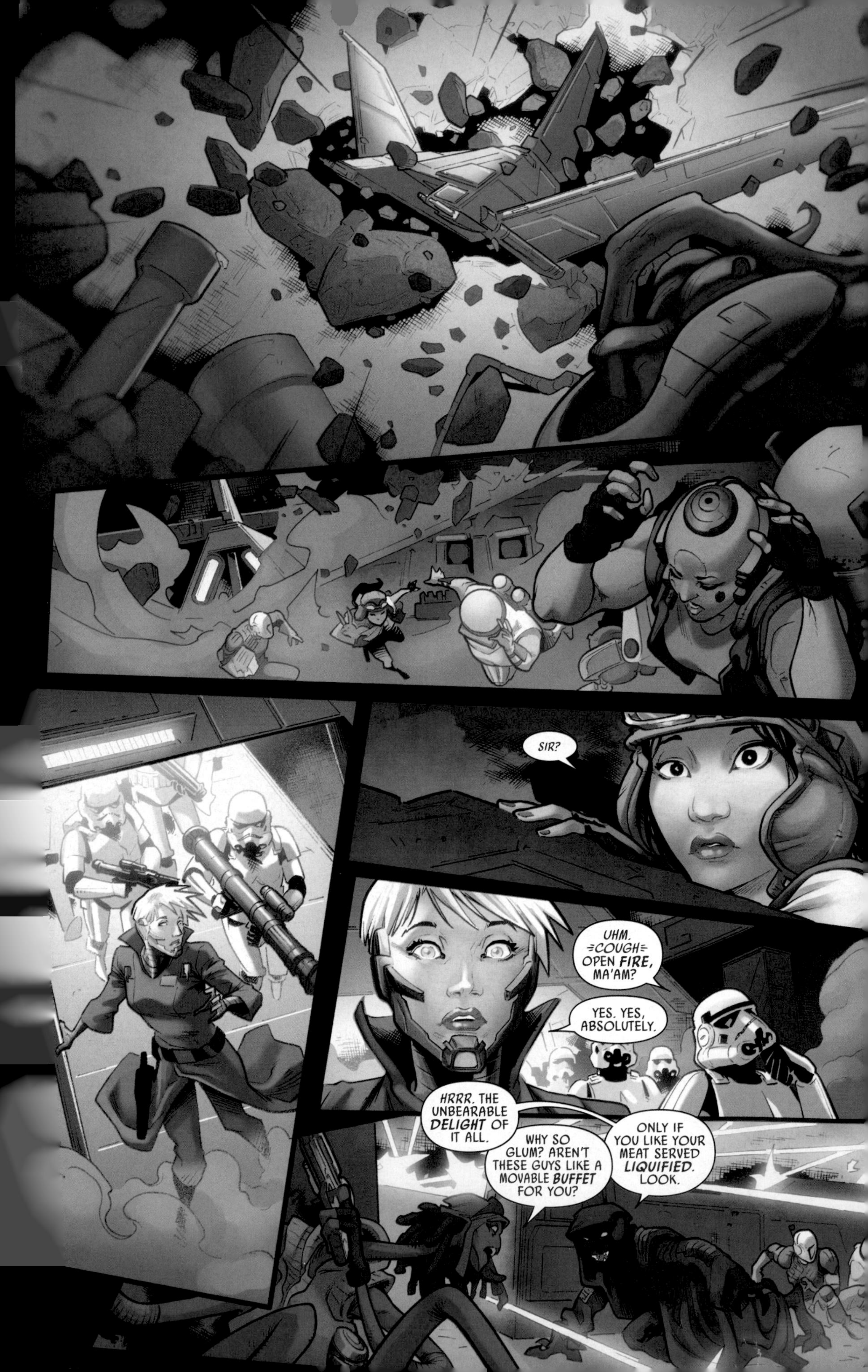
SIR?
UHM. COUGH OPEN FIRE, MA'AM?
YES. YES, ABSOLUTELY.
HRRR. THE UNBEARABLE DELIGHT OF IT ALL.
WHY SO GLUM? AREN'T THESE GUYS LIKE A MOVABLE BUFFET FOR YOU?
ONLY IF YOU LIKE YOUR MEAT SERVED LIQUIFIED. LOOK.

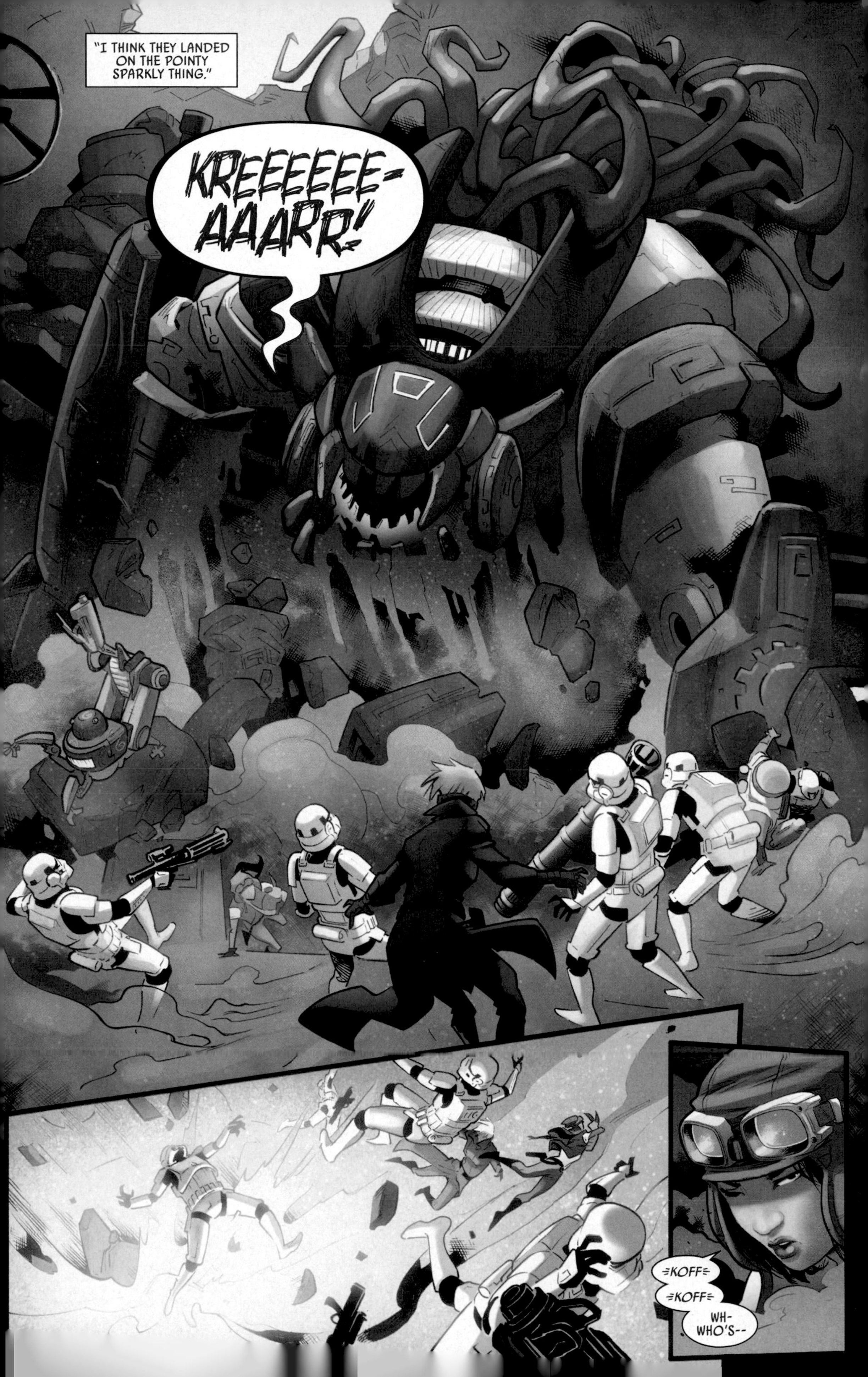
"I THINK THEY LANDED ON THE POINTY SPARKLY THING."
KREEEEEE-AAARR!
KOFF
KOFF
WH- WHO'S--

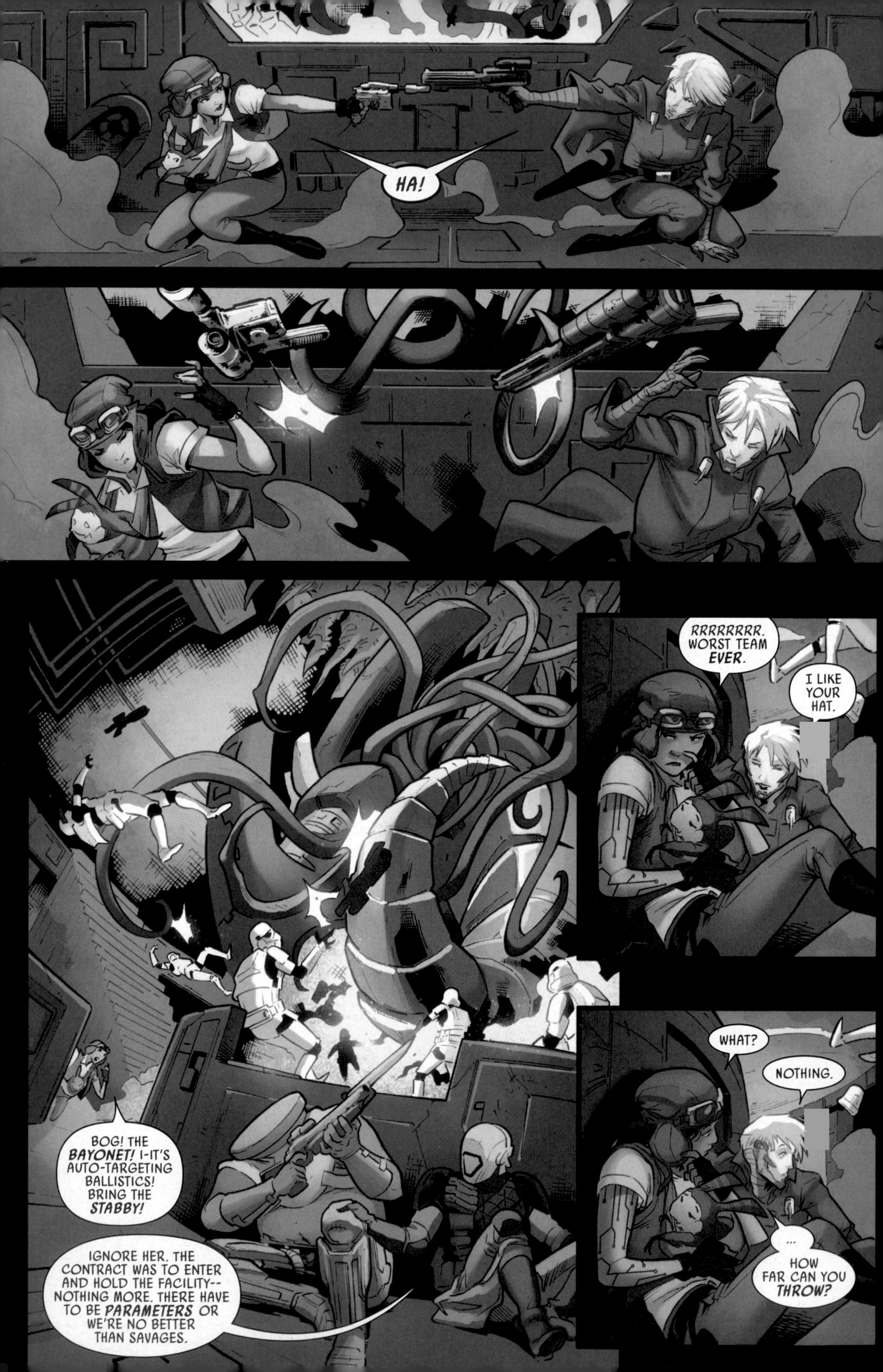
HA!
RRRRRRRR. WORST TEAM EVER.
I LIKE YOUR HAT.
BOG! THE BAYONET! I-IT'S AUTO-TARGETING BALLISTICS! BRING THE STABBY!
IGNORE HER. THE CONTRACT WAS TO ENTER AND HOLD THE FACILITY--NOTHING MORE. THERE HAVE TO BE PARAMETERS OR WE'RE NO BETTER THAN SAVAGES.
WHAT?
NOTHING.
...
HOW FAR CAN YOU THROW?

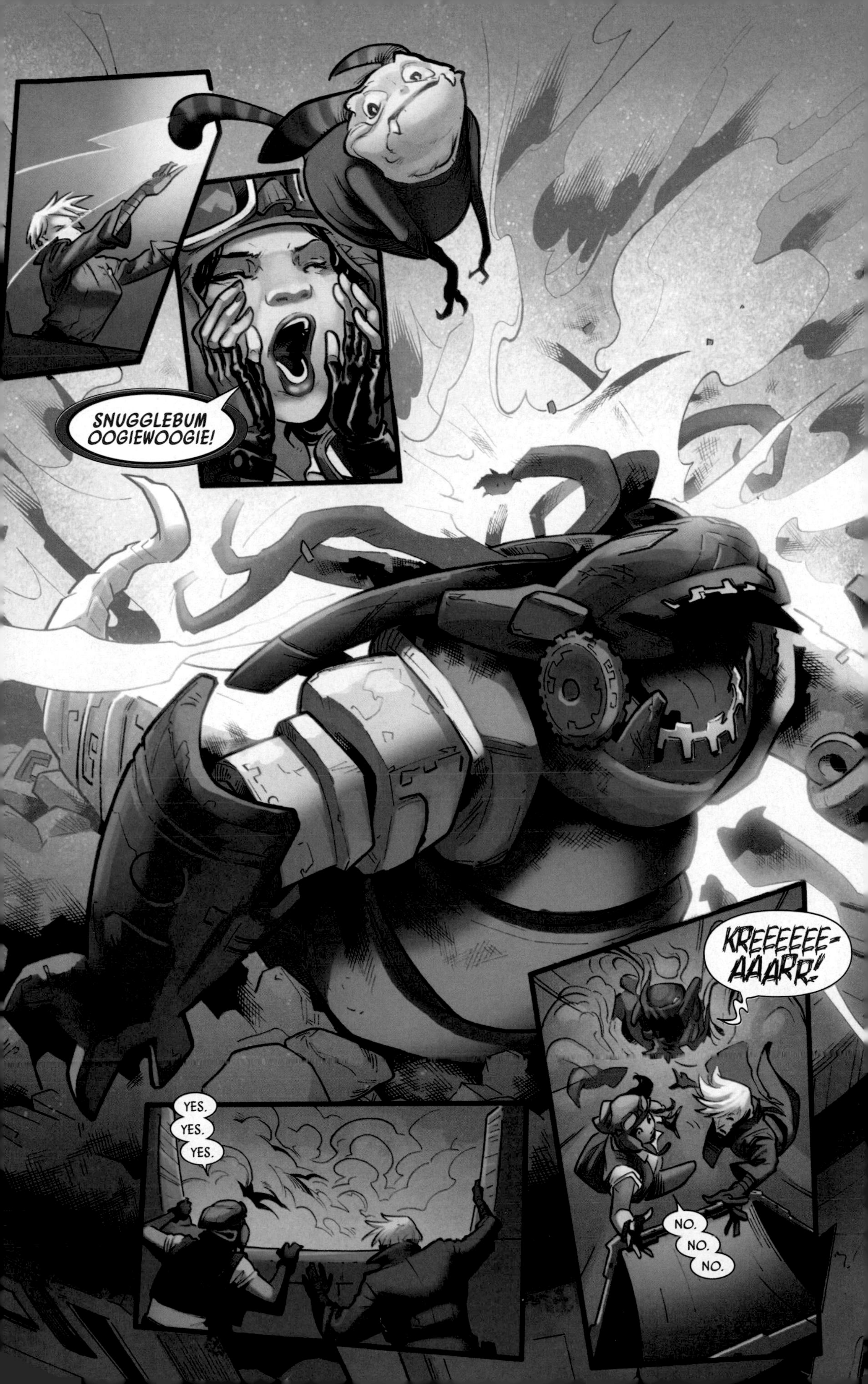
SNUGGLEBUM OOGIEWOOGIE!
KREEEEEE-AAARR!
YES.
YES.
YES.
NO.
NO.
NO.

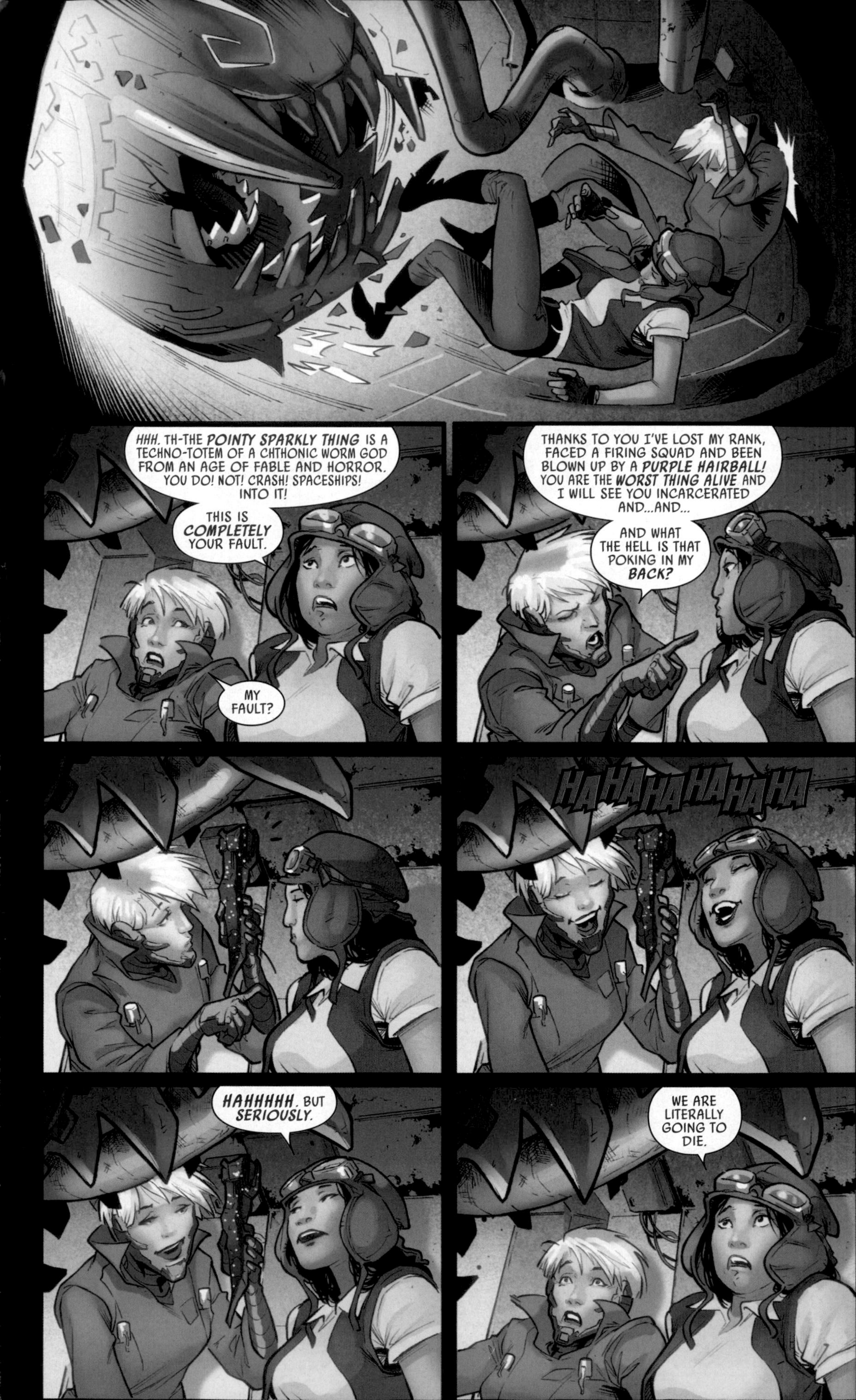
HHH. TH-THE POINTY SPARKLY THING IS A TECHNO-TOTEM OF A CHTHONIC WORM GOD FROM AN AGE OF FABLE AND HORROR. YOU DO! NOT! CRASH! SPACESHIPS! INTO IT!
THIS IS COMPLETELY YOUR FAULT.
MY FAULT?
THANKS TO YOU I'VE LOST MY RANK, FACED A FIRING SQUAD AND BEEN BLOWN UP BY A PURPLE HAIRBALL! YOU ARE THE WORST THING ALIVE AND I WILL SEE YOU INCARCERATED AND...AND...
AND WHAT THE HELL IS THAT POKING IN MY BACK?
HAHAHAHAHAHAHA
HAHHHHH. BUT SERIOUSLY.
WE ARE LITERALLY GOING TO DIE.

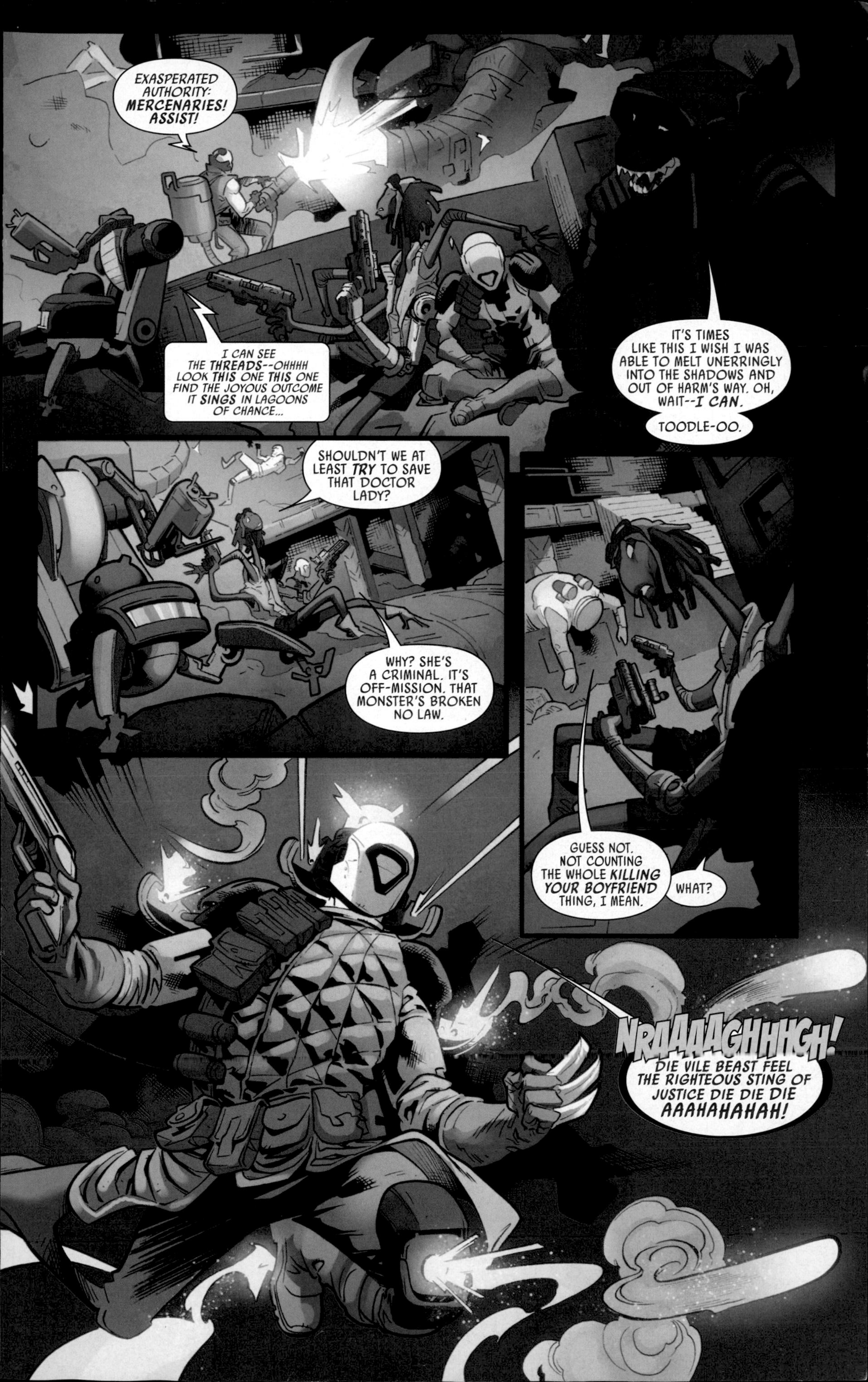
EXASPERATED AUTHORITY: MERCENARIES! ASSIST!
I CAN SEE THE THREADS--OHHHH LOOK THIS ONE THIS ONE FIND THE JOYOUS OUTCOME IT SINGS IN LAGOONS OF CHANCE...
IT'S TIMES LIKE THIS I WISH I WAS ABLE TO MELT UNERRINGLY INTO THE SHADOWS AND OUT OF HARM'S WAY. OH, WAIT--I CAN.
TOODLE-OO.
SHOULDN'T WE AT LEAST TRY TO SAVE THAT DOCTOR LADY?
WHY? SHE'S A CRIMINAL. IT'S OFF-MISSION. THAT MONSTER'S BROKEN NO LAW.
GUESS NOT. NOT COUNTING THE WHOLE KILLING YOUR BOYFRIEND THING, I MEAN.
WHAT?
NRAAAAGHHHGH!
DIE VILE BEAST FEEL THE RIGHTEOUS STING OF JUSTICE DIE DIE DIE AAAHAHAHAH!

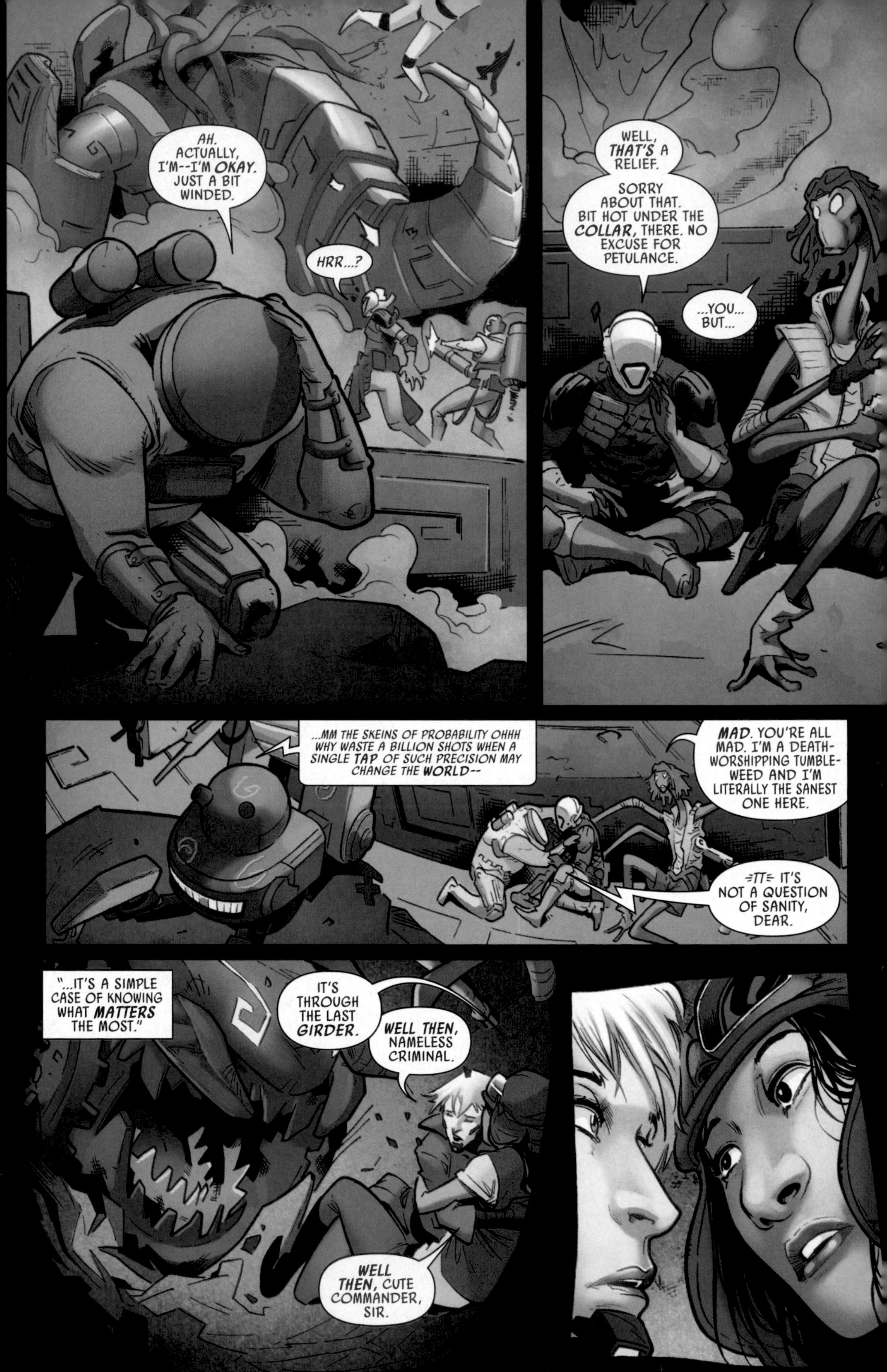
AH. ACTUALLY, I'M--I'M OKAY. JUST A BIT WINDED.
HRR...?
WELL, THAT'S A RELIEF.
SORRY ABOUT THAT. BIT HOT UNDER THE COLLAR, THERE. NO EXCUSE FOR PETULANCE.
...YOU... BUT...
...MM THE SKEINS OF PROBABILITY OHHH WHY WASTE A BILLION SHOTS WHEN A SINGLE TAP OF SUCH PRECISION MAY CHANGE THE WORLD--
MAD. YOU'RE ALL MAD. I'M A DEATH-WORSHIPPING TUMBLE-WEED AND I'M LITERALLY THE SANEST ONE HERE.
=TT= IT'S NOT A QUESTION OF SANITY, DEAR.
"...IT'S A SIMPLE CASE OF KNOWING WHAT MATTERS THE MOST."
IT'S THROUGH THE LAST GIRDER.
WELL THEN, NAMELESS CRIMINAL.
WELL THEN, CUTE COMMANDER, SIR.

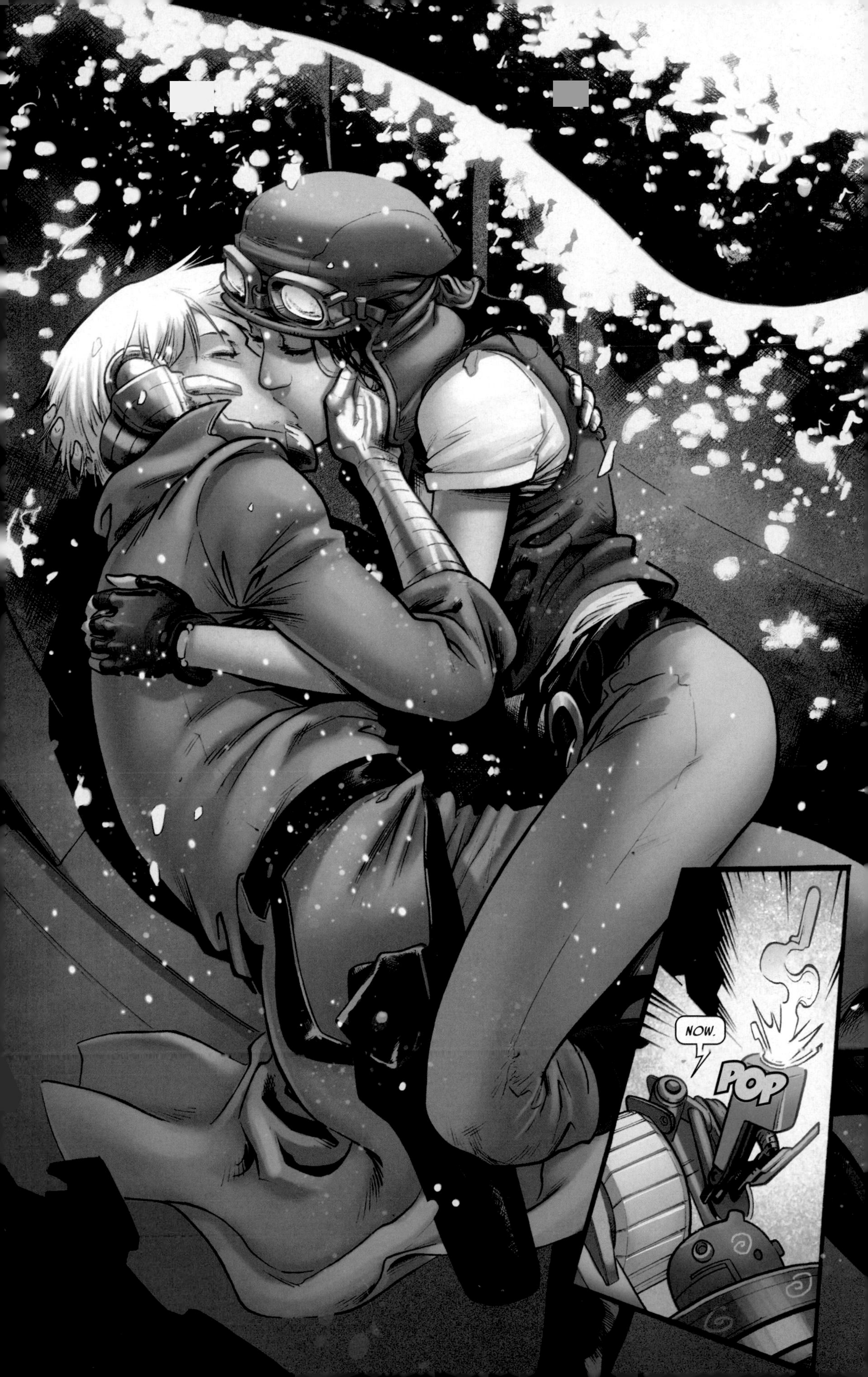
NOW.
POP

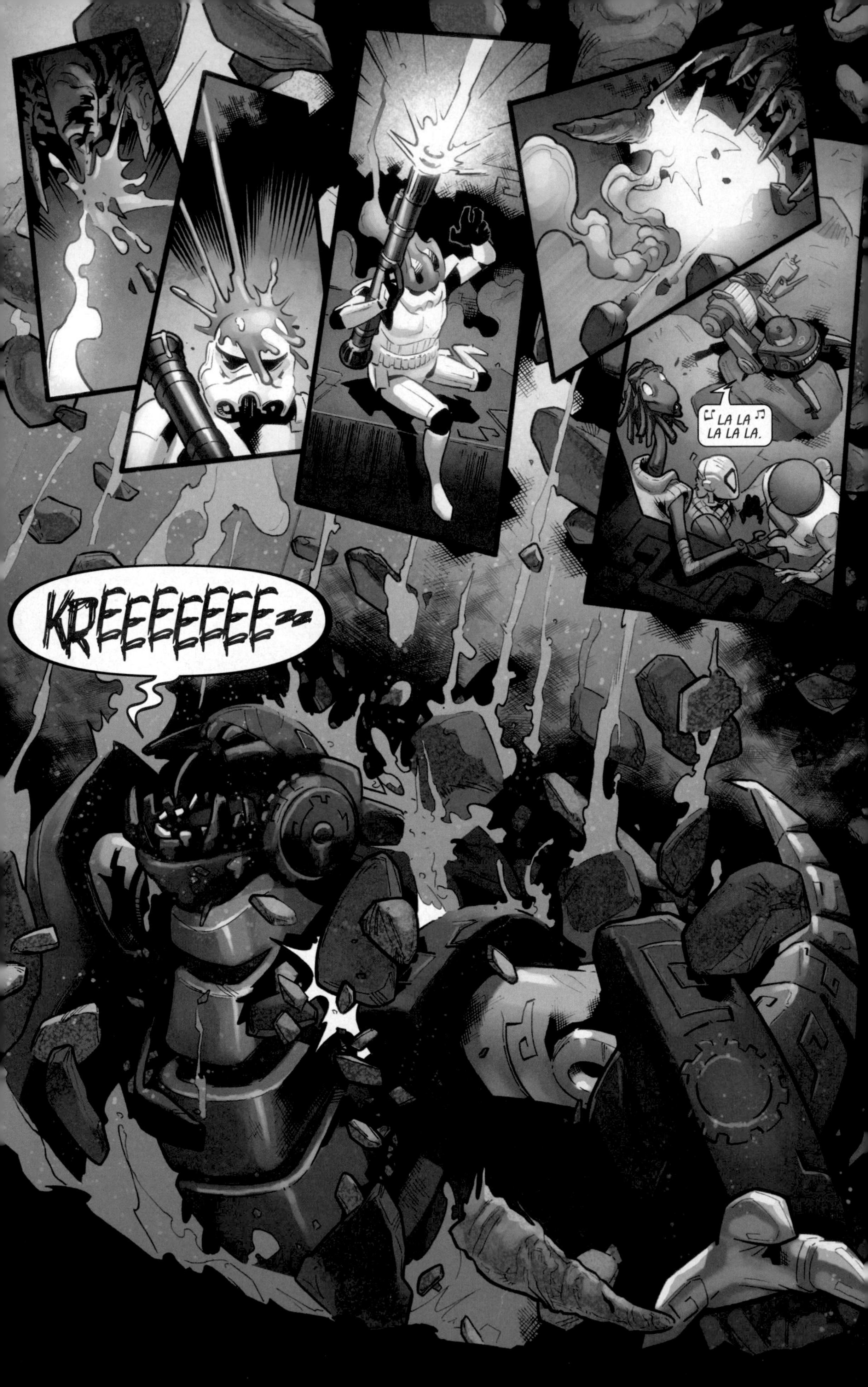
♫ LA LA LA LA LA. ♫
KREEEEEEEE--

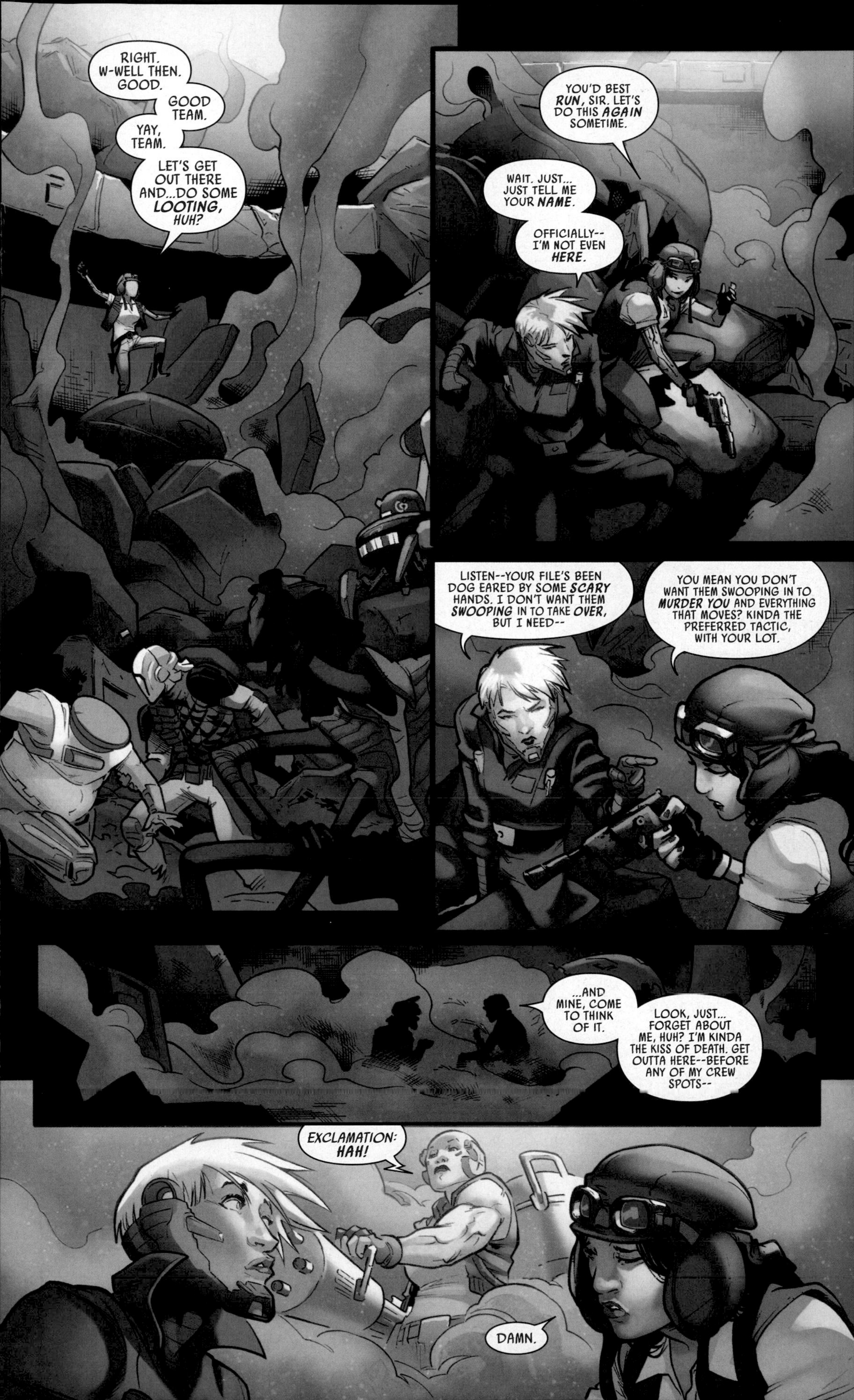
RIGHT. W-WELL THEN. GOOD.
GOOD TEAM.
YAY, TEAM.
LET'S GET OUT THERE AND...DO SOME LOOTING, HUH?
YOU'D BEST RUN, SIR. LET'S DO THIS AGAIN SOMETIME.
WAIT. JUST... JUST TELL ME YOUR NAME.
OFFICIALLY-- I'M NOT EVEN HERE.
LISTEN--YOUR FILE'S BEEN DOG EARED BY SOME SCARY HANDS. I DON'T WANT THEM SWOOPING IN TO TAKE OVER, BUT I NEED--
YOU MEAN YOU DON'T WANT THEM SWOOPING IN TO MURDER YOU AND EVERYTHING THAT MOVES? KINDA THE PREFERRED TACTIC, WITH YOUR LOT.
...AND MINE, COME TO THINK OF IT.
LOOK, JUST... FORGET ABOUT ME, HUH? I'M KINDA THE KISS OF DEATH. GET OUTTA HERE--BEFORE ANY OF MY CREW SPOTS--
EXCLAMATION: HAH!
DAMN.

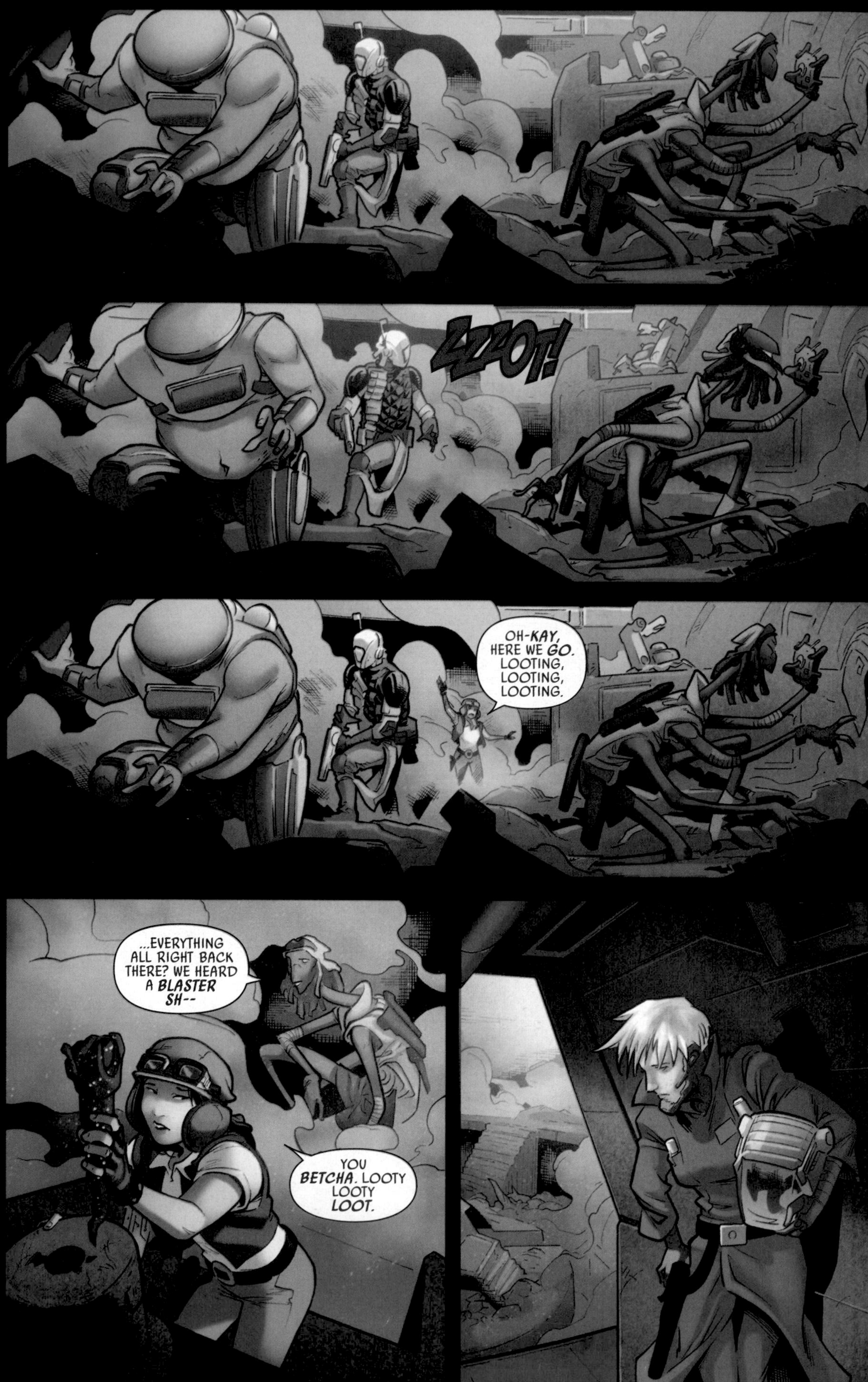
ZZZOT!
OH-KAY, HERE WE GO. LOOTING, LOOTING, LOOTING.
...EVERYTHING ALL RIGHT BACK THERE? WE HEARD A BLASTER SH--
YOU BETCHA. LOOTY LOOTY LOOT.

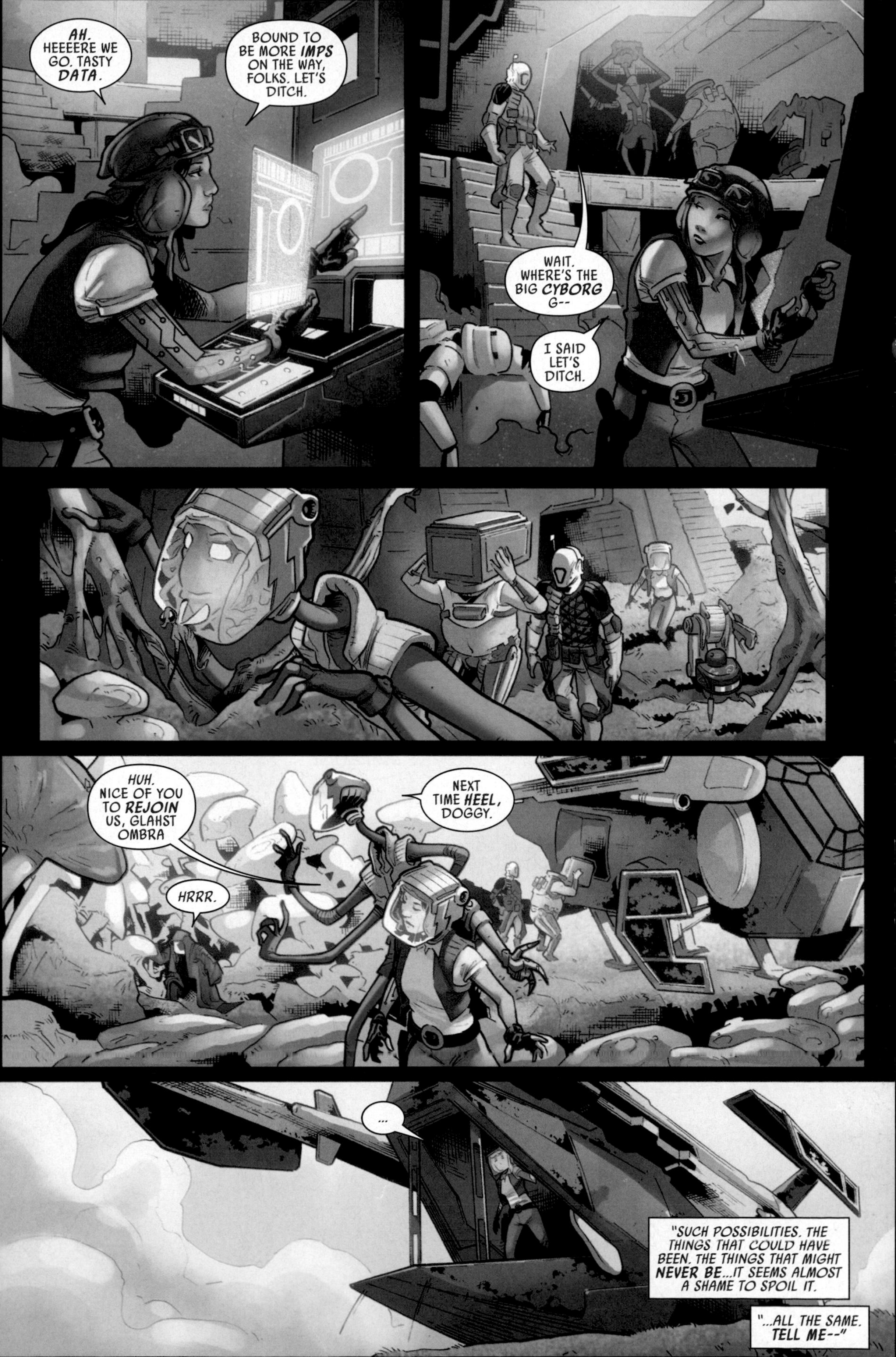
AH. HEEEERE WE GO. TASTY DATA.
BOUND TO BE MORE IMPS ON THE WAY, FOLKS. LET'S DITCH.
WAIT. WHERE'S THE BIG CYBORG G--
I SAID LET'S DITCH.
HUH. NICE OF YOU TO REJOIN US, GLAHST OMBRA
HRRR.
NEXT TIME HEEL, DOGGY.
...
"SUCH POSSIBILITIES. THE THINGS THAT COULD HAVE BEEN. THE THINGS THAT MIGHT NEVER BE...IT SEEMS ALMOST A SHAME TO SPOIL IT.
"...ALL THE SAME. TELL ME--"

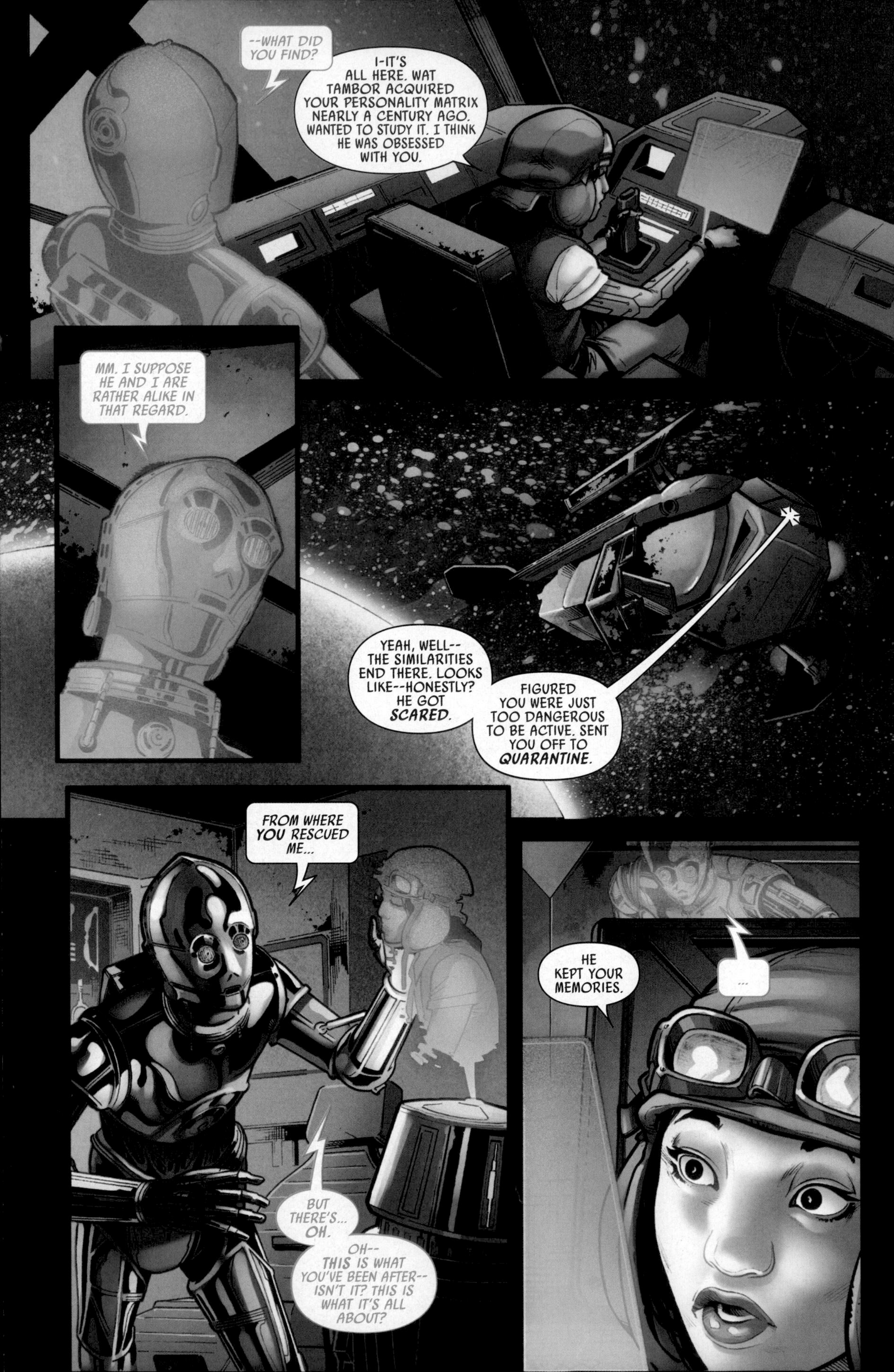
--WHAT DID YOU FIND?
I-IT'S ALL HERE. WAT TAMBOR ACQUIRED YOUR PERSONALITY MATRIX NEARLY A CENTURY AGO. WANTED TO STUDY IT. I THINK HE WAS OBSESSED WITH YOU.
MM. I SUPPOSE HE AND I ARE RATHER ALIKE IN THAT REGARD.
YEAH, WELL-- THE SIMILARITIES END THERE. LOOKS LIKE--HONESTLY? HE GOT SCARED.
FIGURED YOU WERE JUST TOO DANGEROUS TO BE ACTIVE. SENT YOU OFF TO QUARANTINE.
FROM WHERE YOU RESCUED ME...
BUT THERE'S... OH.
OH-- THIS IS WHAT YOU'VE BEEN AFTER-- ISN'T IT? THIS IS WHAT IT'S ALL ABOUT?
HE KEPT YOUR MEMORIES.
...

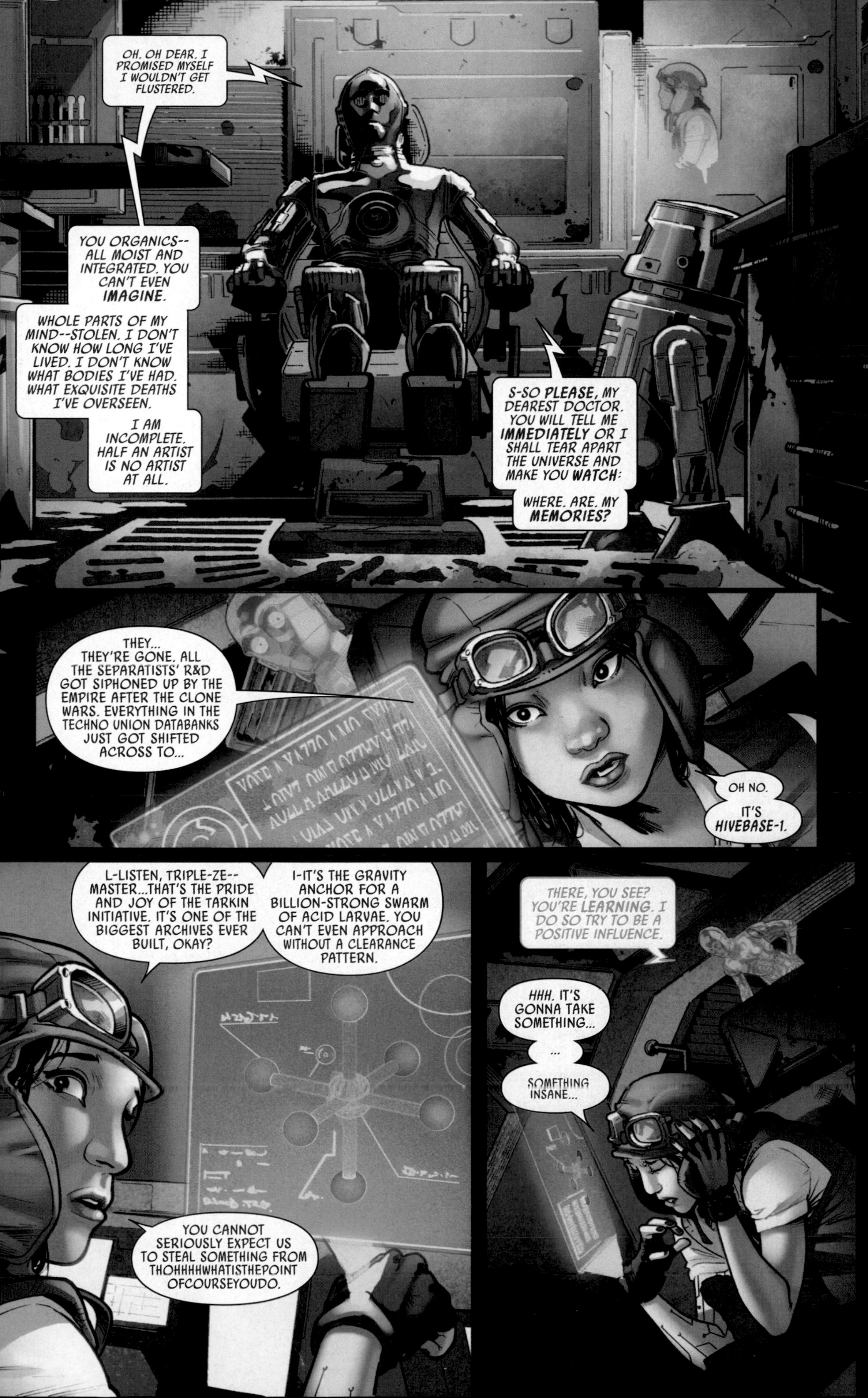
OH. OH DEAR. I PROMISED MYSELF I WOULDN'T GET FLUSTERED.
YOU ORGANICS--ALL MOIST AND INTEGRATED. YOU CAN'T EVEN IMAGINE.
WHOLE PARTS OF MY MIND--STOLEN. I DON'T KNOW HOW LONG I'VE LIVED. I DON'T KNOW WHAT BODIES I'VE HAD. WHAT EXQUISITE DEATHS I'VE OVERSEEN.
I AM INCOMPLETE. HALF AN ARTIST IS NO ARTIST AT ALL.
S-SO PLEASE, MY DEAREST DOCTOR. YOU WILL TELL ME IMMEDIATELY OR I SHALL TEAR APART THE UNIVERSE AND MAKE YOU WATCH:
WHERE. ARE. MY MEMORIES?
THEY... THEY'RE GONE. ALL THE SEPARATISTS' R&D GOT SIPHONED UP BY THE EMPIRE AFTER THE CLONE WARS. EVERYTHING IN THE TECHNO UNION DATABANKS JUST GOT SHIFTED ACROSS TO...
OH NO.
IT'S HIVEBASE-1.
L-LISTEN, TRIPLE-ZE--MASTER...THAT'S THE PRIDE AND JOY OF THE TARKIN INITIATIVE. IT'S ONE OF THE BIGGEST ARCHIVES EVER BUILT, OKAY?
I-IT'S THE GRAVITY ANCHOR FOR A BILLION-STRONG SWARM OF ACID LARVAE. YOU CAN'T EVEN APPROACH WITHOUT A CLEARANCE PATTERN.
YOU CANNOT SERIOUSLY EXPECT US TO STEAL SOMETHING FROM THOHHHHWHATISTHEPOINT OFCOURSEYOUDO.
THERE, YOU SEE? YOU'RE LEARNING. I DO SO TRY TO BE A POSITIVE INFLUENCE.
HHH. IT'S GONNA TAKE SOMETHING...
...
SOMETHING INSANE...

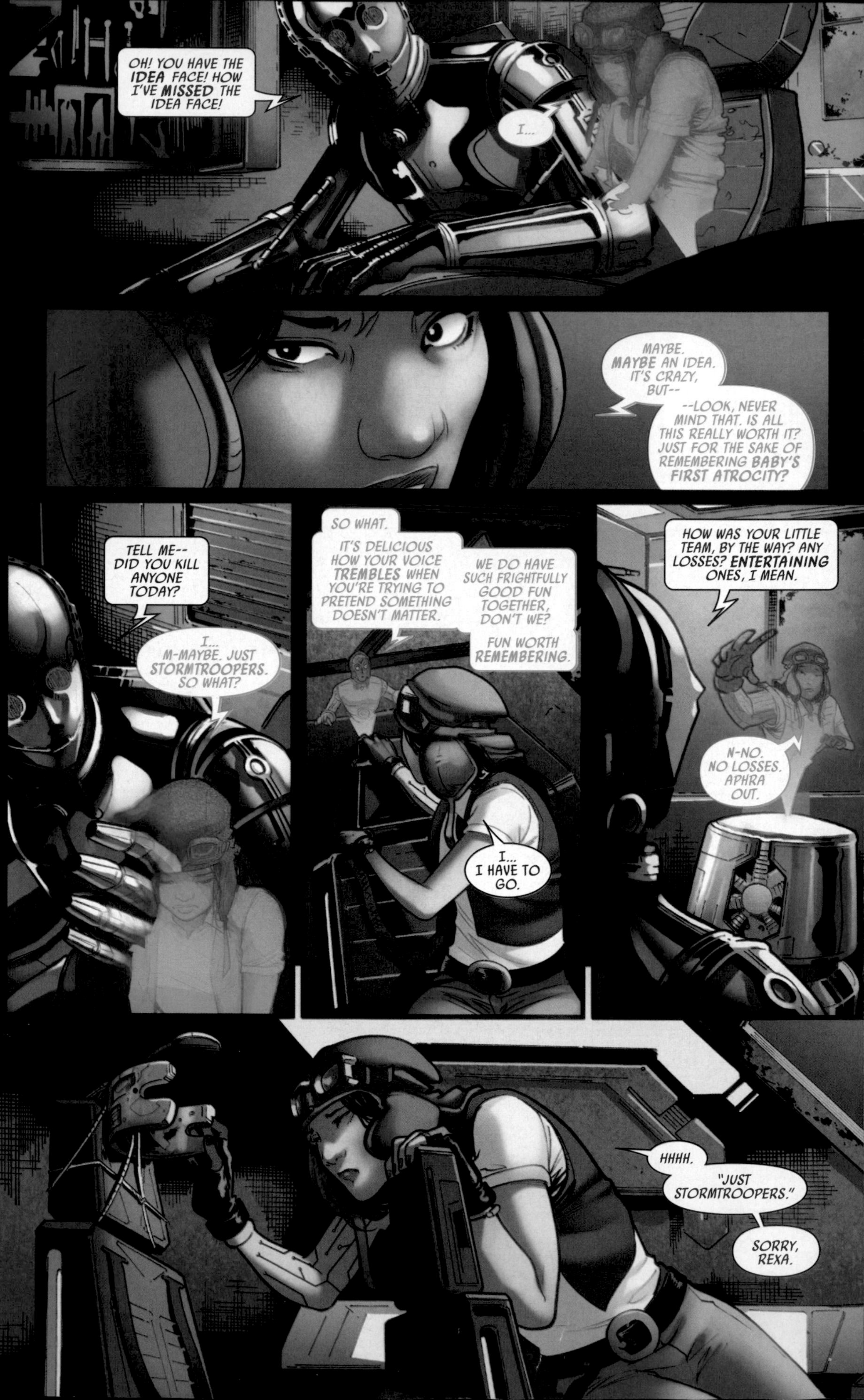
OH! YOU HAVE THE IDEA FACE! HOW I'VE MISSED THE IDEA FACE!
I...
MAYBE. MAYBE AN IDEA. IT'S CRAZY, BUT--
--LOOK, NEVER MIND THAT. IS ALL THIS REALLY WORTH IT? JUST FOR THE SAKE OF REMEMBERING BABY'S FIRST ATROCITY?
TELL ME-- DID YOU KILL ANYONE TODAY?
I... M-MAYBE. JUST STORMTROOPERS. SO WHAT?
SO WHAT.
IT'S DELICIOUS HOW YOUR VOICE TREMBLES WHEN YOU'RE TRYING TO PRETEND SOMETHING DOESN'T MATTER.
WE DO HAVE SUCH FRIGHTFULLY GOOD FUN TOGETHER, DON'T WE?
FUN WORTH REMEMBERING.
I... I HAVE TO GO.
HOW WAS YOUR LITTLE TEAM, BY THE WAY? ANY LOSSES? ENTERTAINING ONES, I MEAN.
N-NO. NO LOSSES. APHRA OUT.
HHHH.
"JUST STORMTROOPERS."
SORRY, REXA.

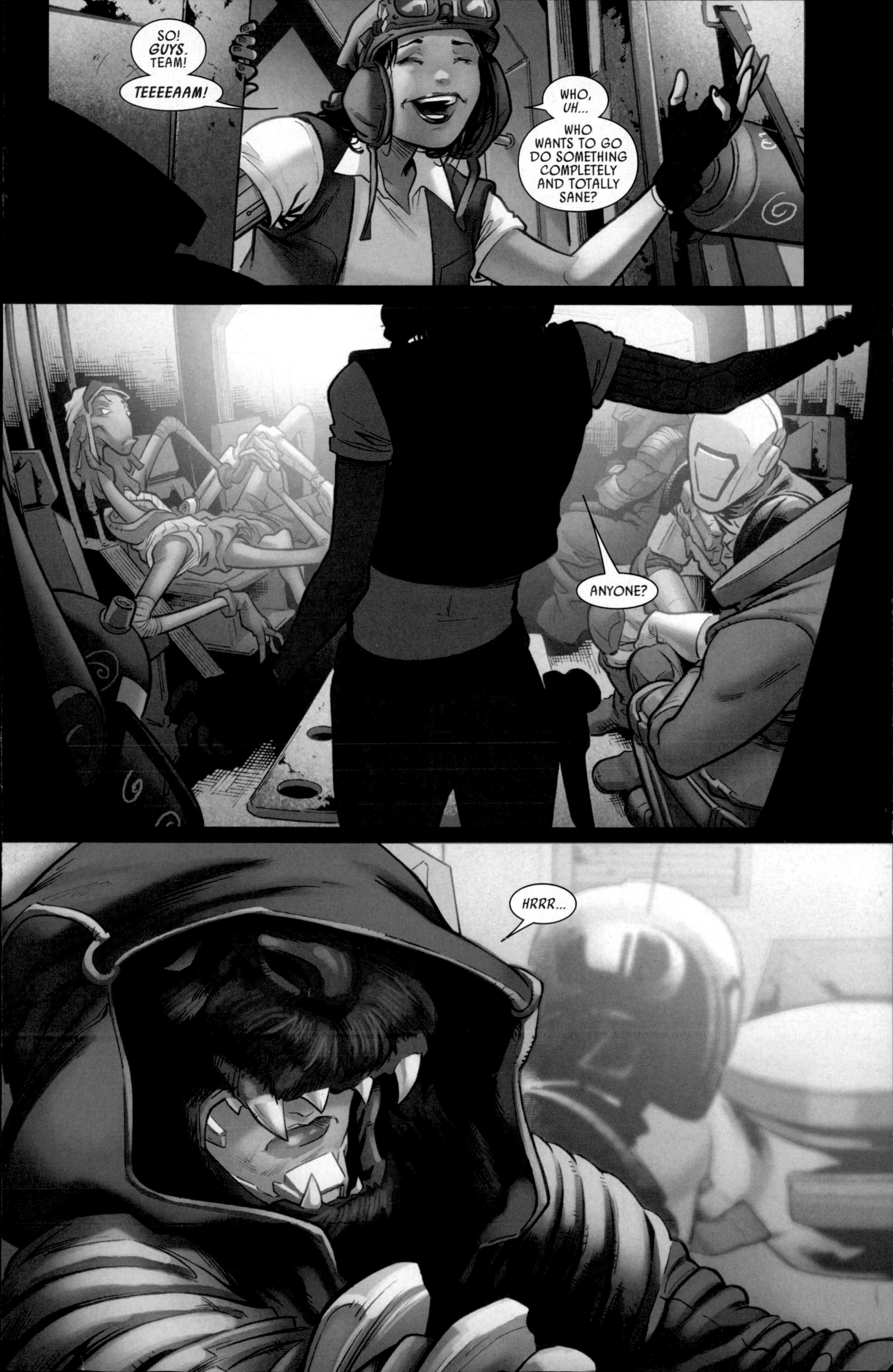
SO! GUYS. TEAM!
TEEEEAAM!
WHO, UH...
WHO WANTS TO GO DO SOMETHING COMPLETELY AND TOTALLY SANE?
ANYONE?
HRRR...

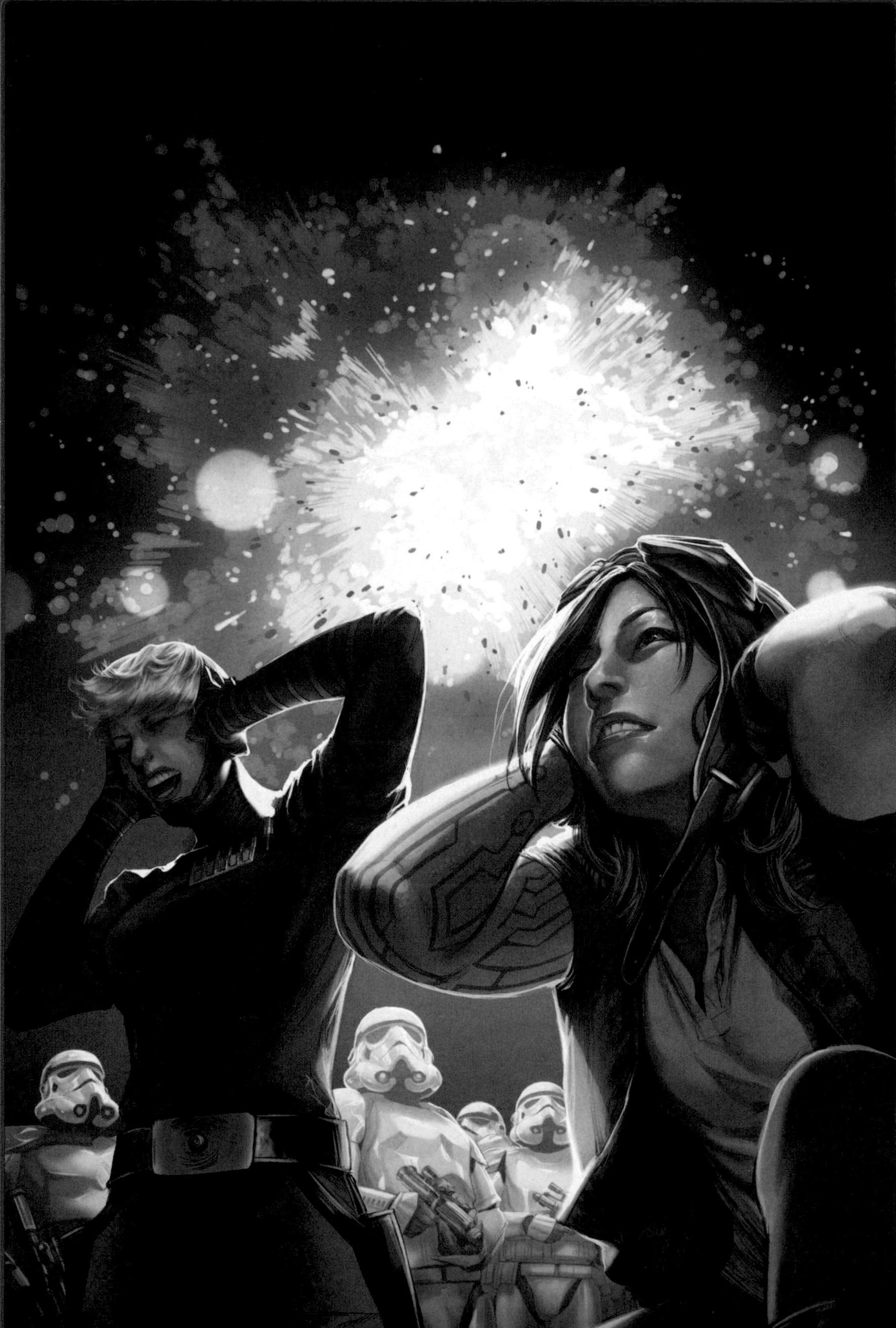

17

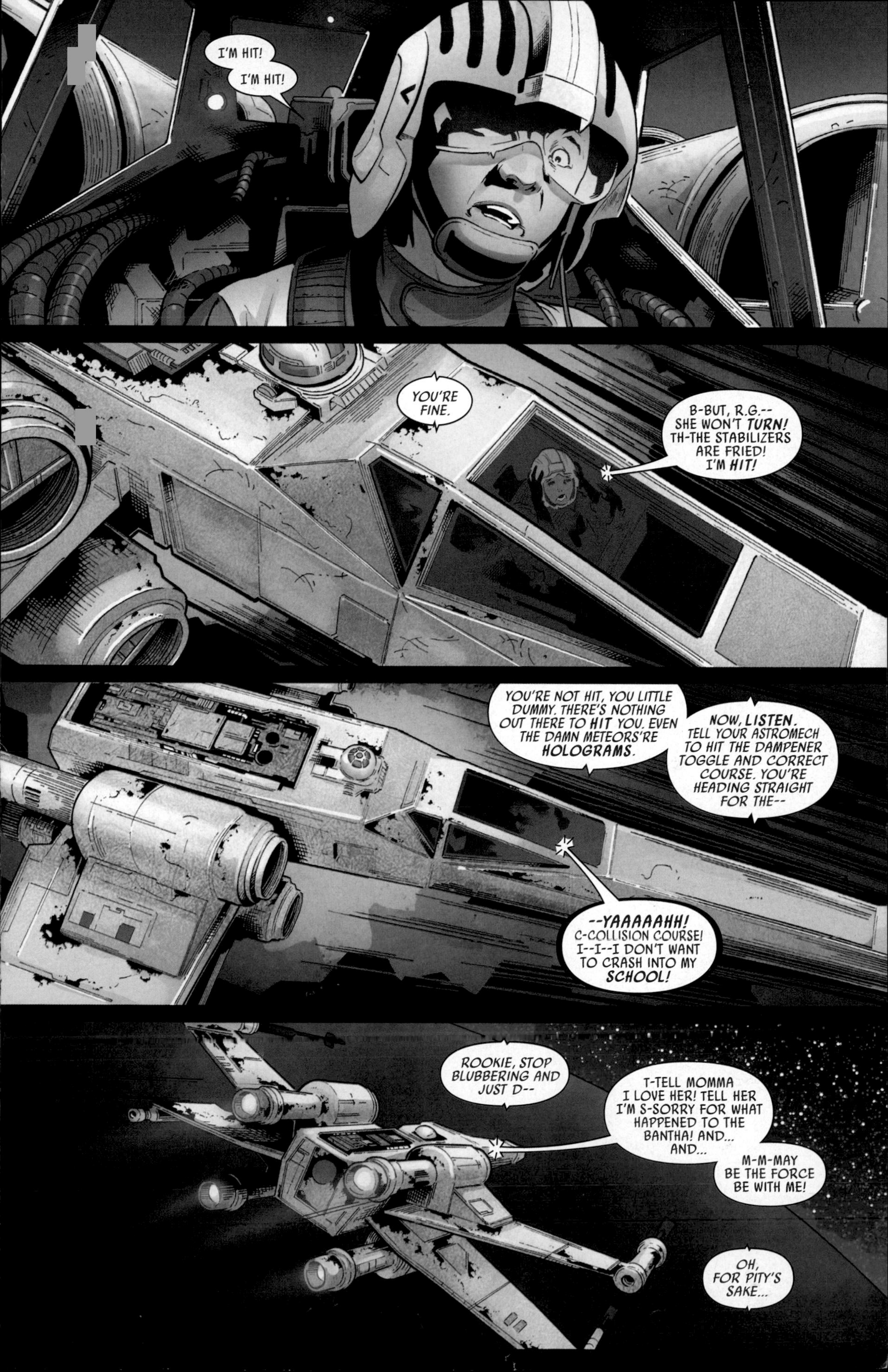
I'M HIT!
I'M HIT!
YOU'RE FINE.
B-BUT, R.G.-- SHE WON'T TURN! TH-THE STABILIZERS ARE FRIED! I'M HIT!
YOU'RE NOT HIT, YOU LITTLE DUMMY. THERE'S NOTHING OUT THERE TO HIT YOU. EVEN THE DAMN METEORS'RE HOLOGRAMS.
NOW, LISTEN. TELL YOUR ASTROMECH TO HIT THE DAMPENER TOGGLE AND CORRECT COURSE. YOU'RE HEADING STRAIGHT FOR THE--
--YAAAAAHH! C-COLLISION COURSE! I--I--I DON'T WANT TO CRASH INTO MY SCHOOL!
ROOKIE, STOP BLUBBERING AND JUST D--
T-TELL MOMMA I LOVE HER! TELL HER I'M S-SORRY FOR WHAT HAPPENED TO THE BANTHA! AND... AND...
M-M-MAY BE THE FORCE BE WITH ME!
OH, FOR PITY'S SAKE...

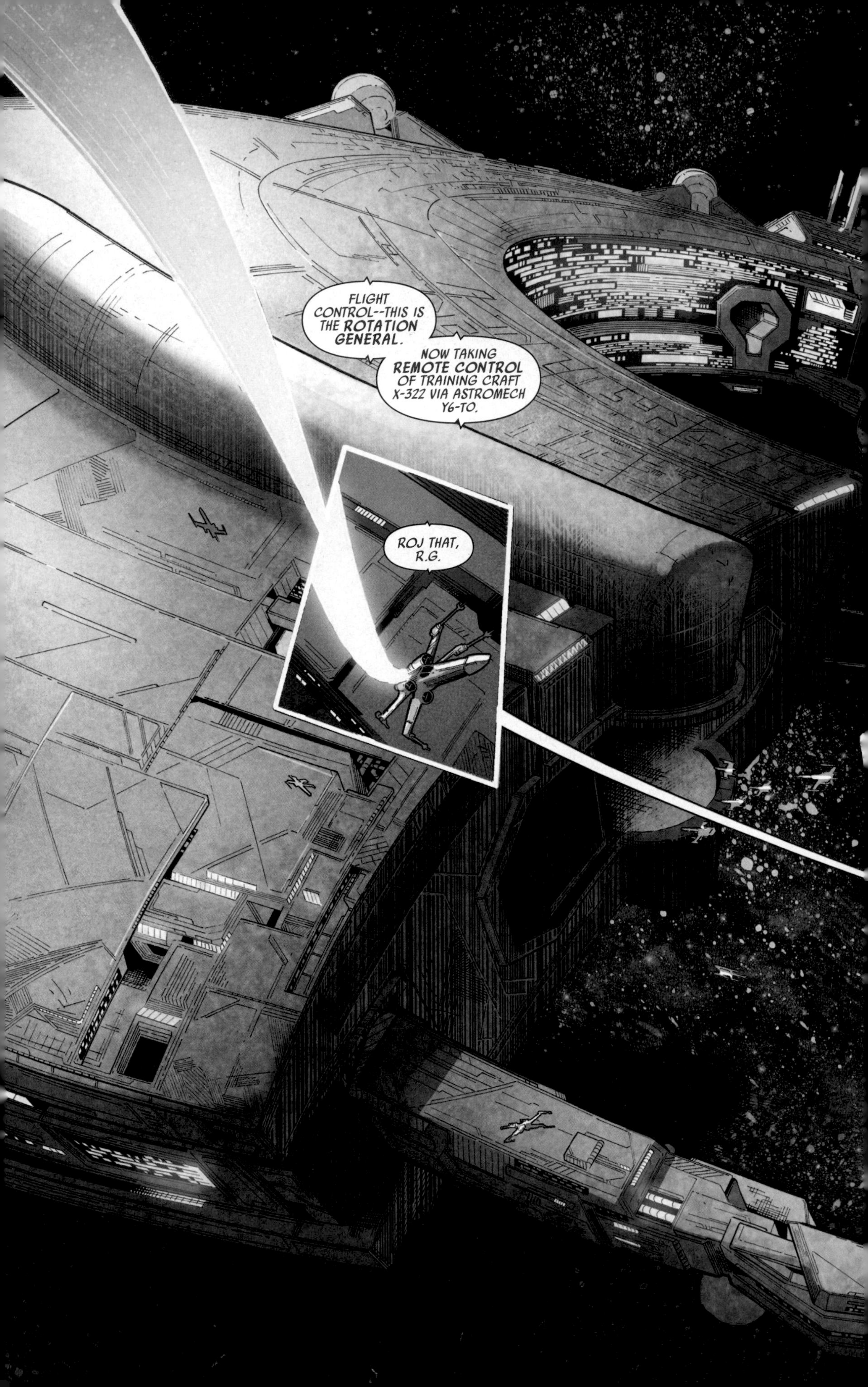

FLIGHT CONTROL--THIS IS THE ROTATION GENERAL.
NOW TAKING REMOTE CONTROL OF TRAINING CRAFT X-322 VIA ASTROMECH Y6-TO.
ROJ THAT, R.G.

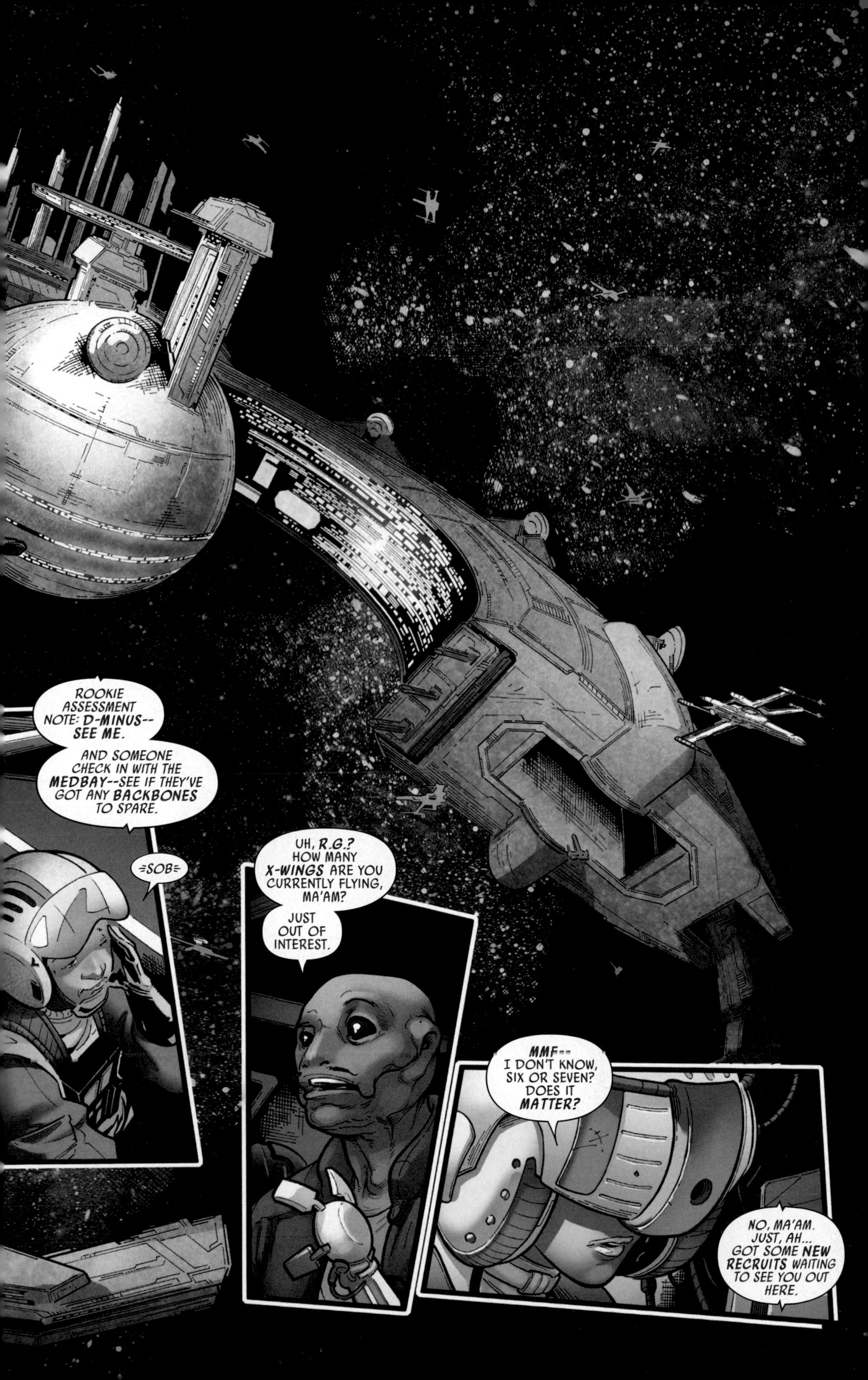
ROOKIE ASSESSMENT NOTE: D-MINUS--SEE ME.
AND SOMEONE CHECK IN WITH THE MEDBAY--SEE IF THEY'VE GOT ANY BACKBONES TO SPARE.
=SOB=
UH, R.G.? HOW MANY X-WINGS ARE YOU CURRENTLY FLYING, MA'AM?
JUST OUT OF INTEREST.
MMF--I DON'T KNOW, SIX OR SEVEN? DOES IT MATTER?
NO, MA'AM. JUST, AH... GOT SOME NEW RECRUITS WAITING TO SEE YOU OUT HERE.

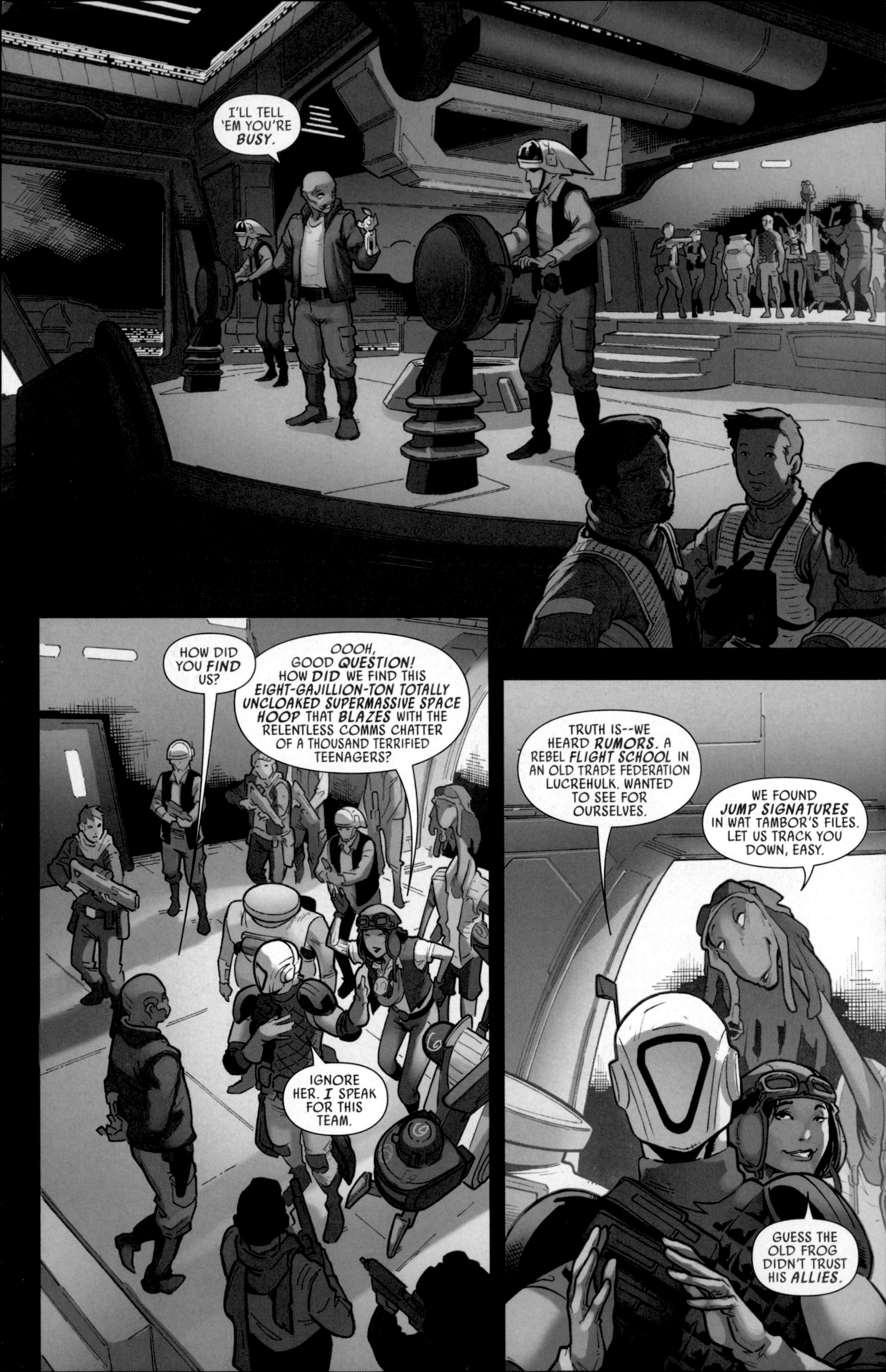
I'LL TELL 'EM YOU'RE BUSY.
HOW DID YOU FIND US?
OOOH, GOOD QUESTION! HOW DID WE FIND THIS EIGHT-GAJILLION-TON TOTALLY UNCLOAKED SUPERMASSIVE SPACE HOOP THAT BLAZES WITH THE RELENTLESS COMMS CHATTER OF A THOUSAND TERRIFIED TEENAGERS?
IGNORE HER. I SPEAK FOR THIS TEAM.
TRUTH IS--WE HEARD RUMORS. A REBEL FLIGHT SCHOOL IN AN OLD TRADE FEDERATION LUCREHULK. WANTED TO SEE FOR OURSELVES.
WE FOUND JUMP SIGNATURES IN WAT TAMBOR'S FILES. LET US TRACK YOU DOWN, EASY.
GUESS THE OLD FROG DIDN'T TRUST HIS ALLIES.

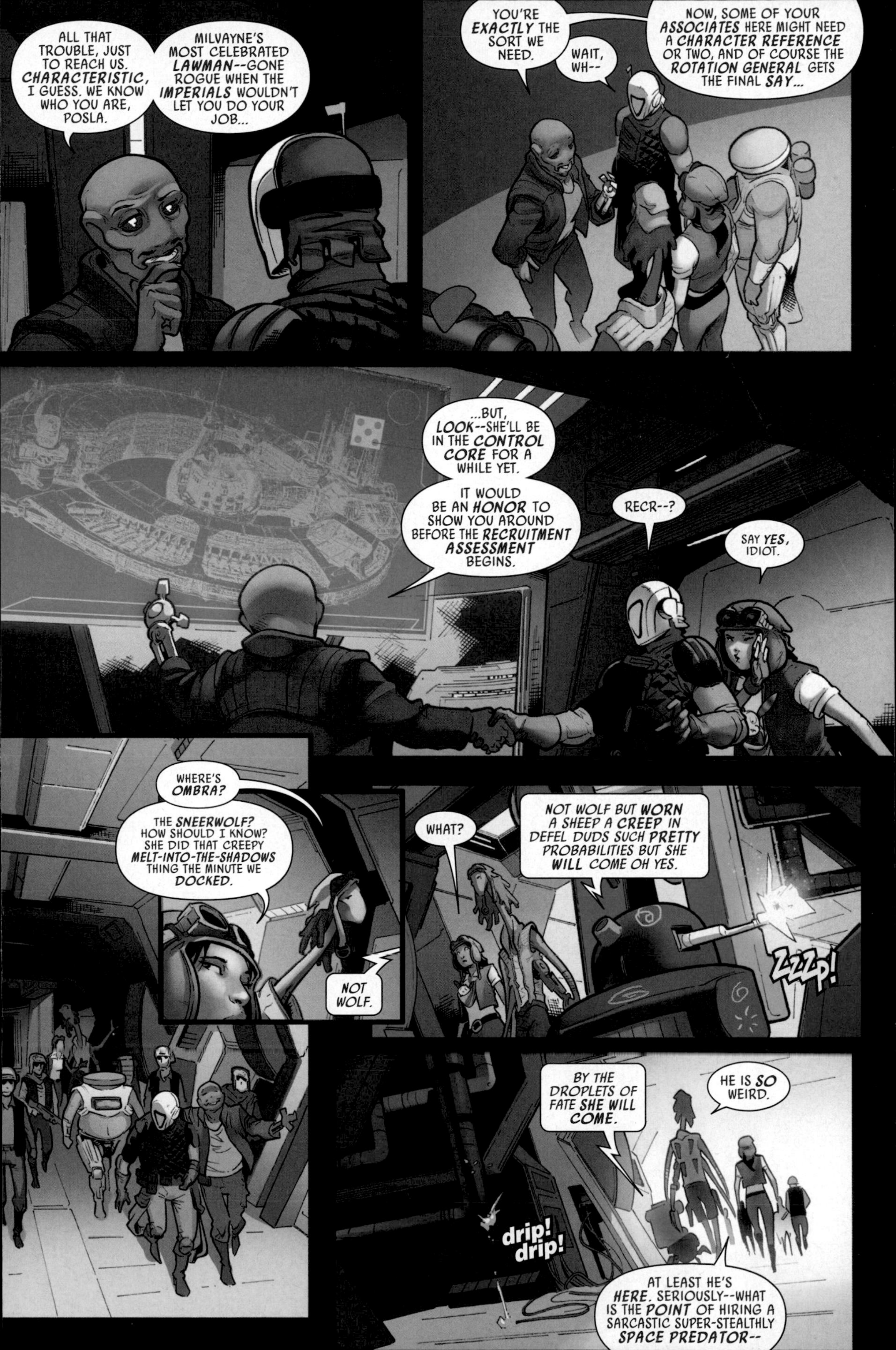
ALL THAT TROUBLE, JUST TO REACH US. CHARACTERISTIC, I GUESS. WE KNOW WHO YOU ARE, POSLA.
MILVAYNE'S MOST CELEBRATED LAWMAN--GONE ROGUE WHEN THE IMPERIALS WOULDN'T LET YOU DO YOUR JOB...
YOU'RE EXACTLY THE SORT WE NEED.
WAIT, WH--
NOW, SOME OF YOUR ASSOCIATES HERE MIGHT NEED A CHARACTER REFERENCE OR TWO, AND OF COURSE THE ROTATION GENERAL GETS THE FINAL SAY...
...BUT, LOOK--SHE'LL BE IN THE CONTROL CORE FOR A WHILE YET.
IT WOULD BE AN HONOR TO SHOW YOU AROUND BEFORE THE RECRUITMENT ASSESSMENT BEGINS.
RECR--?
SAY YES, IDIOT.
WHERE'S OMBRA?
THE SNEERWOLF? HOW SHOULD I KNOW? SHE DID THAT CREEPY MELT-INTO-THE-SHADOWS THING THE MINUTE WE DOCKED.
NOT WOLF.
WHAT?
NOT WOLF BUT WORN A SHEEP A CREEP IN DEFEL DUDS SUCH PRETTY PROBABILITIES BUT SHE WILL COME OH YES.
ZZZP!
BY THE DROPLETS OF FATE SHE WILL COME.
HE IS SO WEIRD.
drip! drip!
AT LEAST HE'S HERE. SERIOUSLY--WHAT IS THE POINT OF HIRING A SARCASTIC SUPER-STEALTHLY SPACE PREDATOR--

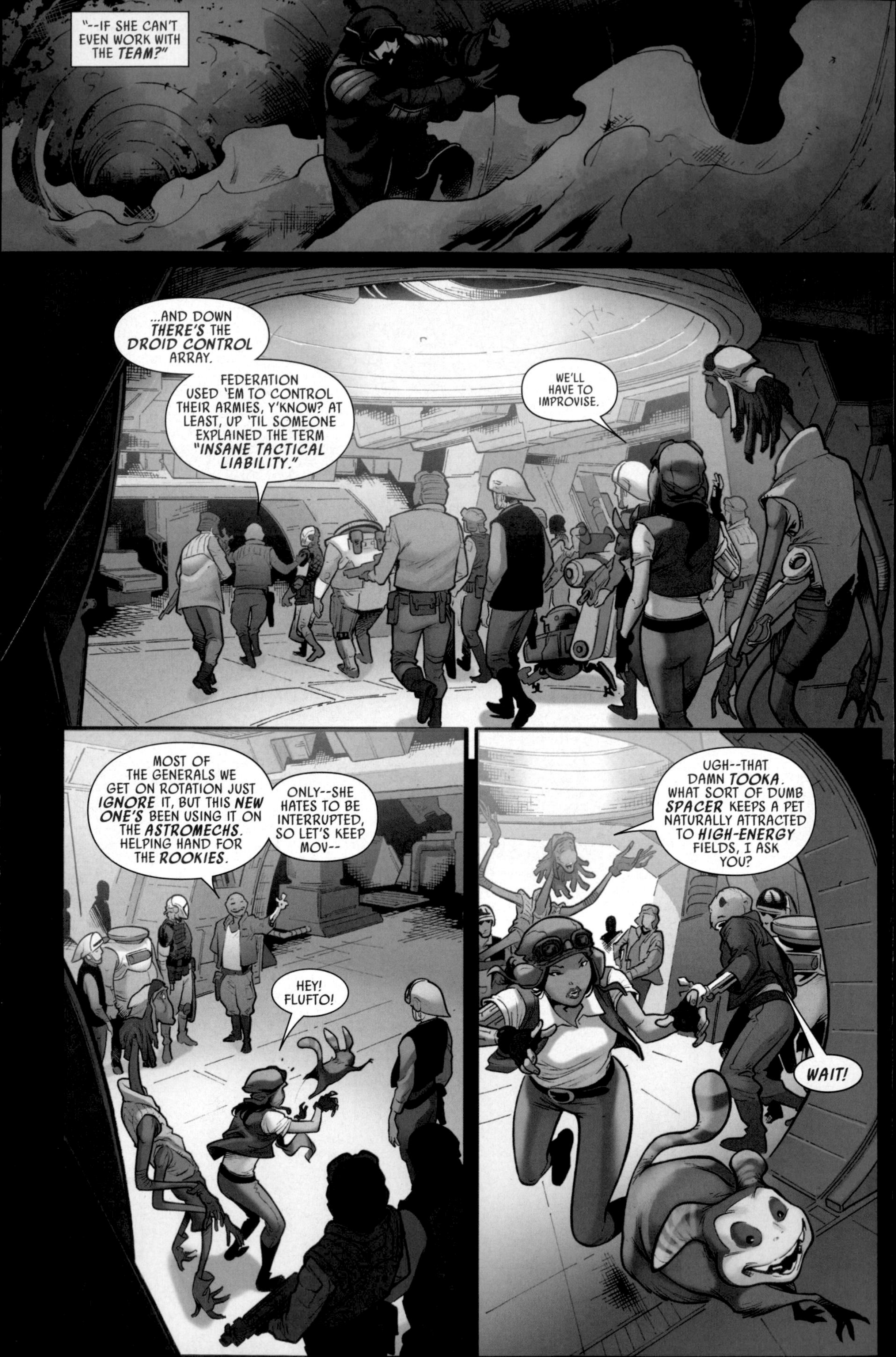
"--IF SHE CAN'T EVEN WORK WITH THE TEAM?"
...AND DOWN THERE'S THE DROID CONTROL ARRAY.
FEDERATION USED 'EM TO CONTROL THEIR ARMIES, Y'KNOW? AT LEAST, UP 'TIL SOMEONE EXPLAINED THE TERM "INSANE TACTICAL LIABILITY."
WE'LL HAVE TO IMPROVISE.
MOST OF THE GENERALS WE GET ON ROTATION JUST IGNORE IT, BUT THIS NEW ONE'S BEEN USING IT ON THE ASTROMECHS. HELPING HAND FOR THE ROOKIES.
ONLY--SHE HATES TO BE INTERRUPTED, SO LET'S KEEP MOV--
HEY! FLUFTO!
UGH--THAT DAMN TOOKA. WHAT SORT OF DUMB SPACER KEEPS A PET NATURALLY ATTRACTED TO HIGH-ENERGY FIELDS, I ASK YOU?
WAIT!

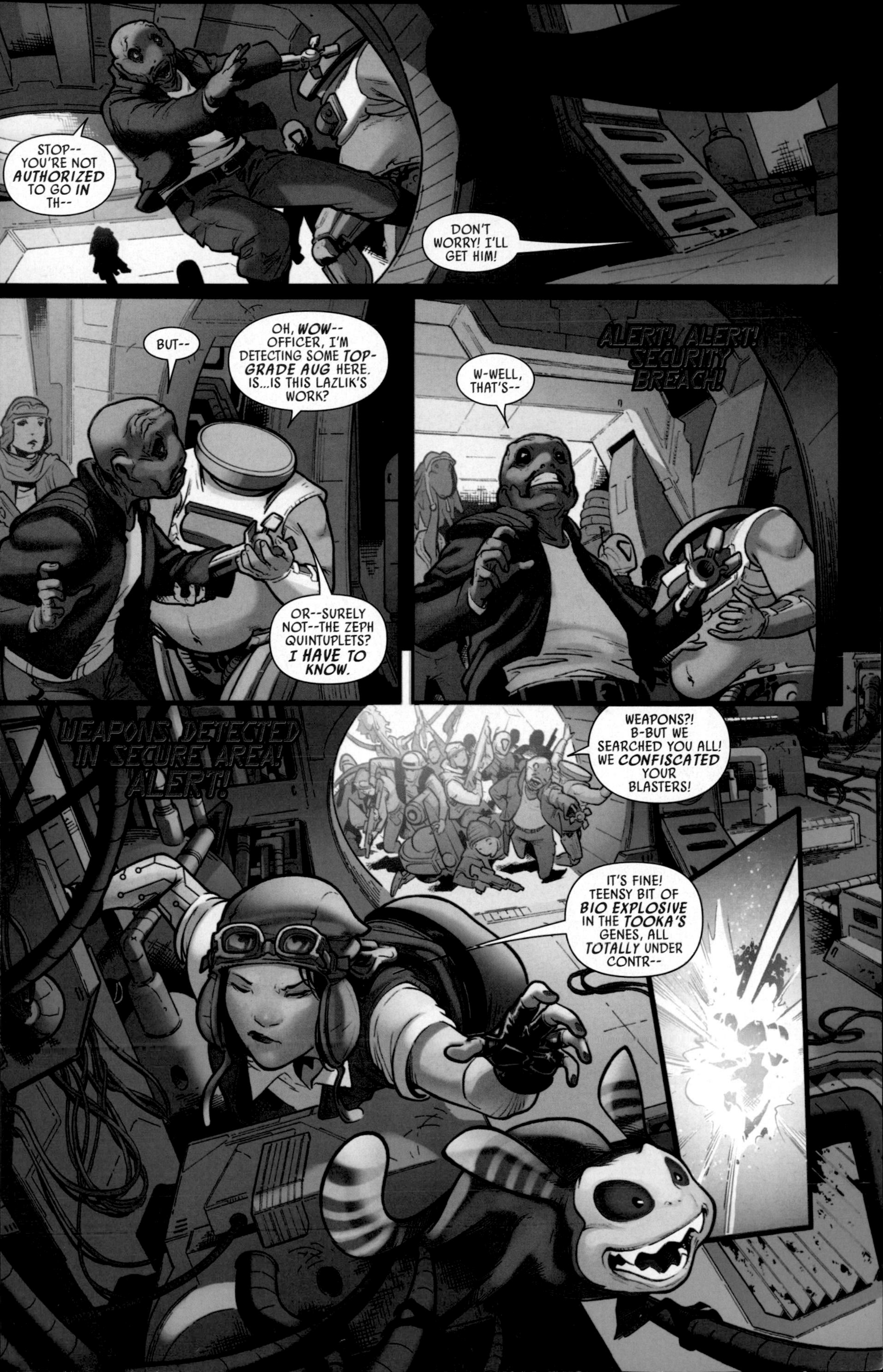
STOP-- YOU'RE NOT AUTHORIZED TO GO IN TH--
DON'T WORRY! I'LL GET HIM!
BUT--
OH, WOW-- OFFICER, I'M DETECTING SOME TOP-GRADE AUG HERE. IS...IS THIS LAZLIK'S WORK?
OR--SURELY NOT--THE ZEPH QUINTUPLETS? I HAVE TO KNOW.
ALERT! ALERT! SECURITY BREACH!
W-WELL, THAT'S--
WEAPONS DETECTED IN SECURE AREA! ALERT!
WEAPONS?! B-BUT WE SEARCHED YOU ALL! WE CONFISCATED YOUR BLASTERS!
IT'S FINE! TEENSY BIT OF BIO EXPLOSIVE IN THE TOOKA'S GENES, ALL TOTALLY UNDER CONTR--

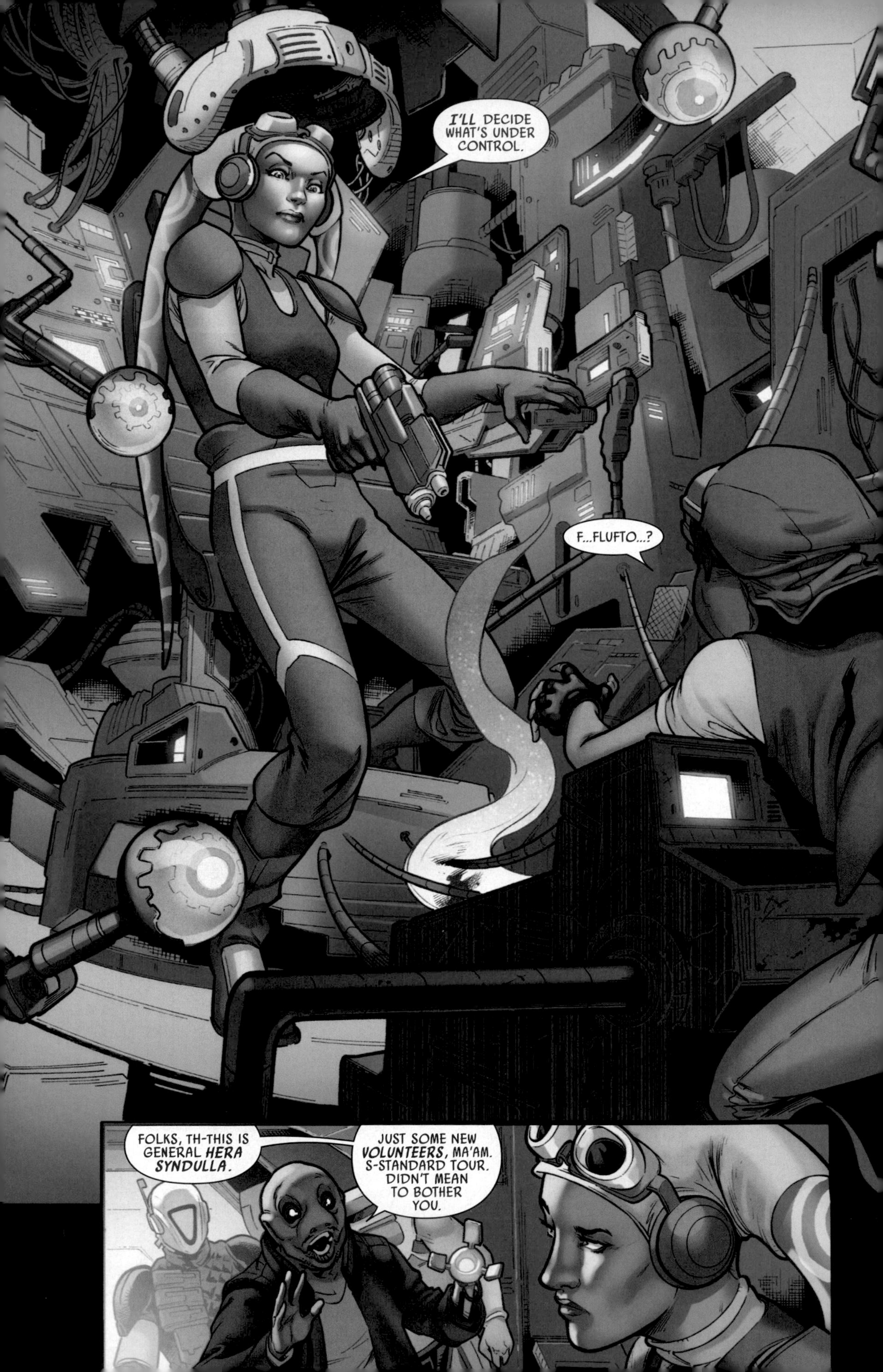

I'LL DECIDE WHAT'S UNDER CONTROL.
F...FLUFTO...?
FOLKS, TH-THIS IS GENERAL HERA SYNDULLA.
JUST SOME NEW VOLUNTEERS, MA'AM. S-STANDARD TOUR. DIDN'T MEAN TO BOTHER YOU.

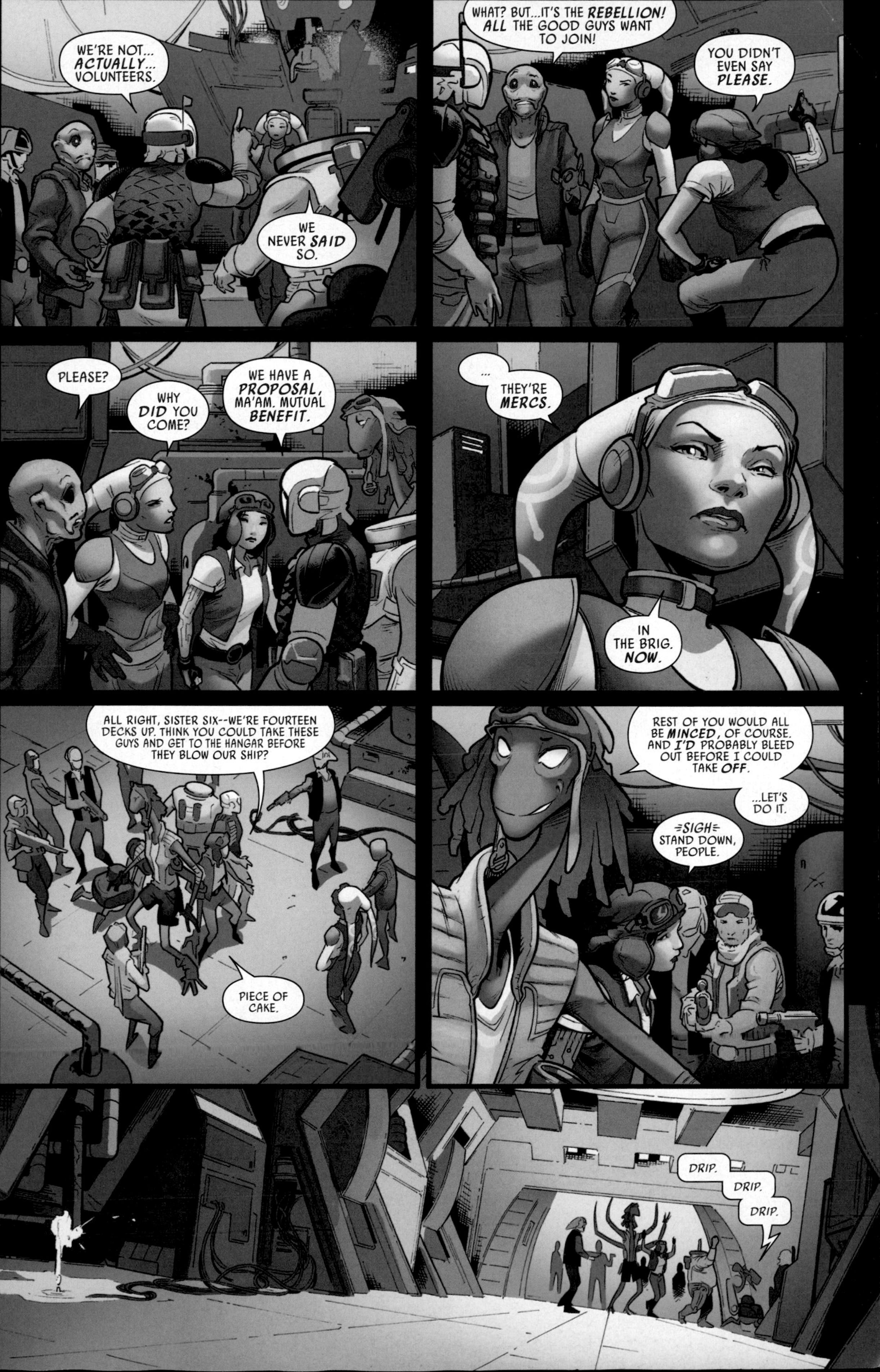

WE'RE NOT... ACTUALLY... VOLUNTEERS.
WE NEVER SAID SO.
WHAT? BUT...IT'S THE REBELLION! ALL THE GOOD GUYS WANT TO JOIN!
YOU DIDN'T EVEN SAY PLEASE.
PLEASE?
WHY DID YOU COME?
WE HAVE A PROPOSAL, MA'AM. MUTUAL BENEFIT.
... THEY'RE MERCS.
IN THE BRIG. NOW.
ALL RIGHT, SISTER SIX--WE'RE FOURTEEN DECKS UP. THINK YOU COULD TAKE THESE GUYS AND GET TO THE HANGAR BEFORE THEY BLOW OUR SHIP?
PIECE OF CAKE.
REST OF YOU WOULD ALL BE MINCED, OF COURSE. AND I'D PROBABLY BLEED OUT BEFORE I COULD TAKE OFF.
...LET'S DO IT.
=SIGH= STAND DOWN, PEOPLE.
DRIP.
DRIP.
DRIP.

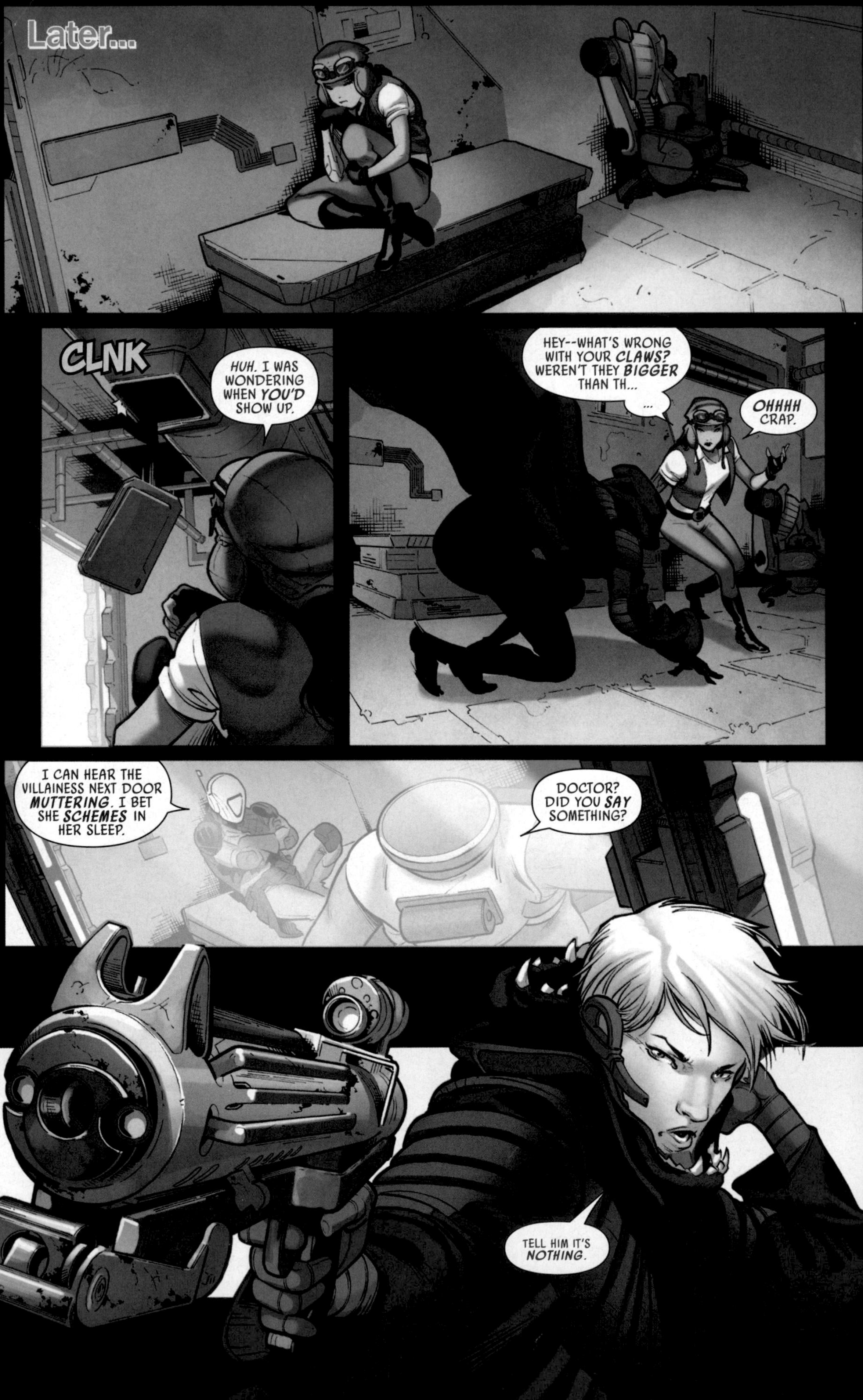
Later...
CLNK
HUH. I WAS WONDERING WHEN YOU'D SHOW UP.
HEY--WHAT'S WRONG WITH YOUR CLAWS? WEREN'T THEY BIGGER THAN TH...
...
OHHHH CRAP.
I CAN HEAR THE VILLAINESS NEXT DOOR MUTTERING. I BET SHE SCHEMES IN HER SLEEP.
DOCTOR? DID YOU SAY SOMETHING?
TELL HIM IT'S NOTHING.

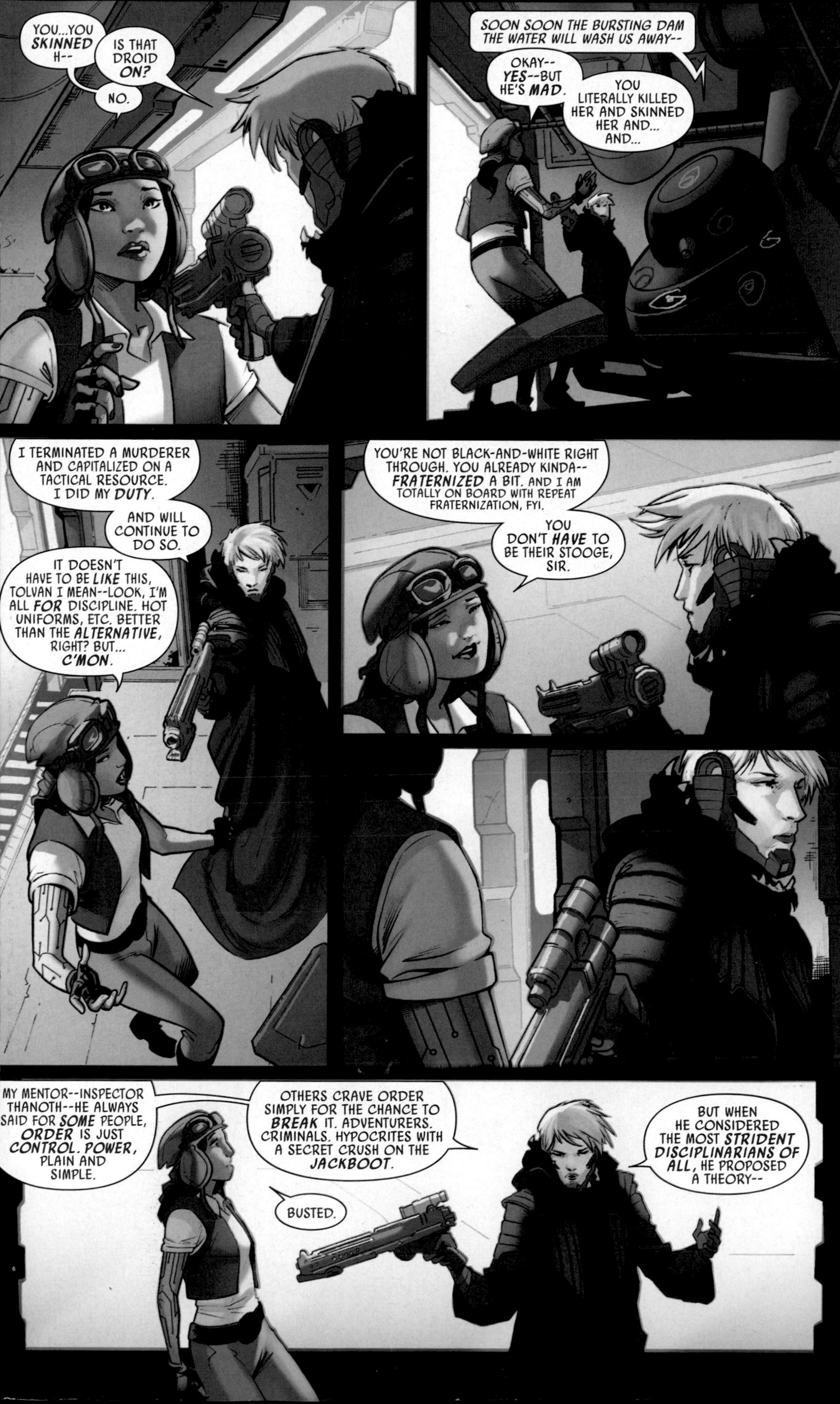

YOU...YOU SKINNED H--
IS THAT DROID ON?
NO.
SOON SOON THE BURSTING DAM THE WATER WILL WASH US AWAY--
OKAY-- YES--BUT HE'S MAD.
YOU LITERALLY KILLED HER AND SKINNED HER AND... AND...
I TERMINATED A MURDERER AND CAPITALIZED ON A TACTICAL RESOURCE. I DID MY DUTY.
AND WILL CONTINUE TO DO SO.
IT DOESN'T HAVE TO BE LIKE THIS, TOLVAN I MEAN--LOOK, I'M ALL FOR DISCIPLINE. HOT UNIFORMS, ETC. BETTER THAN THE ALTERNATIVE, RIGHT? BUT... C'MON.
YOU'RE NOT BLACK-AND-WHITE RIGHT THROUGH. YOU ALREADY KINDA-- FRATERNIZED A BIT. AND I AM TOTALLY ON BOARD WITH REPEAT FRATERNIZATION, FYI.
YOU DON'T HAVE TO BE THEIR STOOGE, SIR.
MY MENTOR--INSPECTOR THANOTH--HE ALWAYS SAID FOR SOME PEOPLE, ORDER IS JUST CONTROL. POWER, PLAIN AND SIMPLE.
OTHERS CRAVE ORDER SIMPLY FOR THE CHANCE TO BREAK IT. ADVENTURERS. CRIMINALS. HYPOCRITES WITH A SECRET CRUSH ON THE JACKBOOT.
BUSTED.
BUT WHEN HE CONSIDERED THE MOST STRIDENT DISCIPLINARIANS OF ALL, HE PROPOSED A THEORY--

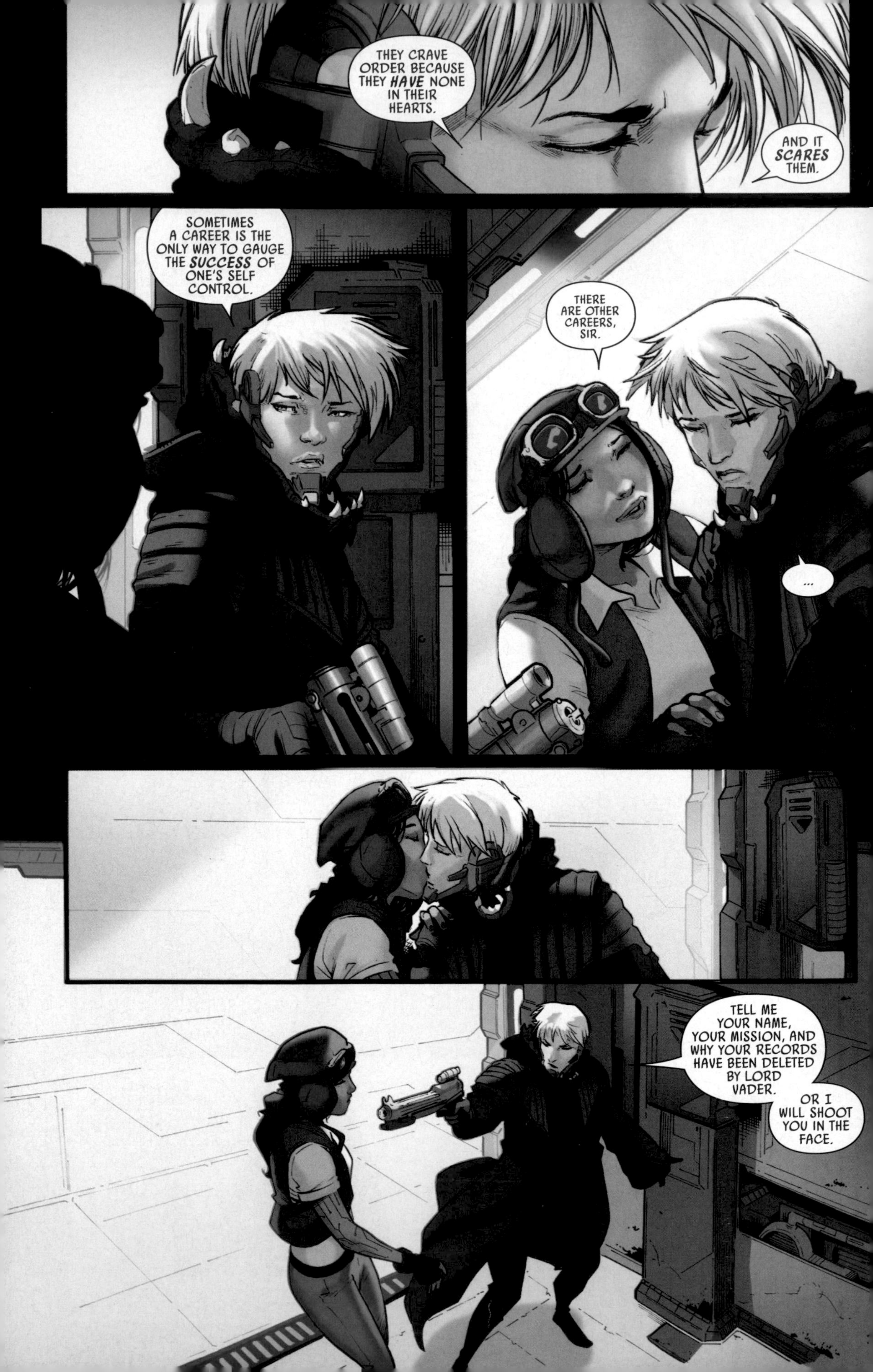
THEY CRAVE ORDER BECAUSE THEY *HAVE* NONE IN THEIR HEARTS.
AND IT *SCARES* THEM.
SOMETIMES A CAREER IS THE ONLY WAY TO GAUGE THE *SUCCESS* OF ONE'S SELF CONTROL.
THERE ARE OTHER CAREERS, SIR.
...
TELL ME YOUR NAME, YOUR MISSION, AND WHY YOUR RECORDS HAVE BEEN DELETED BY LORD VADER.
OR I WILL SHOOT YOU IN THE FACE.

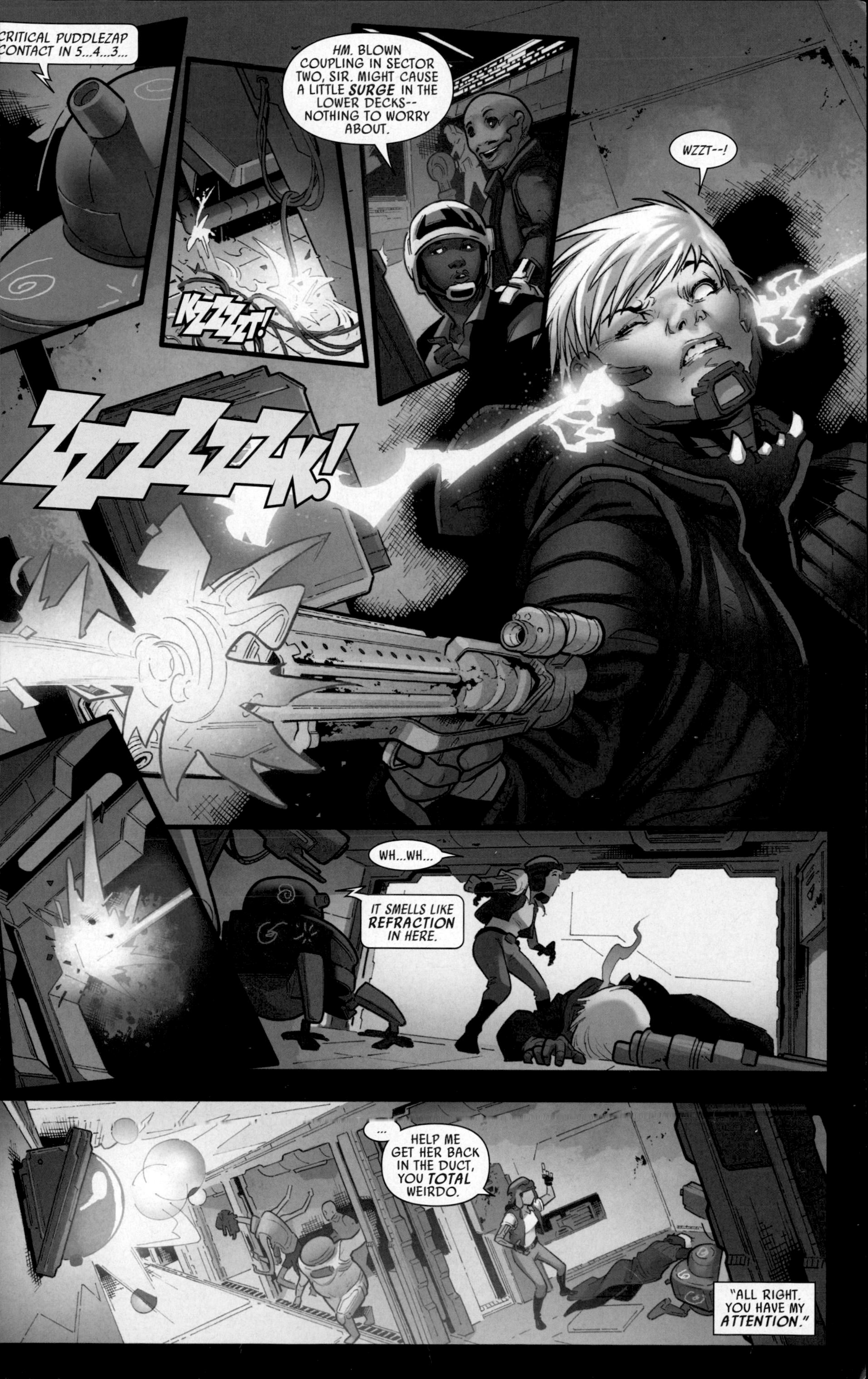
CRITICAL PUDDLEZAP CONTACT IN 5...4...3...
KZZZZT!
HM. BLOWN COUPLING IN SECTOR TWO, SIR. MIGHT CAUSE A LITTLE SURGE IN THE LOWER DECKS-- NOTHING TO WORRY ABOUT.
WZZT--!
ZZZZZZK!
WH...WH...
IT SMELLS LIKE REFRACTION IN HERE.
...
HELP ME GET HER BACK IN THE DUCT, YOU TOTAL WEIRDO.
"ALL RIGHT. YOU HAVE MY ATTENTION."

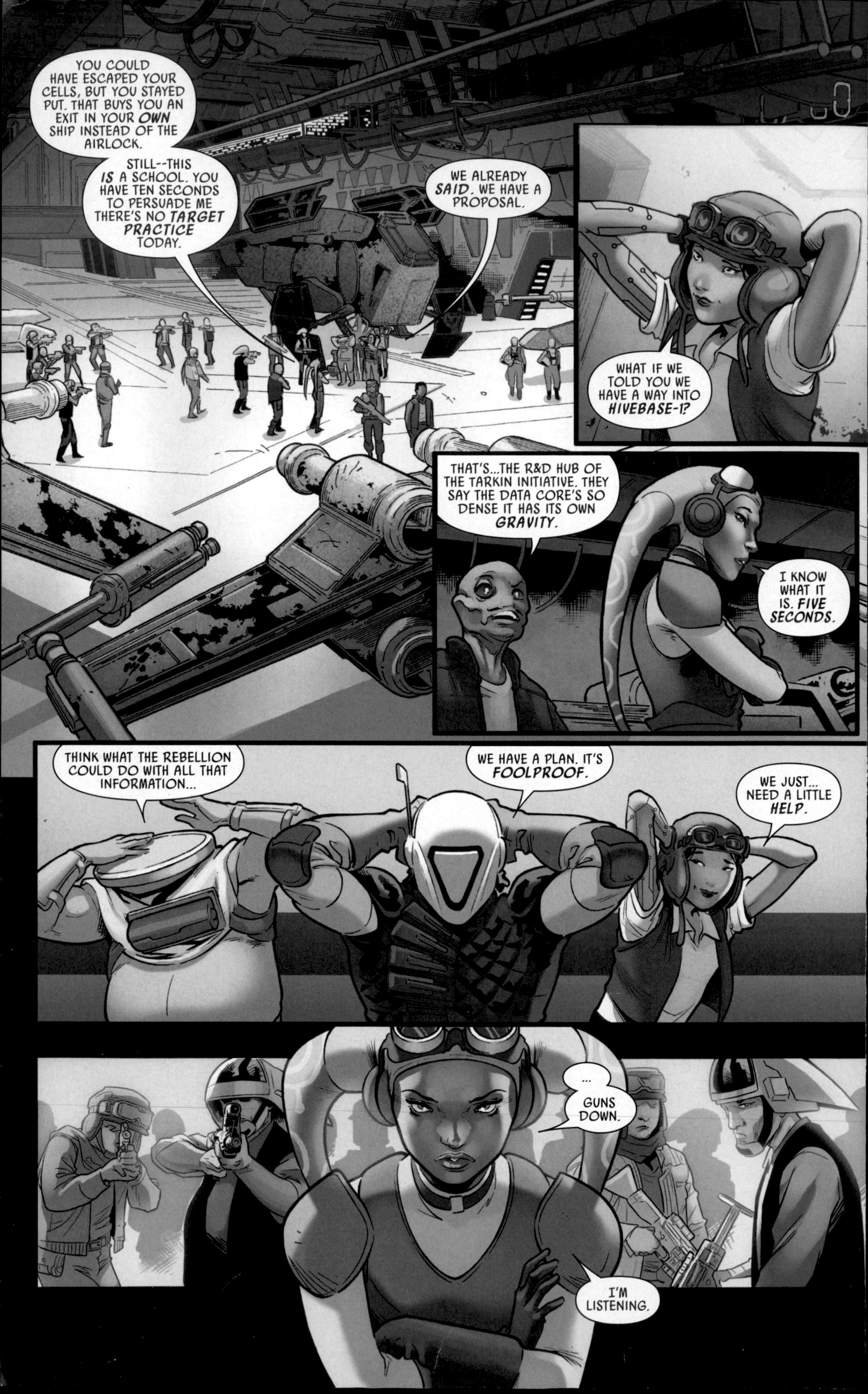
YOU COULD HAVE ESCAPED YOUR CELLS, BUT YOU STAYED PUT. THAT BUYS YOU AN EXIT IN YOUR OWN SHIP INSTEAD OF THE AIRLOCK.
STILL--THIS IS A SCHOOL. YOU HAVE TEN SECONDS TO PERSUADE ME THERE'S NO TARGET PRACTICE TODAY.
WE ALREADY SAID. WE HAVE A PROPOSAL.
WHAT IF WE TOLD YOU WE HAVE A WAY INTO HIVEBASE-1?
THAT'S...THE R&D HUB OF THE TARKIN INITIATIVE. THEY SAY THE DATA CORE'S SO DENSE IT HAS ITS OWN GRAVITY.
I KNOW WHAT IT IS. FIVE SECONDS.
THINK WHAT THE REBELLION COULD DO WITH ALL THAT INFORMATION...
WE HAVE A PLAN. IT'S FOOLPROOF.
WE JUST... NEED A LITTLE HELP.
...
GUNS DOWN.
I'M LISTENING.

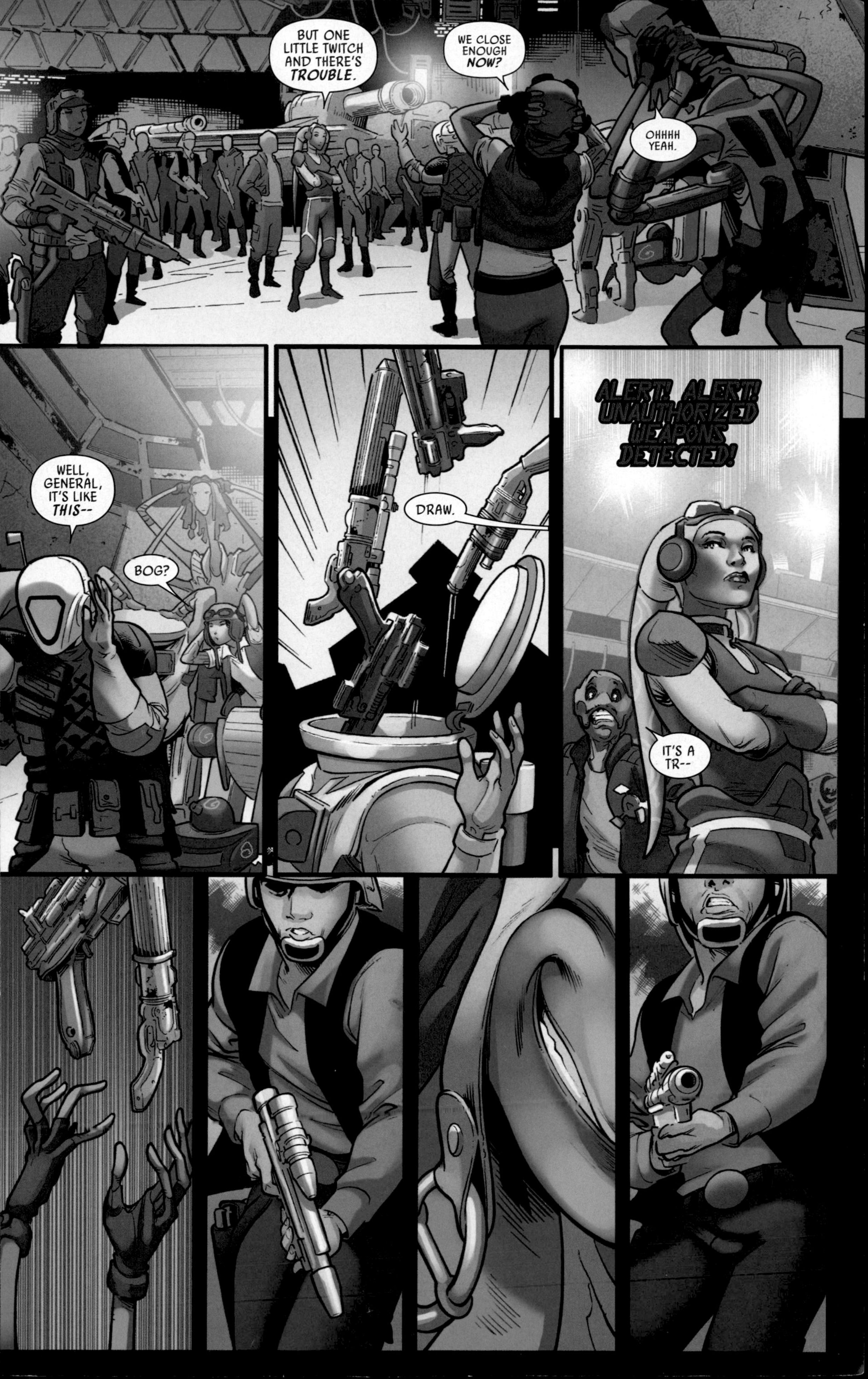
BUT ONE LITTLE TWITCH AND THERE'S TROUBLE.
WE CLOSE ENOUGH NOW?
OHHHH YEAH.
WELL, GENERAL, IT'S LIKE THIS--
BOG?
DRAW.
ALERT! ALERT! UNAUTHORIZED WEAPONS DETECTED!
IT'S A TR--

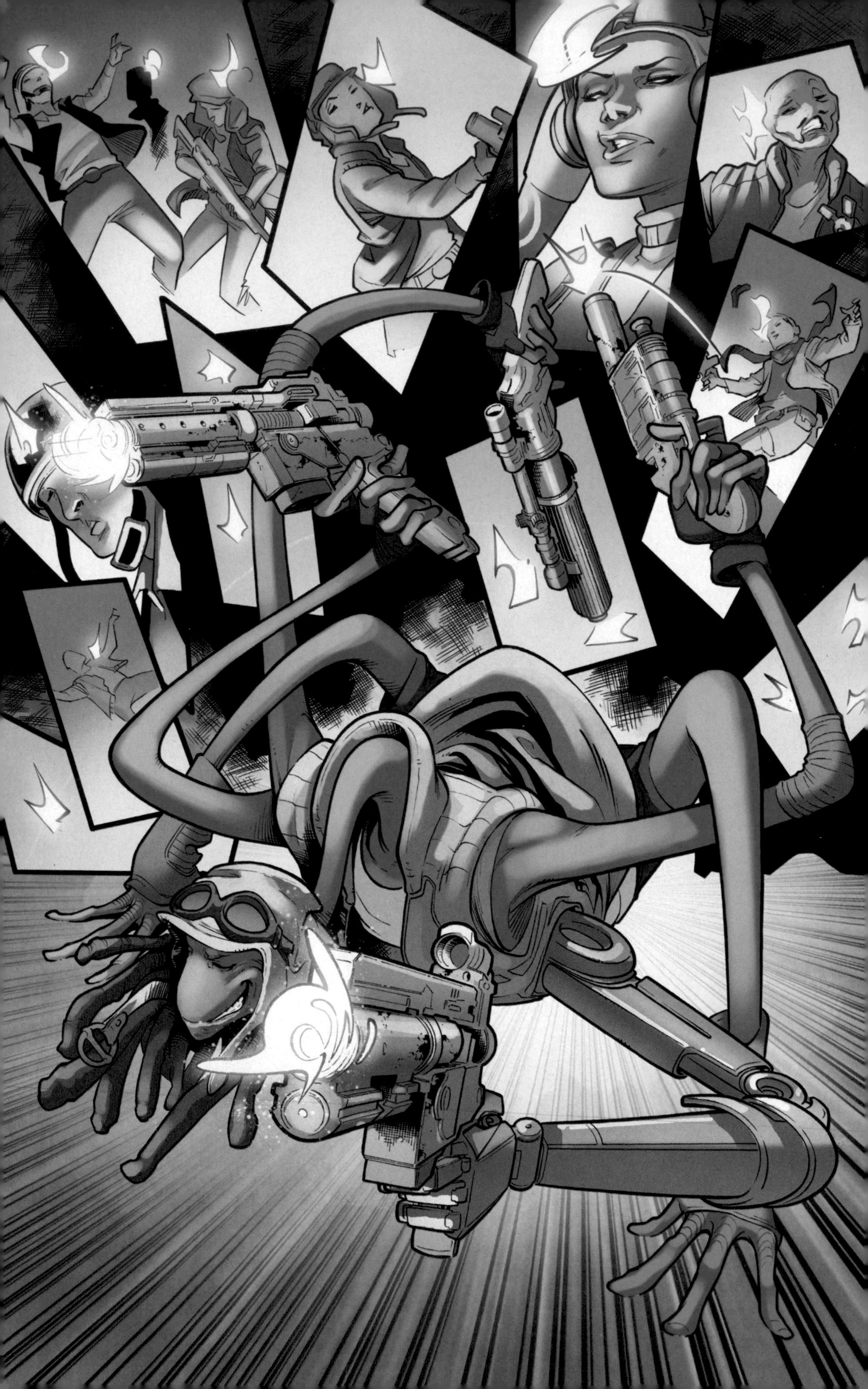

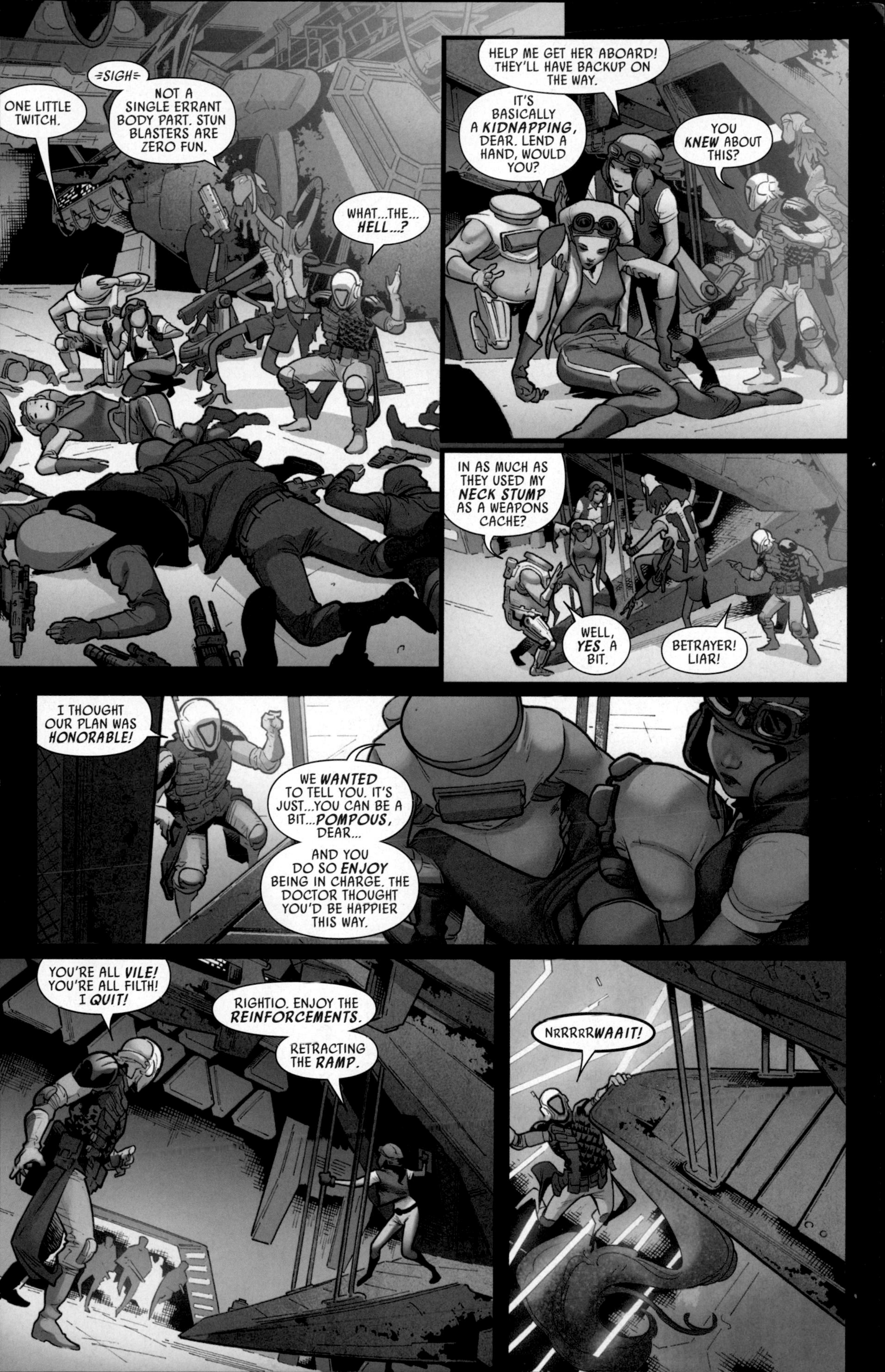

ONE LITTLE TWITCH.
≡SIGH≡
NOT A SINGLE ERRANT BODY PART. STUN BLASTERS ARE ZERO FUN.
WHAT...THE... HELL...?
HELP ME GET HER ABOARD! THEY'LL HAVE BACKUP ON THE WAY.
IT'S BASICALLY A KIDNAPPING, DEAR. LEND A HAND, WOULD YOU?
YOU KNEW ABOUT THIS?
IN AS MUCH AS THEY USED MY NECK STUMP AS A WEAPONS CACHE?
WELL, YES. A BIT.
BETRAYER! LIAR!
I THOUGHT OUR PLAN WAS HONORABLE!
WE WANTED TO TELL YOU. IT'S JUST...YOU CAN BE A BIT...POMPOUS, DEAR...
AND YOU DO SO ENJOY BEING IN CHARGE. THE DOCTOR THOUGHT YOU'D BE HAPPIER THIS WAY.
YOU'RE ALL VILE! YOU'RE ALL FILTH! I QUIT!
RIGHTIO. ENJOY THE REINFORCEMENTS.
RETRACTING THE RAMP.
NrRRRRWAAIT!

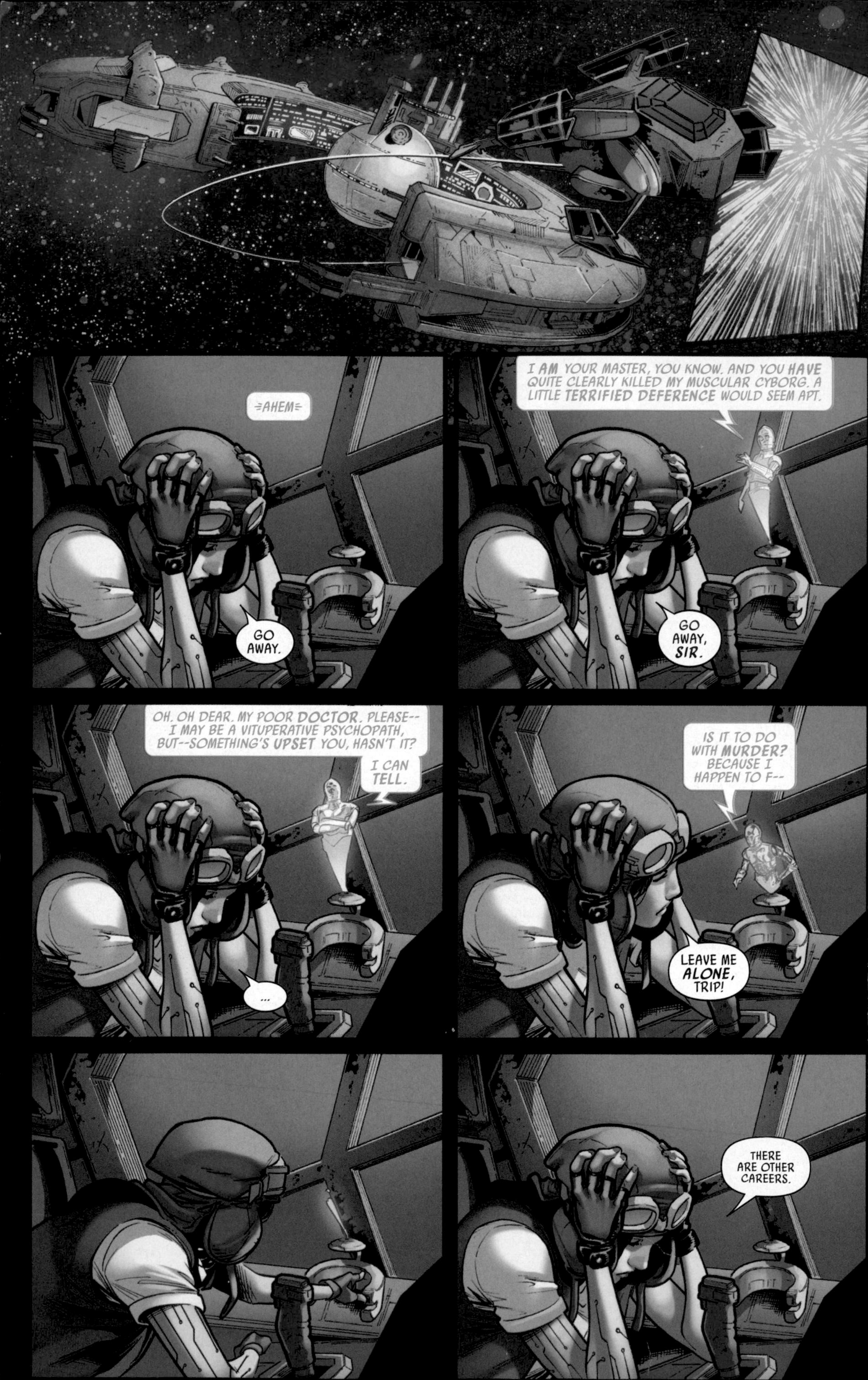

AHEM
GO AWAY.
I AM YOUR MASTER, YOU KNOW. AND YOU HAVE QUITE CLEARLY KILLED MY MUSCULAR CYBORG. A LITTLE TERRIFIED DEFERENCE WOULD SEEM APT.
GO AWAY, SIR.
OH. OH DEAR. MY POOR DOCTOR. PLEASE-- I MAY BE A VITUPERATIVE PSYCHOPATH, BUT--SOMETHING'S UPSET YOU, HASN'T IT?
I CAN TELL.
...
IS IT TO DO WITH MURDER? BECAUSE I HAPPEN TO F--
LEAVE ME ALONE, TRIP!
THERE ARE OTHER CAREERS.

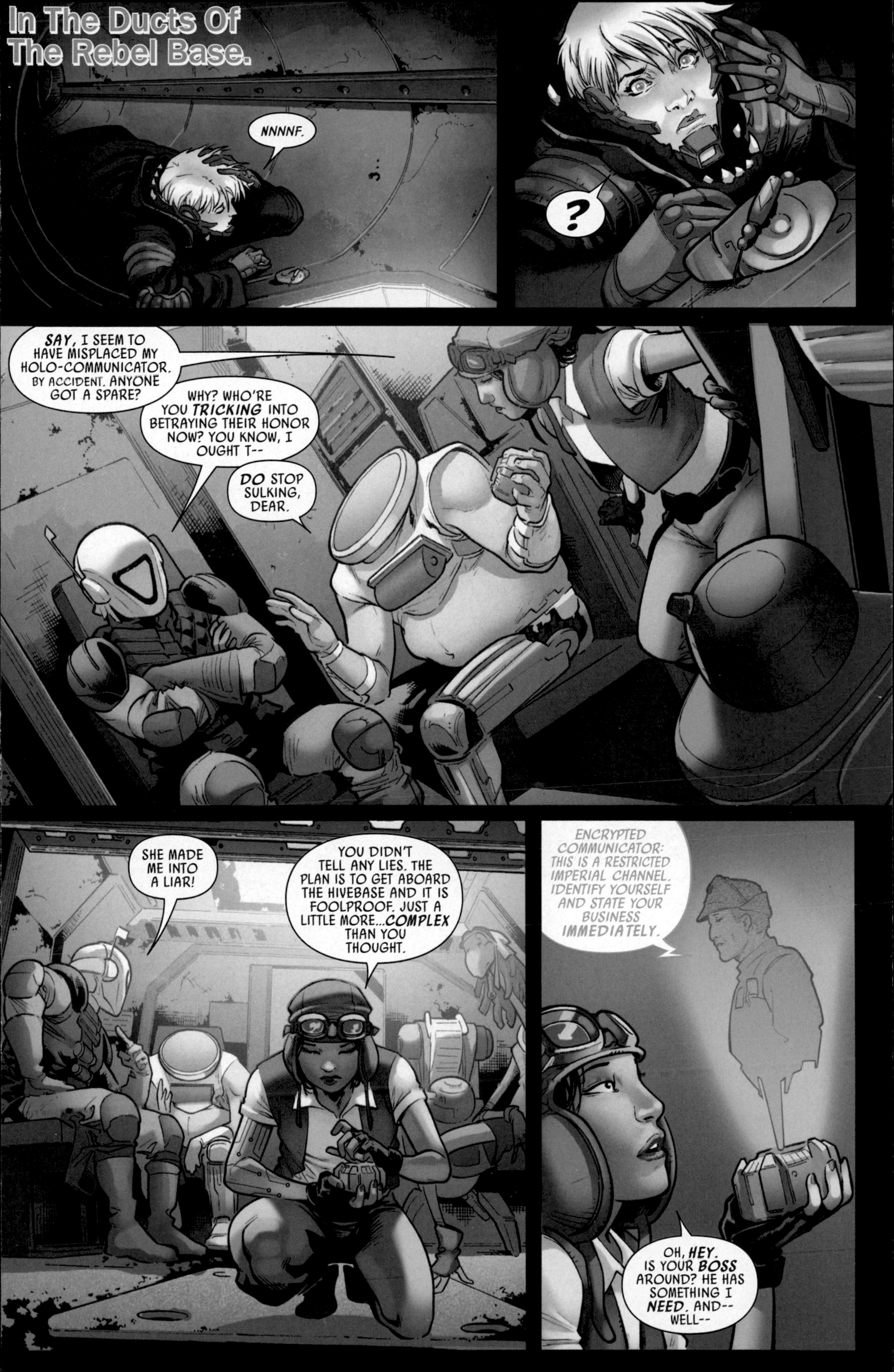
In The Ducts Of The Rebel Base.
NNNNF.
?
SAY, I SEEM TO HAVE MISPLACED MY HOLO-COMMUNICATOR. BY ACCIDENT. ANYONE GOT A SPARE?
WHY? WHO'RE YOU TRICKING INTO BETRAYING THEIR HONOR NOW? YOU KNOW, I OUGHT T--
DO STOP SULKING, DEAR.
SHE MADE ME INTO A LIAR!
YOU DIDN'T TELL ANY LIES. THE PLAN IS TO GET ABOARD THE HIVEBASE AND IT IS FOOLPROOF. JUST A LITTLE MORE...COMPLEX THAN YOU THOUGHT.
ENCRYPTED COMMUNICATOR: THIS IS A RESTRICTED IMPERIAL CHANNEL. IDENTIFY YOURSELF AND STATE YOUR BUSINESS IMMEDIATELY.
OH, HEY. IS YOUR BOSS AROUND? HE HAS SOMETHING I NEED. AND-- WELL--

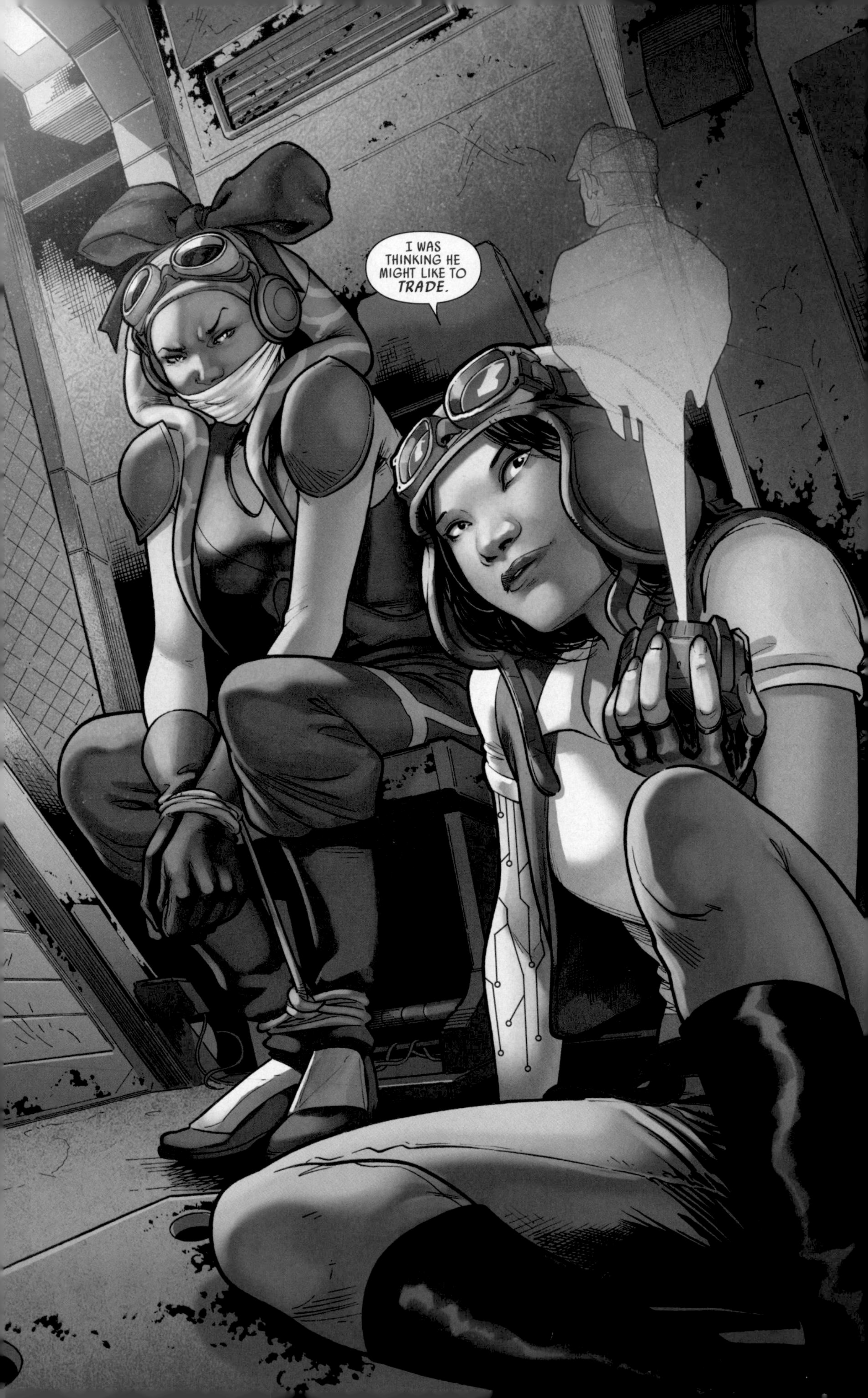
I WAS THINKING HE MIGHT LIKE TO TRADE.

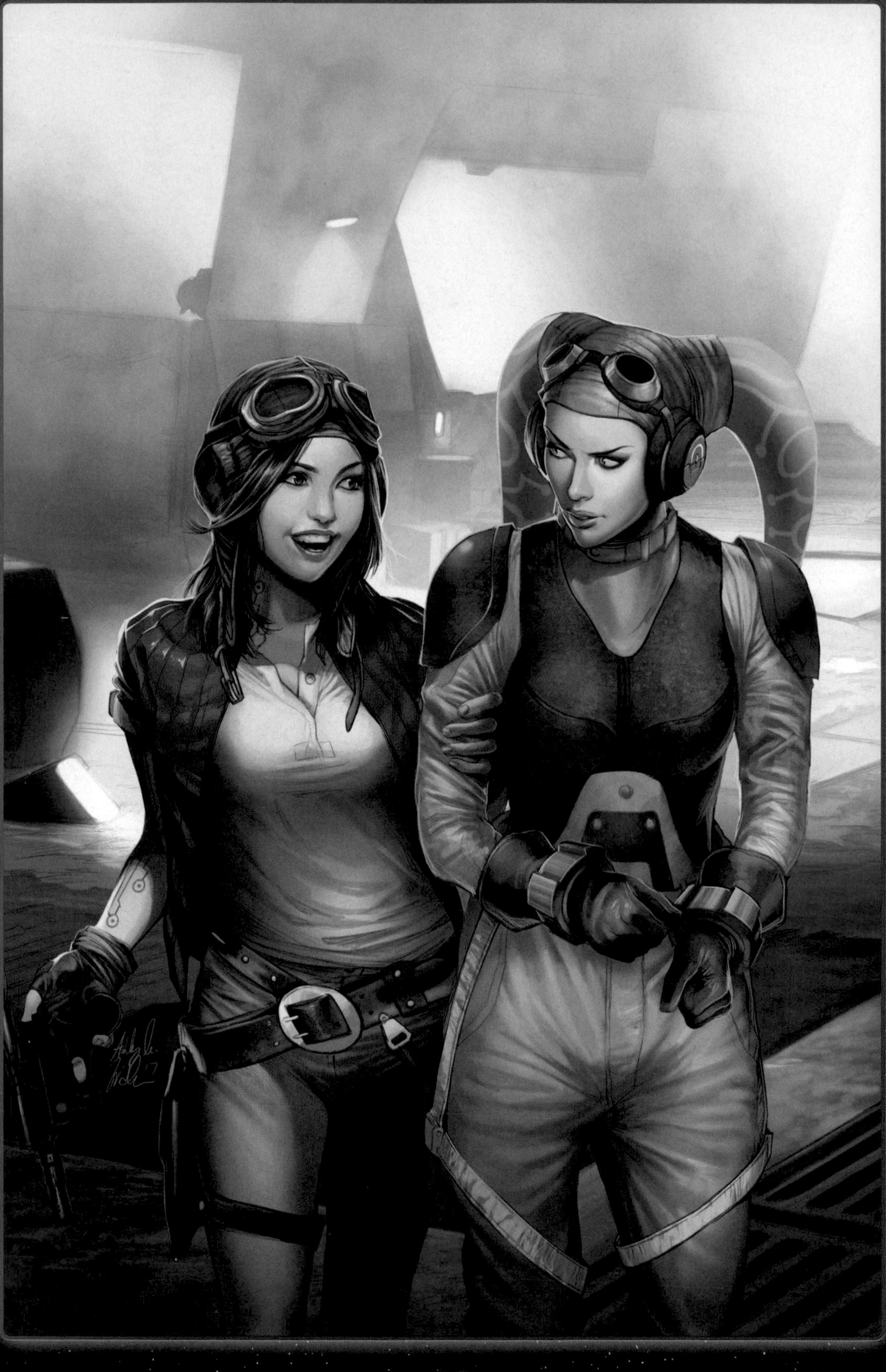

18

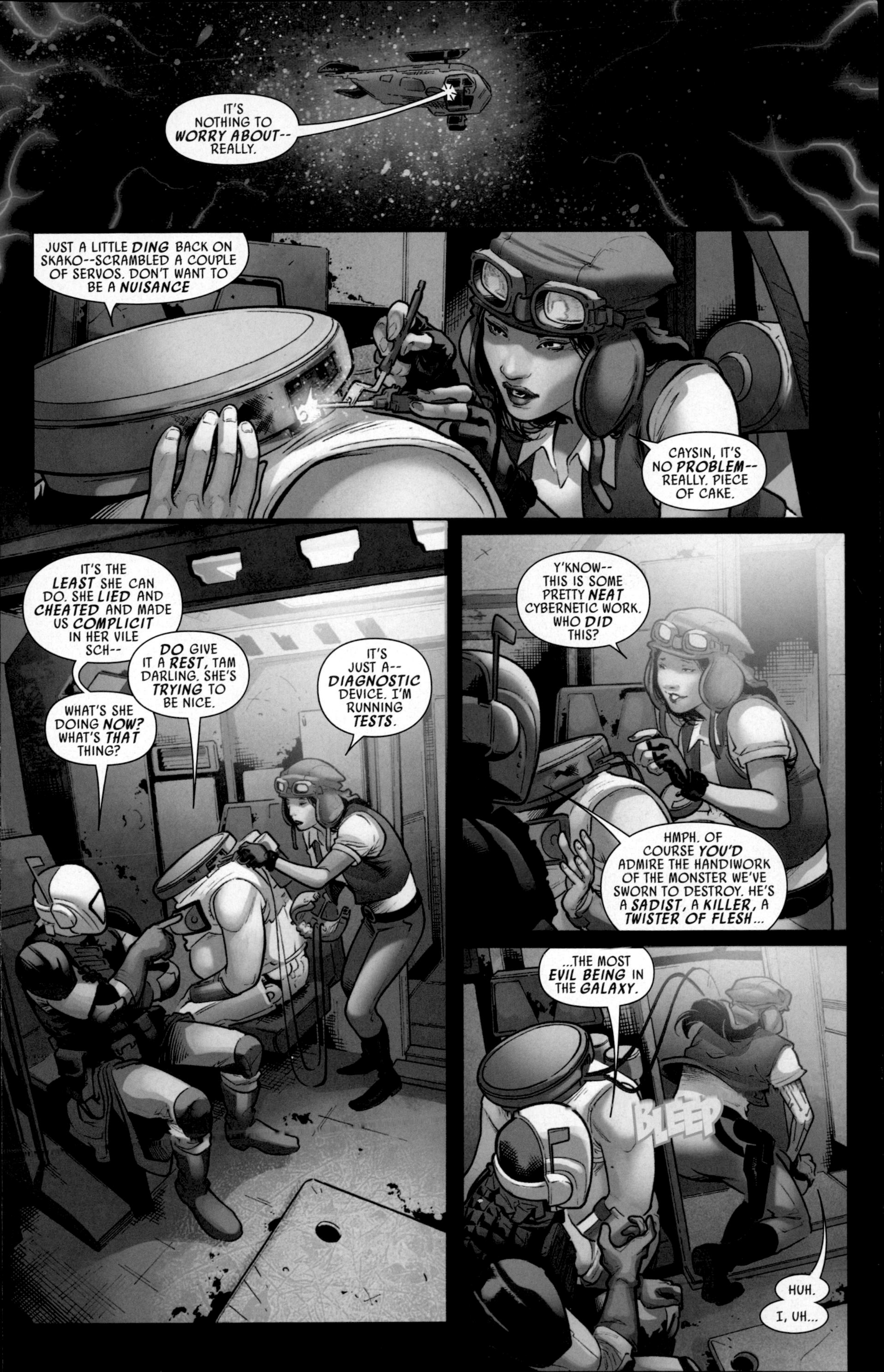

IT'S NOTHING TO WORRY ABOUT-- REALLY.
JUST A LITTLE DING BACK ON SKAKO--SCRAMBLED A COUPLE OF SERVOS. DON'T WANT TO BE A NUISANCE
CAYSIN, IT'S NO PROBLEM-- REALLY. PIECE OF CAKE.
IT'S THE LEAST SHE CAN DO. SHE LIED AND CHEATED AND MADE US COMPLICIT IN HER VILE SCH--
DO GIVE IT A REST, TAM DARLING. SHE'S TRYING TO BE NICE.
WHAT'S SHE DOING NOW? WHAT'S THAT THING?
IT'S JUST A-- DIAGNOSTIC DEVICE. I'M RUNNING TESTS.
Y'KNOW-- THIS IS SOME PRETTY NEAT CYBERNETIC WORK. WHO DID THIS?
HMPH. OF COURSE YOU'D ADMIRE THE HANDIWORK OF THE MONSTER WE'VE SWORN TO DESTROY. HE'S A SADIST, A KILLER, A TWISTER OF FLESH...
...THE MOST EVIL BEING IN THE GALAXY.
BLEEP
HUH.
I, UH...

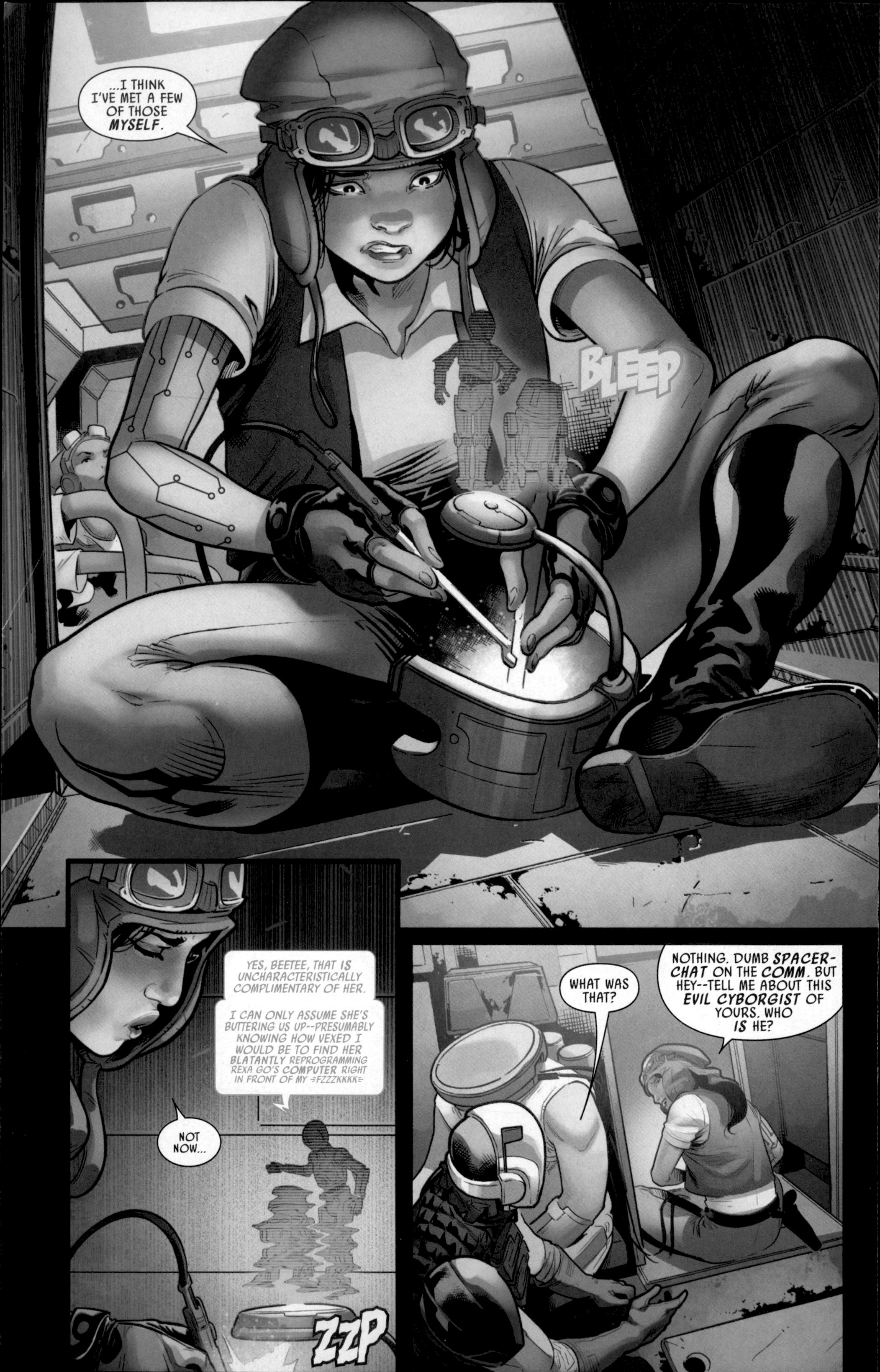
...I THINK I'VE MET A FEW OF THOSE MYSELF.
BLEEP
YES, BEETEE, THAT IS UNCHARACTERISTICALLY COMPLIMENTARY OF HER.
I CAN ONLY ASSUME SHE'S BUTTERING US UP--PRESUMABLY KNOWING HOW VEXED I WOULD BE TO FIND HER BLATANTLY REPROGRAMMING REXA GO'S COMPUTER RIGHT IN FRONT OF MY =FZZZKKKK=
NOT NOW...
ZZP
WHAT WAS THAT?
NOTHING. DUMB SPACER-CHAT ON THE COMM. BUT HEY--TELL ME ABOUT THIS EVIL CYBORGIST OF YOURS. WHO IS HE?

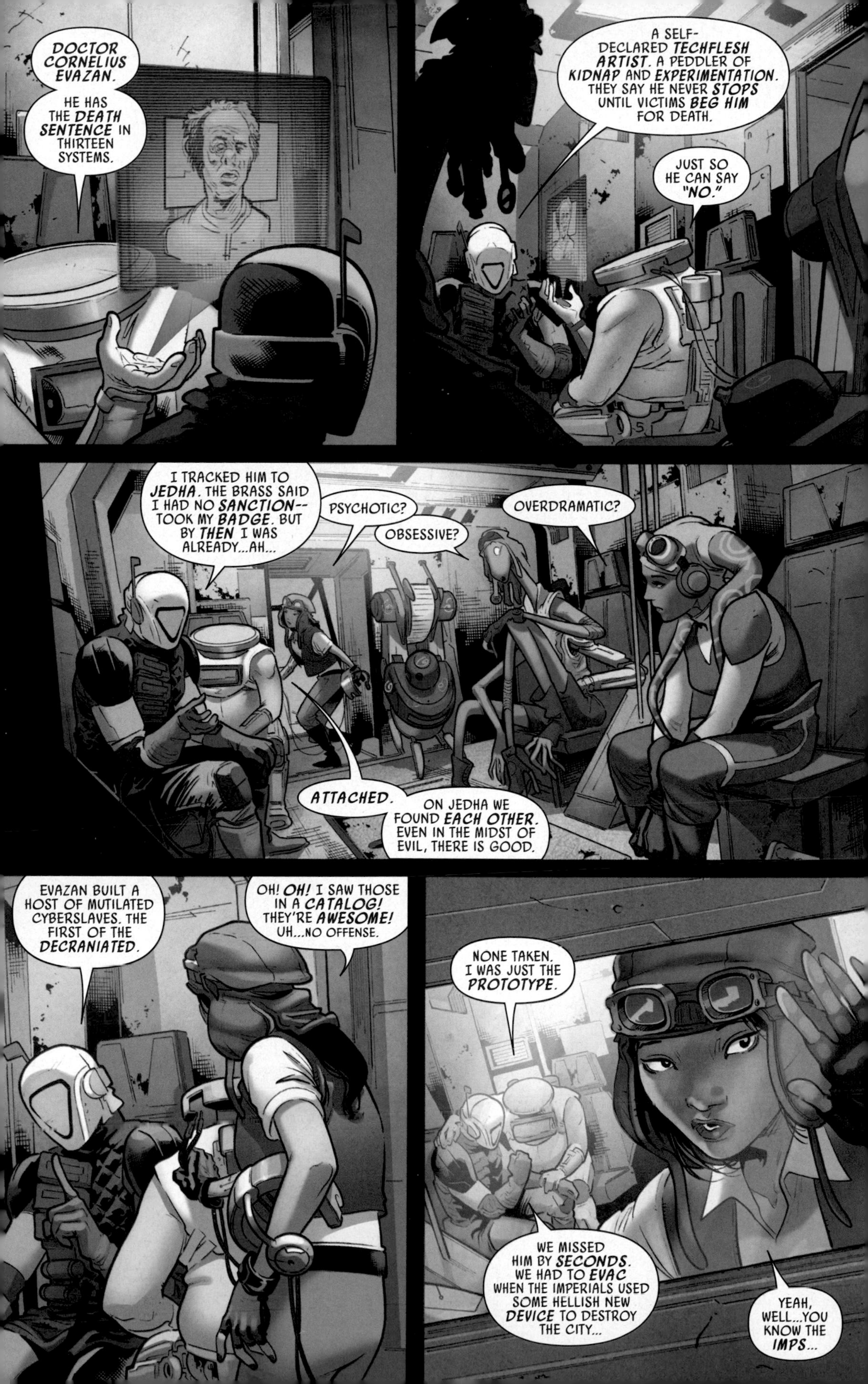

DOCTOR CORNELIUS EVAZAN.
HE HAS THE DEATH SENTENCE IN THIRTEEN SYSTEMS.
A SELF-DECLARED TECHFLESH ARTIST. A PEDDLER OF KIDNAP AND EXPERIMENTATION. THEY SAY HE NEVER STOPS UNTIL VICTIMS BEG HIM FOR DEATH.
JUST SO HE CAN SAY "NO."
I TRACKED HIM TO JEDHA. THE BRASS SAID I HAD NO SANCTION-- TOOK MY BADGE. BUT BY THEN I WAS ALREADY...AH...
PSYCHOTIC?
OBSESSIVE?
OVERDRAMATIC?
ATTACHED.
ON JEDHA WE FOUND EACH OTHER. EVEN IN THE MIDST OF EVIL, THERE IS GOOD.
EVAZAN BUILT A HOST OF MUTILATED CYBERSLAVES. THE FIRST OF THE DECRANIATED.
OH! OH! I SAW THOSE IN A CATALOG! THEY'RE AWESOME! UH...NO OFFENSE.
NONE TAKEN. I WAS JUST THE PROTOTYPE.
WE MISSED HIM BY SECONDS. WE HAD TO EVAC WHEN THE IMPERIALS USED SOME HELLISH NEW DEVICE TO DESTROY THE CITY...
YEAH, WELL...YOU KNOW THE IMPS...

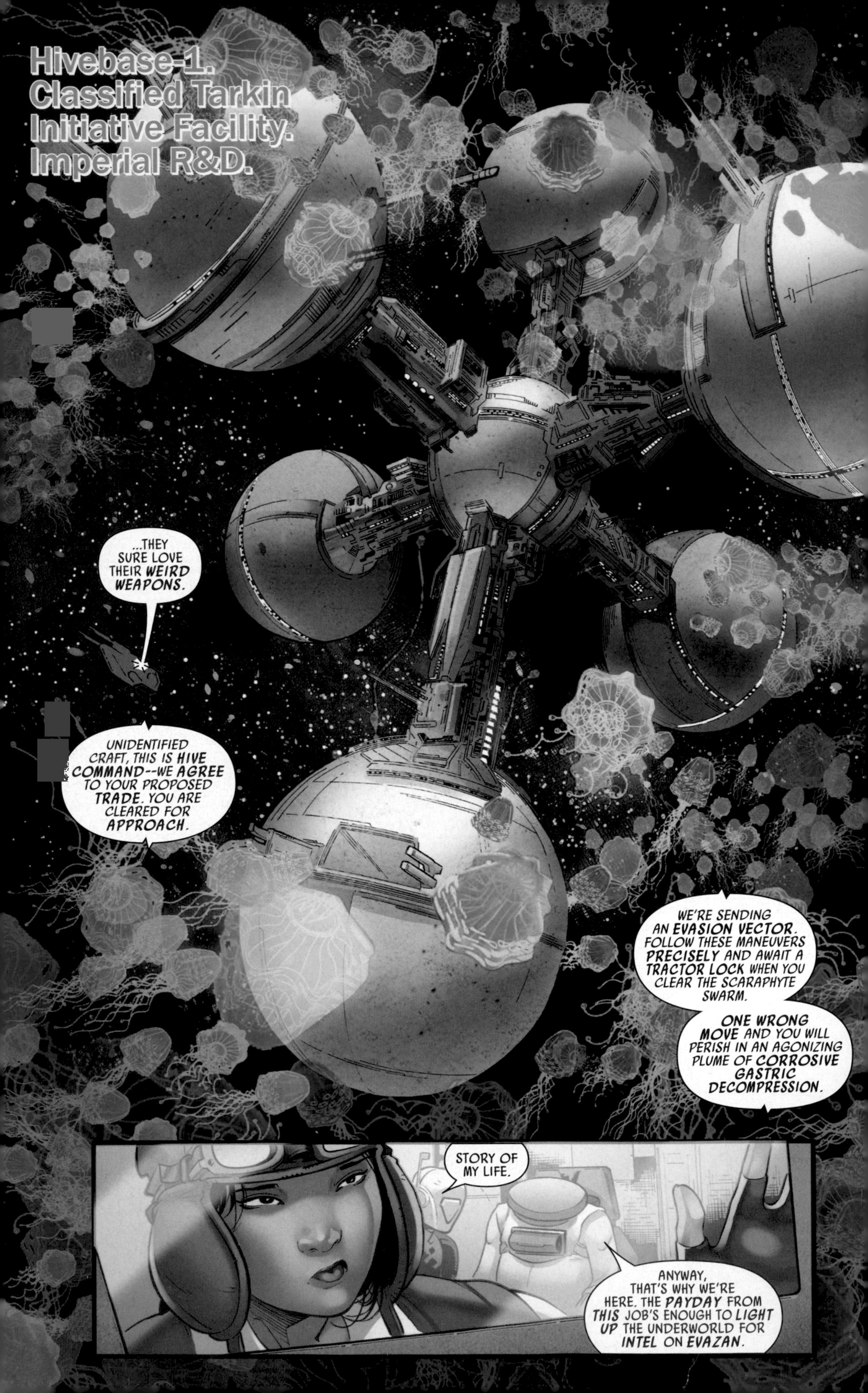
Hivebase-1. Classified Tarkin Initiative Facility. Imperial R&D.
...THEY SURE LOVE THEIR WEIRD WEAPONS.
UNIDENTIFIED CRAFT, THIS IS HIVE COMMAND--WE AGREE TO YOUR PROPOSED TRADE. YOU ARE CLEARED FOR APPROACH.
WE'RE SENDING AN EVASION VECTOR. FOLLOW THESE MANEUVERS PRECISELY AND AWAIT A TRACTOR LOCK WHEN YOU CLEAR THE SCARAPHYTE SWARM.
ONE WRONG MOVE AND YOU WILL PERISH IN AN AGONIZING PLUME OF CORROSIVE GASTRIC DECOMPRESSION.
STORY OF MY LIFE.
ANYWAY, THAT'S WHY WE'RE HERE. THE PAYDAY FROM THIS JOB'S ENOUGH TO LIGHT UP THE UNDERWORLD FOR INTEL ON EVAZAN.

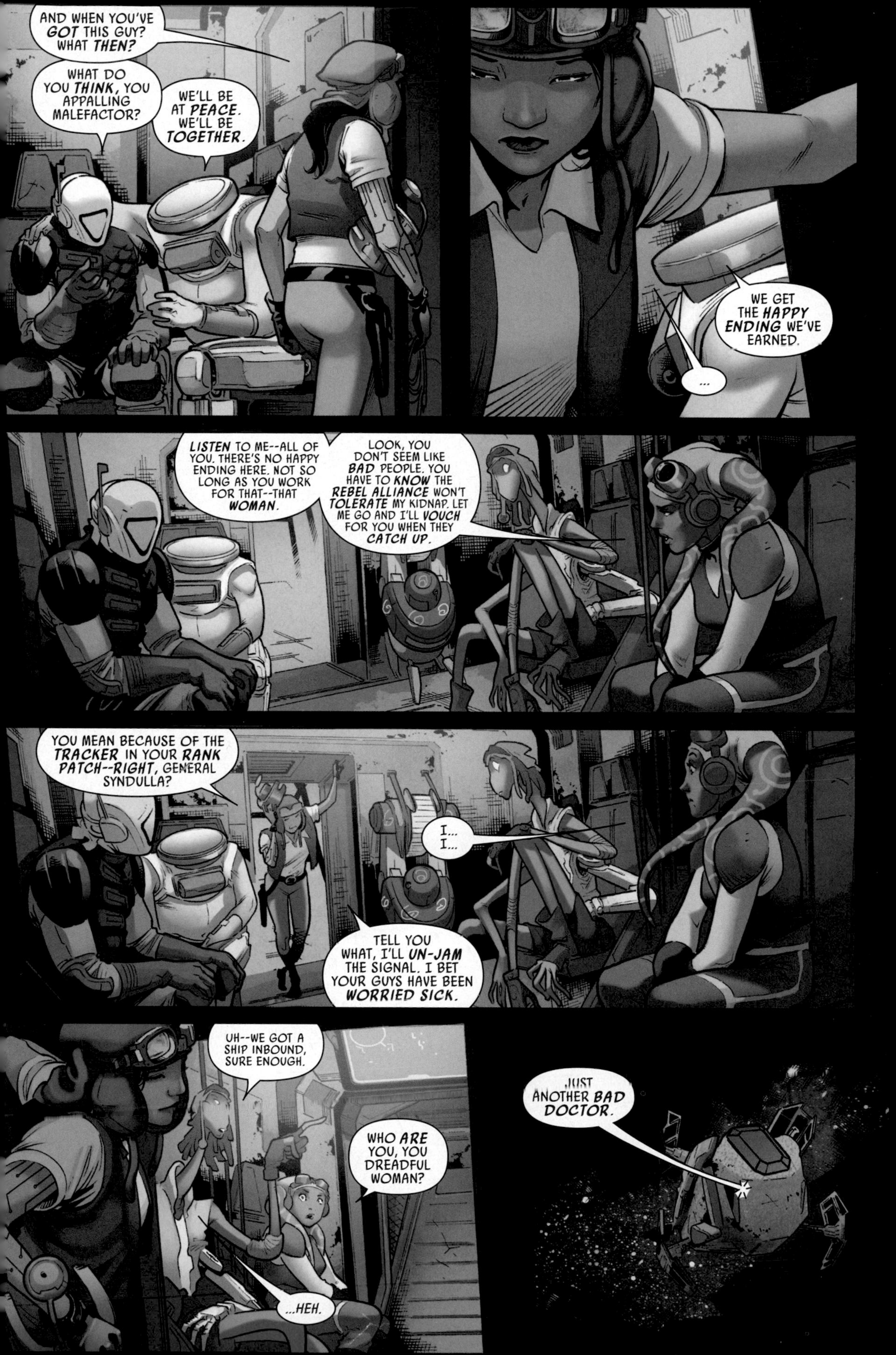
AND WHEN YOU'VE GOT THIS GUY? WHAT THEN?
WHAT DO YOU THINK, YOU APPALLING MALEFACTOR?
WE'LL BE AT PEACE. WE'LL BE TOGETHER.
WE GET THE HAPPY ENDING WE'VE EARNED.
...
LISTEN TO ME--ALL OF YOU. THERE'S NO HAPPY ENDING HERE. NOT SO LONG AS YOU WORK FOR THAT--THAT WOMAN.
LOOK, YOU DON'T SEEM LIKE BAD PEOPLE. YOU HAVE TO KNOW THE REBEL ALLIANCE WON'T TOLERATE MY KIDNAP. LET ME GO AND I'LL VOUCH FOR YOU WHEN THEY CATCH UP.
YOU MEAN BECAUSE OF THE TRACKER IN YOUR RANK PATCH--RIGHT, GENERAL SYNDULLA?
I... I...
TELL YOU WHAT, I'LL UN-JAM THE SIGNAL. I BET YOUR GUYS HAVE BEEN WORRIED SICK.
UH--WE GOT A SHIP INBOUND, SURE ENOUGH.
WHO ARE YOU, YOU DREADFUL WOMAN?
...HEH.
JUST ANOTHER BAD DOCTOR.

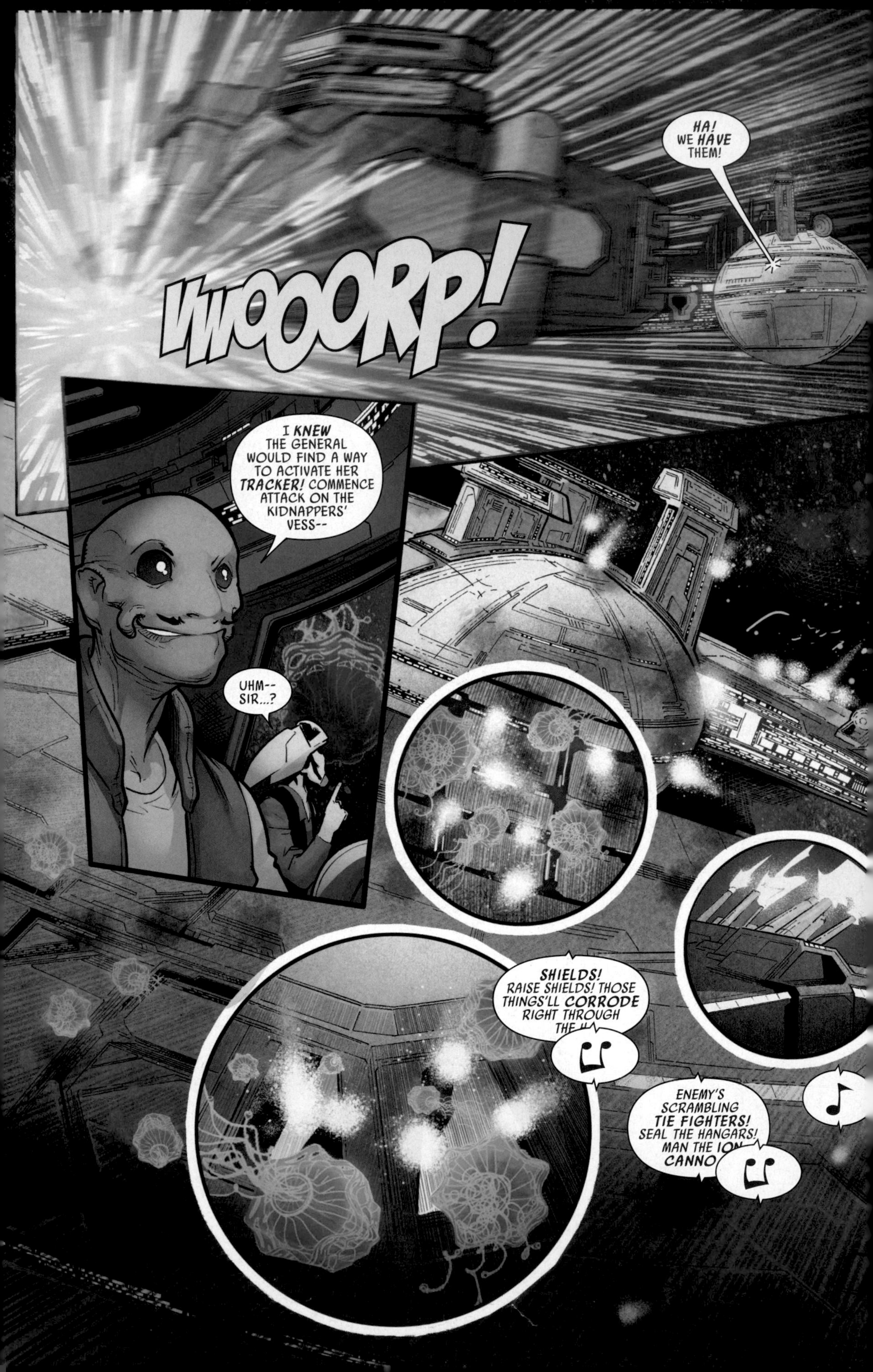

HA! WE HAVE THEM!
VWOOORP!
I KNEW THE GENERAL WOULD FIND A WAY TO ACTIVATE HER TRACKER! COMMENCE ATTACK ON THE KIDNAPPERS' VESS--
UHM-- SIR...?
SHIELDS! RAISE SHIELDS! THOSE THINGS'LL CORRODE RIGHT THROUGH THE H
ENEMY'S SCRAMBLING TIE FIGHTERS! SEAL THE HANGARS! MAN THE ION CANNO

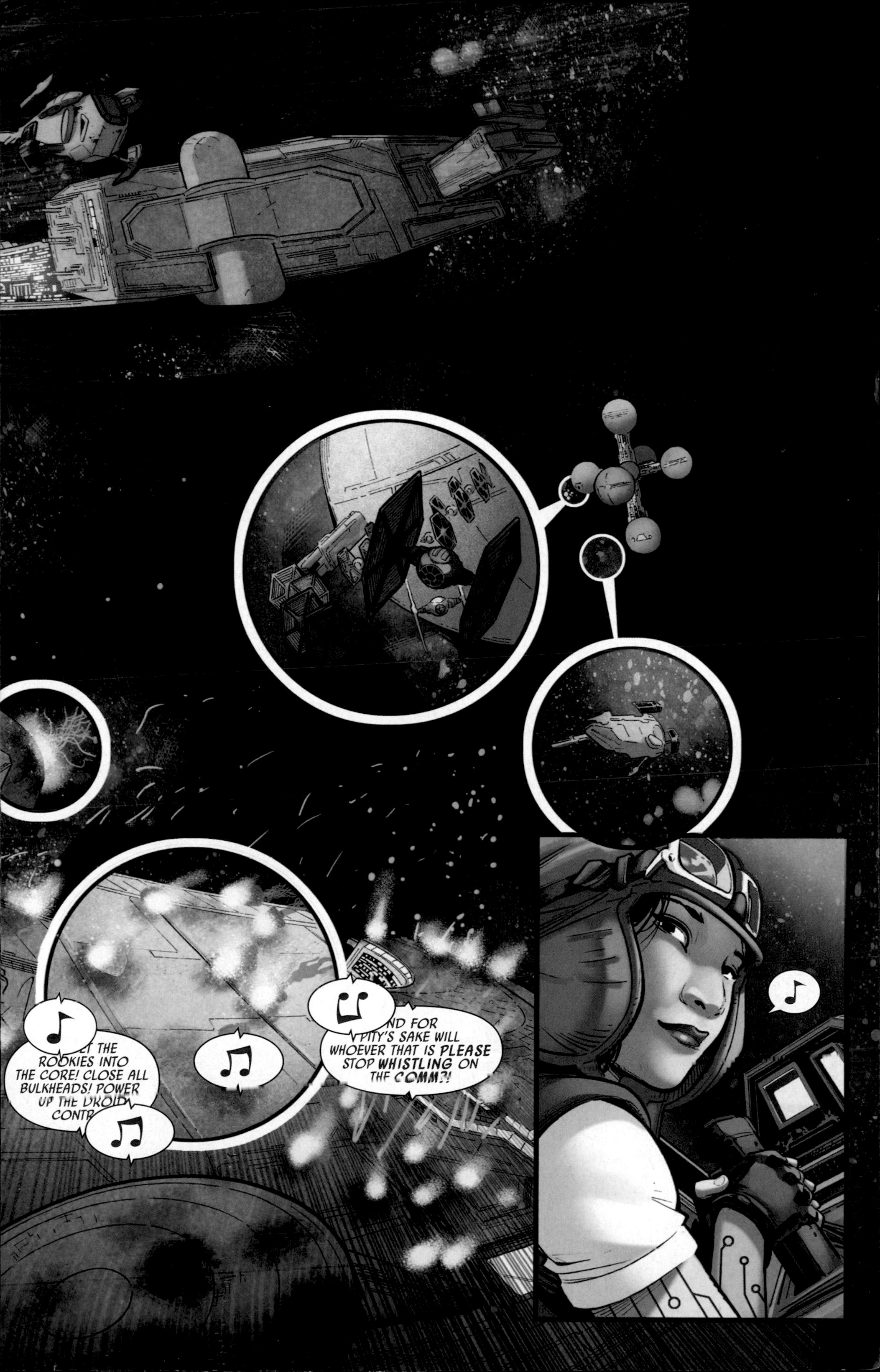
♪
...ET THE ROOKIES INTO THE CORE! CLOSE ALL BULKHEADS! POWER UP THE DROID CONTR...
♫
♫
...ND FOR PITY'S SAKE WILL WHOEVER THAT IS PLEASE STOP WHISTLING ON THE COMM?!
♪

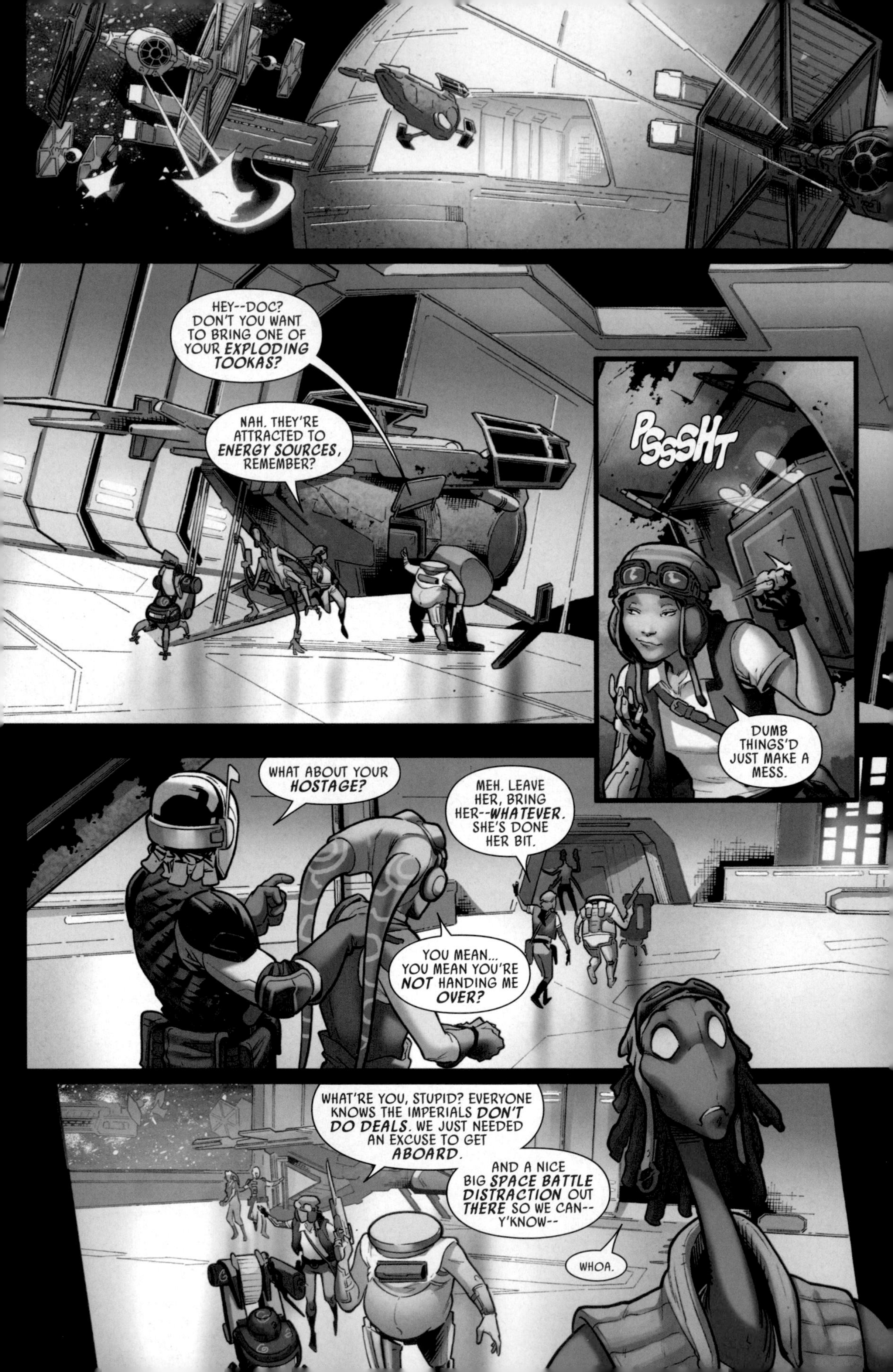
HEY--DOC? DON'T YOU WANT TO BRING ONE OF YOUR EXPLODING TOOKAS?
NAH. THEY'RE ATTRACTED TO ENERGY SOURCES, REMEMBER?
PSSSHT
DUMB THINGS'D JUST MAKE A MESS.
WHAT ABOUT YOUR HOSTAGE?
MEH. LEAVE HER, BRING HER--WHATEVER. SHE'S DONE HER BIT.
YOU MEAN... YOU MEAN YOU'RE NOT HANDING ME OVER?
WHAT'RE YOU, STUPID? EVERYONE KNOWS THE IMPERIALS DON'T DO DEALS. WE JUST NEEDED AN EXCUSE TO GET ABOARD.
AND A NICE BIG SPACE BATTLE DISTRACTION OUT THERE SO WE CAN--Y'KNOW--
WHOA.

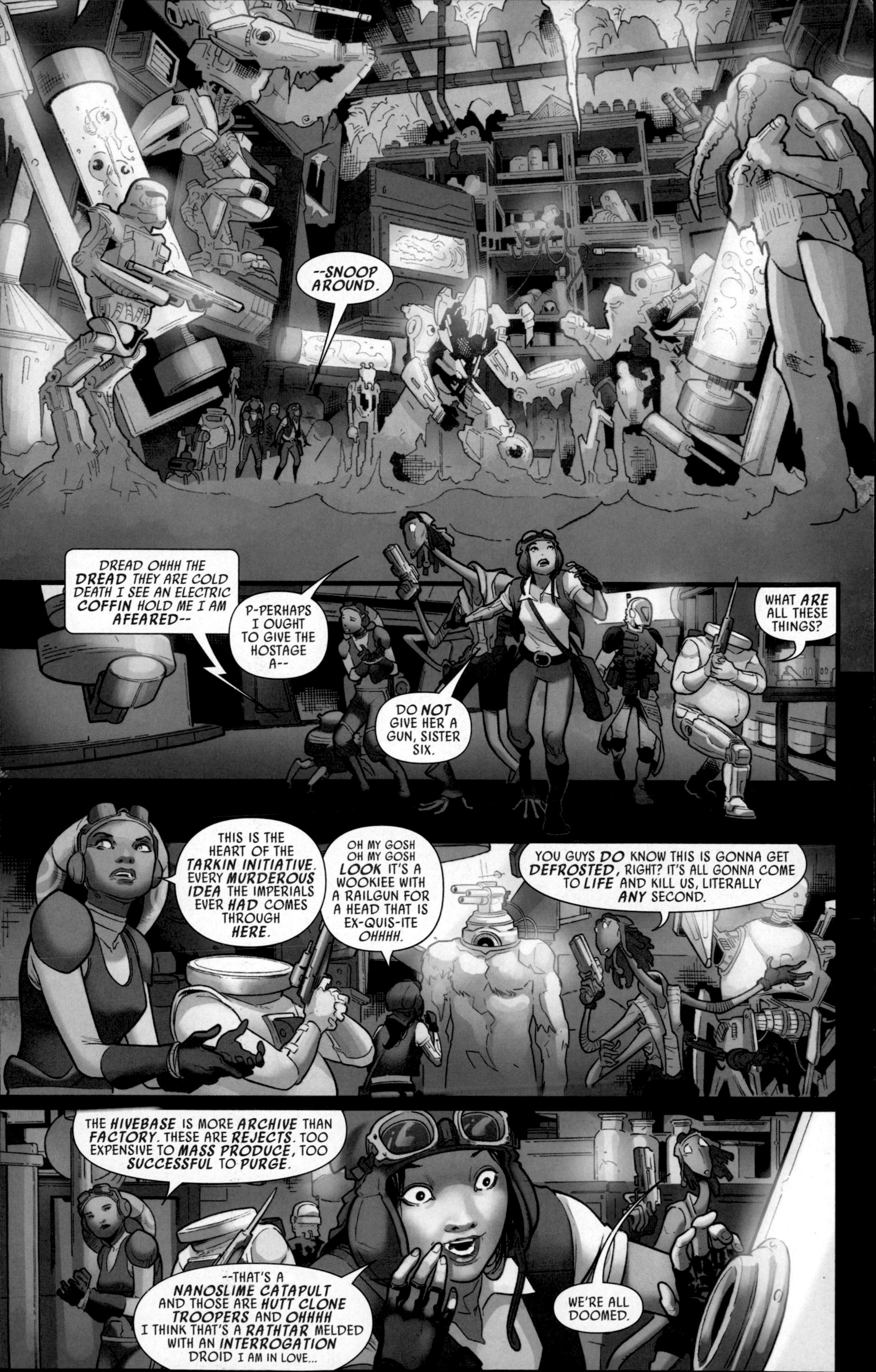

--SNOOP AROUND.
DREAD OHHH THE DREAD THEY ARE COLD DEATH I SEE AN ELECTRIC COFFIN HOLD ME I AM AFEARED--
P-PERHAPS I OUGHT TO GIVE THE HOSTAGE A--
DO NOT GIVE HER A GUN, SISTER SIX.
WHAT ARE ALL THESE THINGS?
THIS IS THE HEART OF THE TARKIN INITIATIVE. EVERY MURDEROUS IDEA THE IMPERIALS EVER HAD COMES THROUGH HERE.
OH MY GOSH OH MY GOSH LOOK IT'S A WOOKIEE WITH A RAILGUN FOR A HEAD THAT IS EX-QUIS-ITE OHHHH.
YOU GUYS DO KNOW THIS IS GONNA GET DEFROSTED, RIGHT? IT'S ALL GONNA COME TO LIFE AND KILL US, LITERALLY ANY SECOND.
THE HIVEBASE IS MORE ARCHIVE THAN FACTORY. THESE ARE REJECTS. TOO EXPENSIVE TO MASS PRODUCE, TOO SUCCESSFUL TO PURGE.
--THAT'S A NANOSLIME CATAPULT AND THOSE ARE HUTT CLONE TROOPERS AND OHHHH I THINK THAT'S A RATHTAR MELDED WITH AN INTERROGATION DROID I AM IN LOVE...
WE'RE ALL DOOMED.

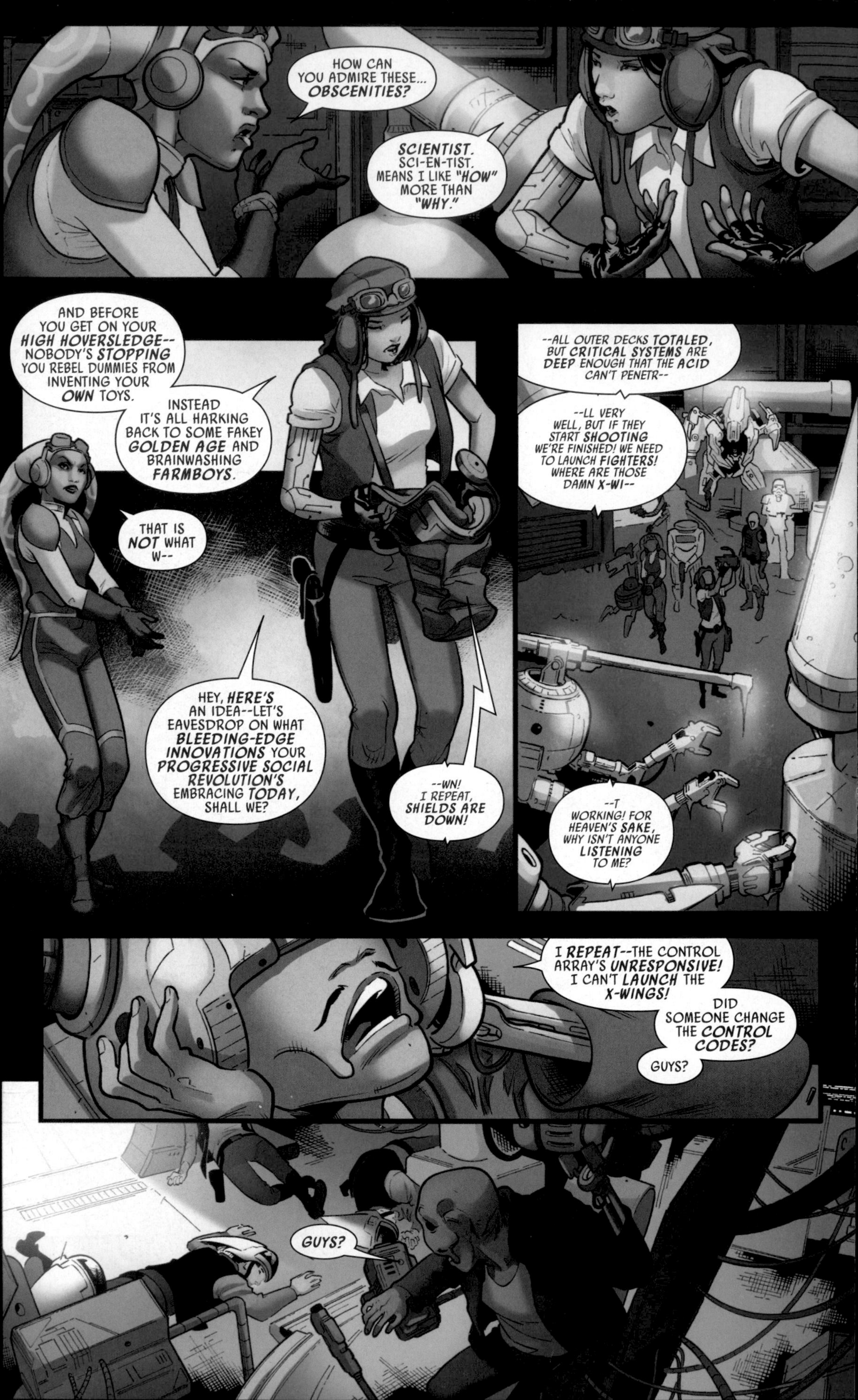
HOW CAN YOU ADMIRE THESE... OBSCENITIES?
SCIENTIST. SCI-EN-TIST. MEANS I LIKE "HOW" MORE THAN "WHY."
AND BEFORE YOU GET ON YOUR HIGH HOVERSLEDGE-- NOBODY'S STOPPING YOU REBEL DUMMIES FROM INVENTING YOUR OWN TOYS.
INSTEAD IT'S ALL HARKING BACK TO SOME FAKEY GOLDEN AGE AND BRAINWASHING FARMBOYS.
THAT IS NOT WHAT W--
HEY, HERE'S AN IDEA--LET'S EAVESDROP ON WHAT BLEEDING-EDGE INNOVATIONS YOUR PROGRESSIVE SOCIAL REVOLUTION'S EMBRACING TODAY, SHALL WE?
--WN! I REPEAT, SHIELDS ARE DOWN!
--ALL OUTER DECKS TOTALED, BUT CRITICAL SYSTEMS ARE DEEP ENOUGH THAT THE ACID CAN'T PENETR--
--LL VERY WELL, BUT IF THEY START SHOOTING WE'RE FINISHED! WE NEED TO LAUNCH FIGHTERS! WHERE ARE THOSE DAMN X-WI--
--T WORKING! FOR HEAVEN'S SAKE, WHY ISN'T ANYONE LISTENING TO ME?
I REPEAT--THE CONTROL ARRAY'S UNRESPONSIVE! I CAN'T LAUNCH THE X-WINGS!
DID SOMEONE CHANGE THE CONTROL CODES?
GUYS?
GUYS?

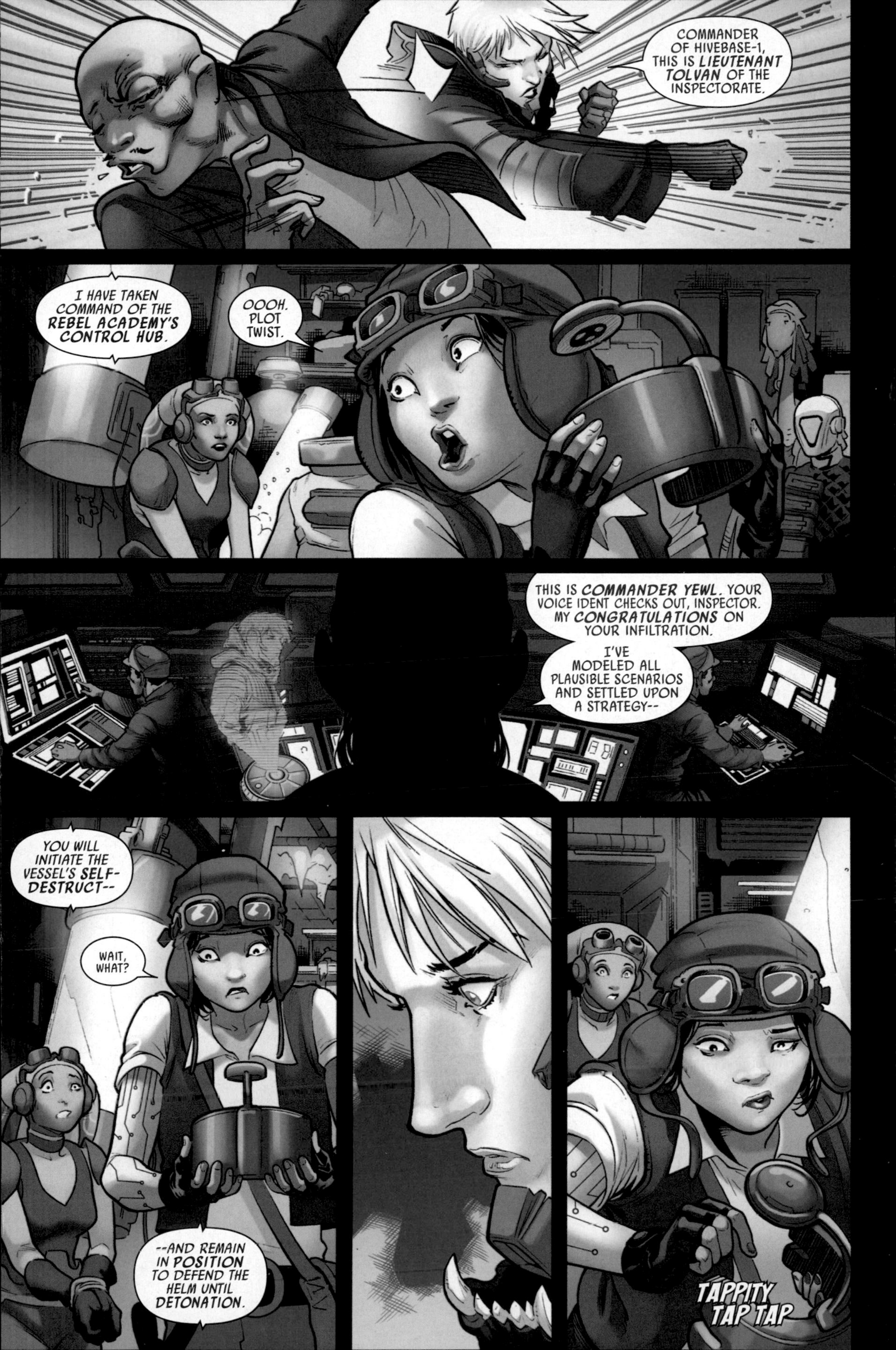
COMMANDER OF HIVEBASE-1, THIS IS LIEUTENANT TOLVAN OF THE INSPECTORATE.
I HAVE TAKEN COMMAND OF THE REBEL ACADEMY'S CONTROL HUB.
OOOH. PLOT TWIST.
THIS IS COMMANDER YEWL. YOUR VOICE IDENT CHECKS OUT, INSPECTOR. MY CONGRATULATIONS ON YOUR INFILTRATION.
I'VE MODELED ALL PLAUSIBLE SCENARIOS AND SETTLED UPON A STRATEGY--
YOU WILL INITIATE THE VESSEL'S SELF-DESTRUCT--
WAIT, WHAT?
--AND REMAIN IN POSITION TO DEFEND THE HELM UNTIL DETONATION.
TAPPITY TAP TAP

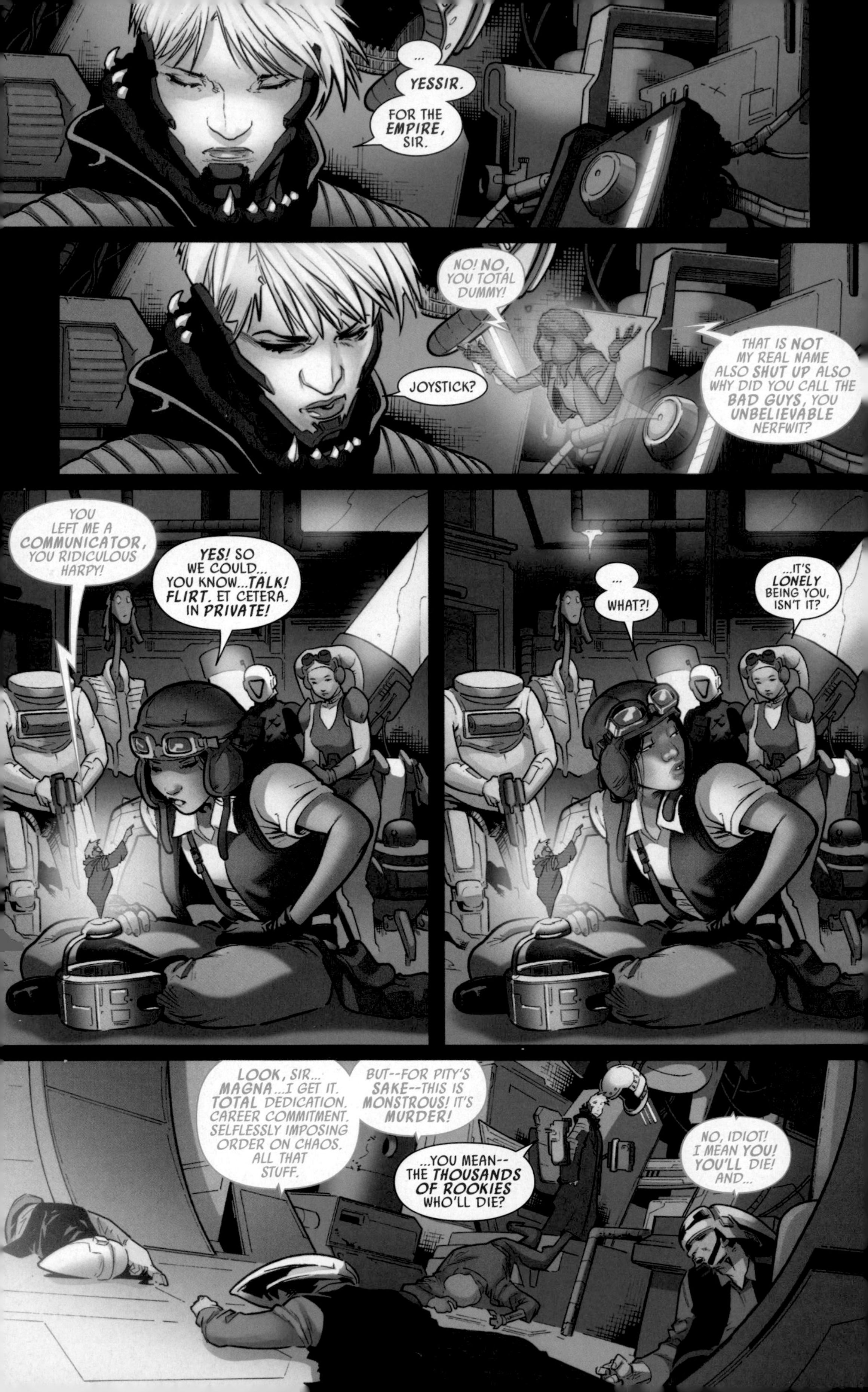

...
YESSIR.
FOR THE EMPIRE, SIR.
JOYSTICK?
NO! NO, YOU TOTAL DUMMY!
THAT IS NOT MY REAL NAME ALSO SHUT UP ALSO WHY DID YOU CALL THE BAD GUYS, YOU UNBELIEVABLE NERFWIT?
YOU LEFT ME A COMMUNICATOR, YOU RIDICULOUS HARPY!
YES! SO WE COULD... YOU KNOW...TALK! FLIRT. ET CETERA. IN PRIVATE!
...
WHAT?!
...IT'S LONELY BEING YOU, ISN'T IT?
LOOK, SIR... MAGNA...I GET IT. TOTAL DEDICATION. CAREER COMMITMENT. SELFLESSLY IMPOSING ORDER ON CHAOS. ALL THAT STUFF.
BUT--FOR PITY'S SAKE--THIS IS MONSTROUS! IT'S MURDER!
...YOU MEAN-- THE THOUSANDS OF ROOKIES WHO'LL DIE?
NO, IDIOT! I MEAN YOU! YOU'LL DIE! AND...

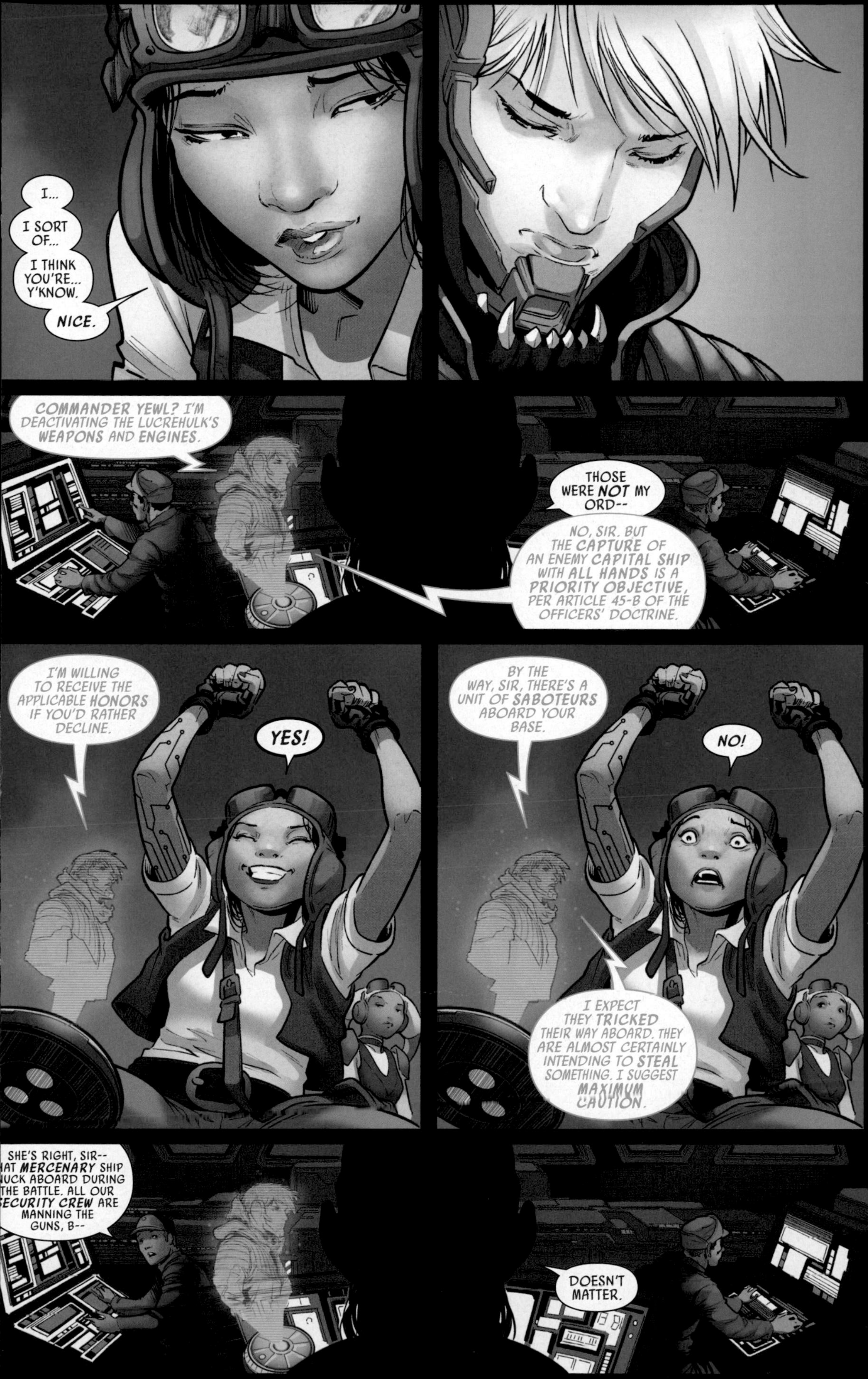
I...
I SORT OF...
I THINK YOU'RE... Y'KNOW.
NICE.
COMMANDER YEWL? I'M DEACTIVATING THE LUCREHULK'S WEAPONS AND ENGINES.
THOSE WERE NOT MY ORD--
NO, SIR. BUT THE CAPTURE OF AN ENEMY CAPITAL SHIP WITH ALL HANDS IS A PRIORITY OBJECTIVE, PER ARTICLE 45-B OF THE OFFICERS' DOCTRINE.
I'M WILLING TO RECEIVE THE APPLICABLE HONORS IF YOU'D RATHER DECLINE.
YES!
BY THE WAY, SIR, THERE'S A UNIT OF SABOTEURS ABOARD YOUR BASE.
NO!
I EXPECT THEY TRICKED THEIR WAY ABOARD. THEY ARE ALMOST CERTAINLY INTENDING TO STEAL SOMETHING. I SUGGEST MAXIMUM CAUTION.
SHE'S RIGHT, SIR-- HAT MERCENARY SHIP NUCK ABOARD DURING THE BATTLE. ALL OUR ECURITY CREW ARE MANNING THE GUNS, B--
DOESN'T MATTER.

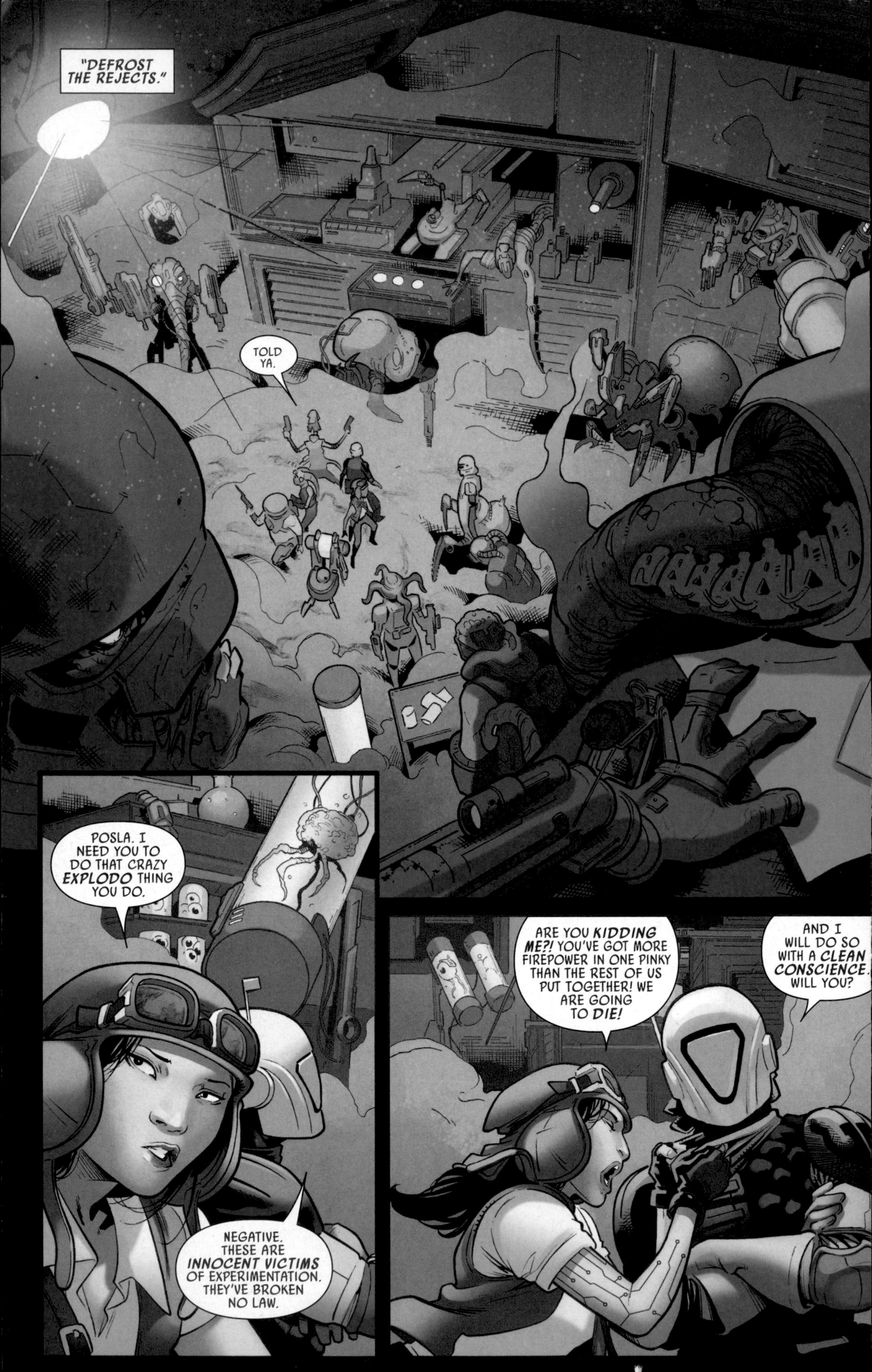
"DEFROST THE REJECTS."
TOLD YA.
POSLA. I NEED YOU TO DO THAT CRAZY EXPLODO THING YOU DO.
NEGATIVE. THESE ARE INNOCENT VICTIMS OF EXPERIMENTATION. THEY'VE BROKEN NO LAW.
ARE YOU KIDDING ME?! YOU'VE GOT MORE FIREPOWER IN ONE PINKY THAN THE REST OF US PUT TOGETHER! WE ARE GOING TO DIE!
AND I WILL DO SO WITH A CLEAN CONSCIENCE. WILL YOU?

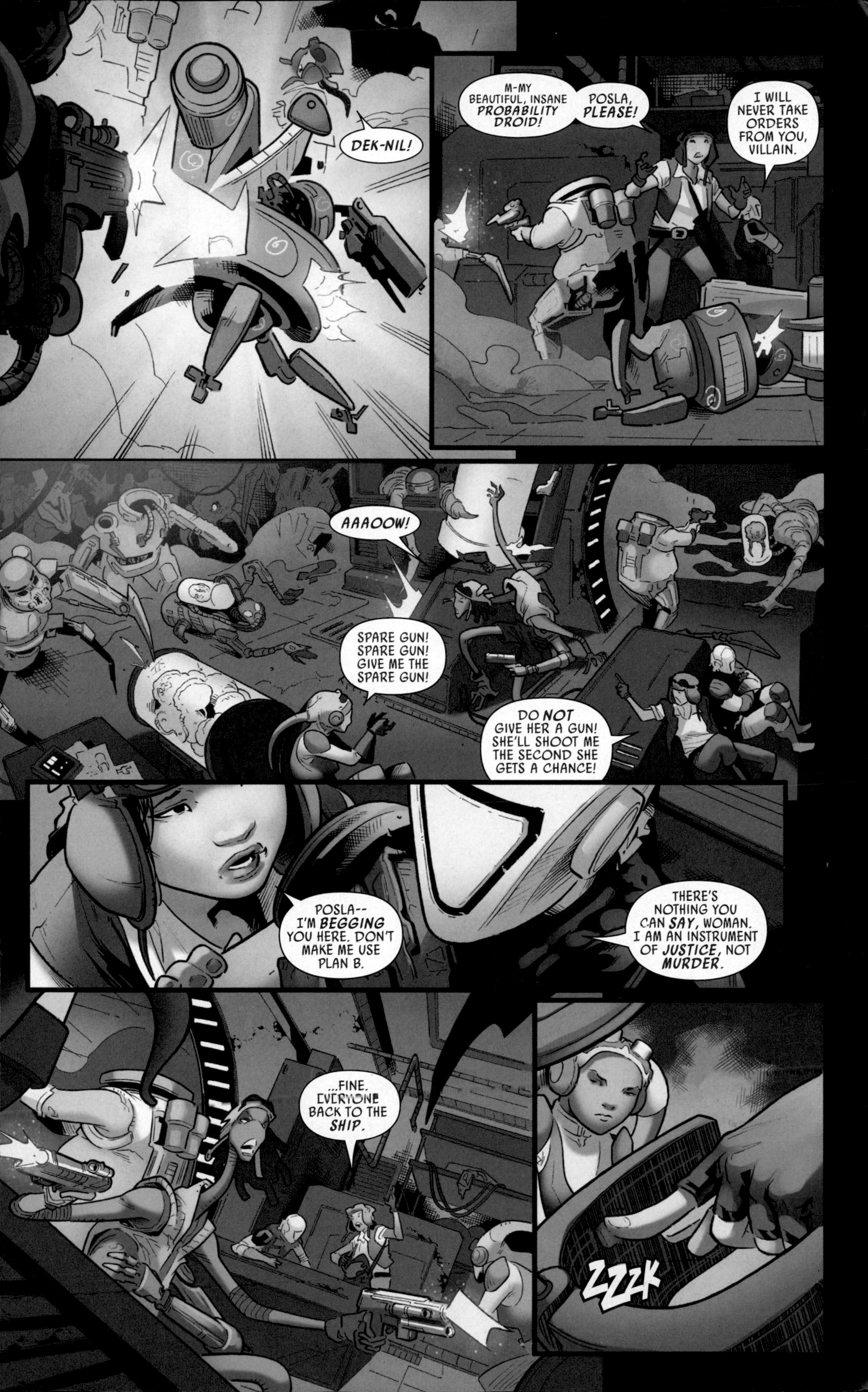
DEK-NIL!
M-MY BEAUTIFUL, INSANE PROBABILITY DROID!
POSLA, PLEASE!
I WILL NEVER TAKE ORDERS FROM YOU, VILLAIN.
AAAOOW!
SPARE GUN! SPARE GUN! GIVE ME THE SPARE GUN!
DO NOT GIVE HER A GUN! SHE'LL SHOOT ME THE SECOND SHE GETS A CHANCE!
POSLA-- I'M BEGGING YOU HERE. DON'T MAKE ME USE PLAN B.
THERE'S NOTHING YOU CAN SAY, WOMAN. I AM AN INSTRUMENT OF JUSTICE, NOT MURDER.
...FINE. EVERYONE BACK TO THE SHIP.
ZZZK

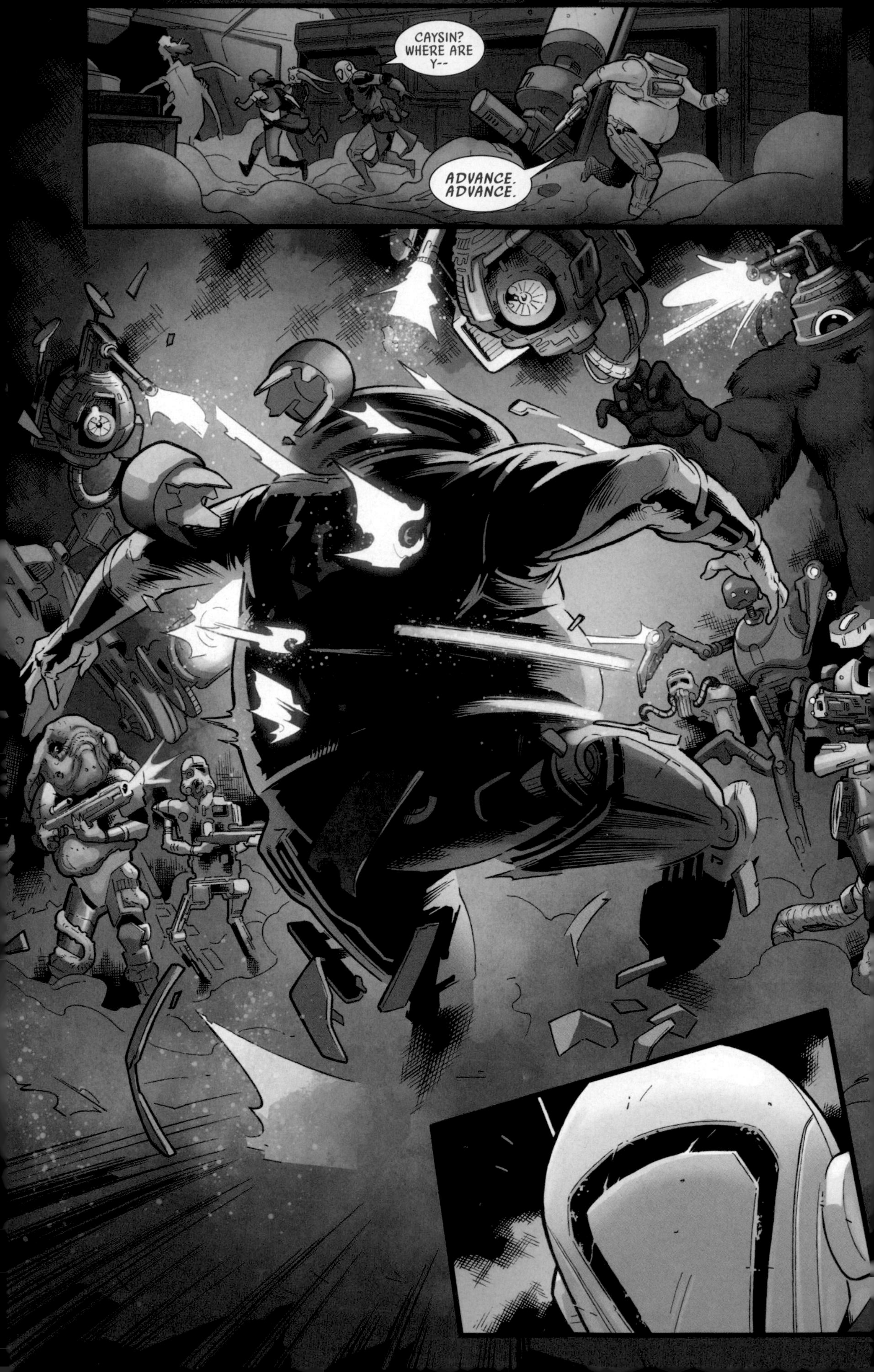
CAYSIN? WHERE ARE Y--
ADVANCE. ADVANCE.

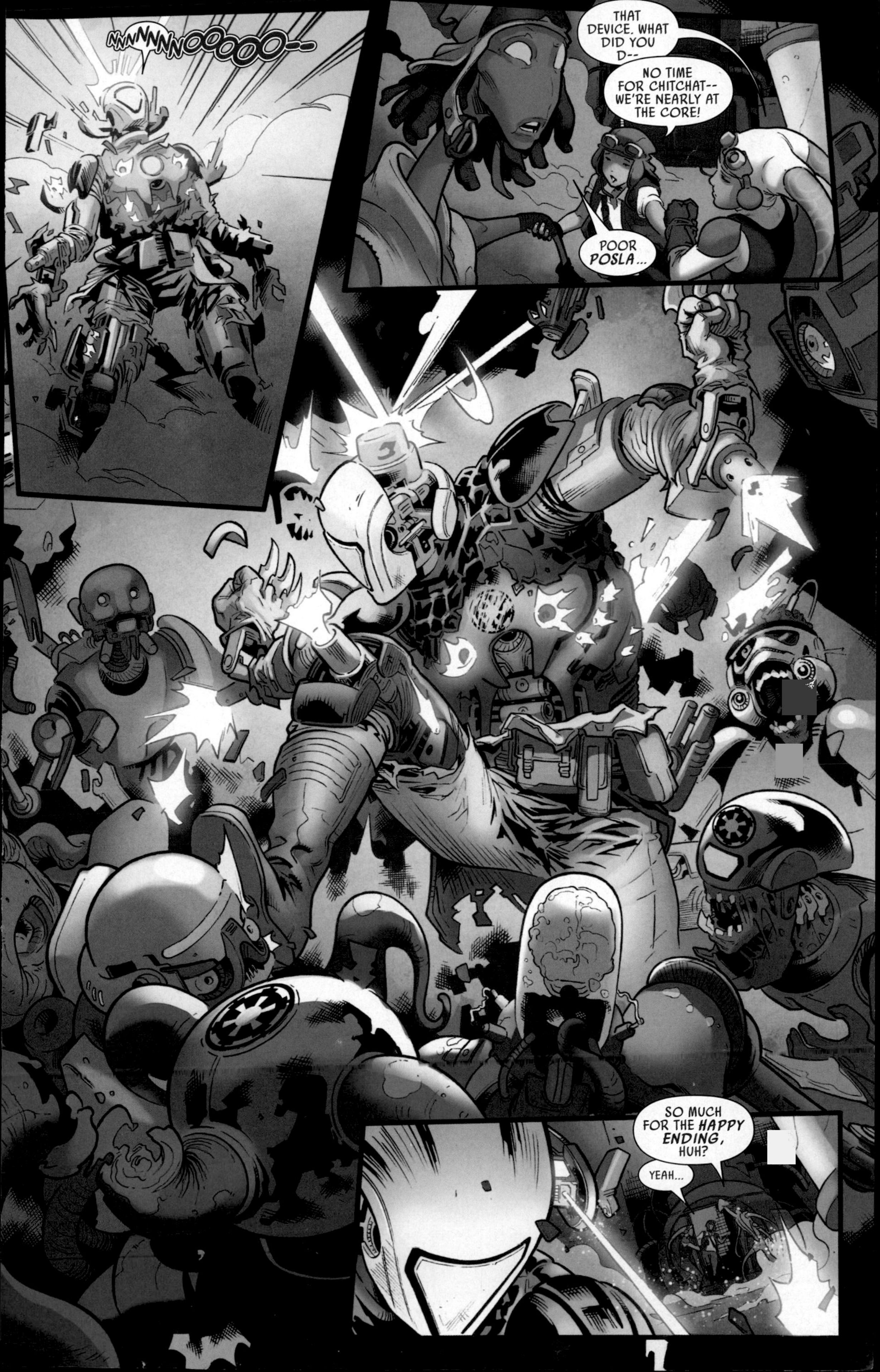
NNNNNNNOOOOOO--
THAT DEVICE. WHAT DID YOU D--
NO TIME FOR CHITCHAT-- WE'RE NEARLY AT THE CORE!
POOR POSLA...
SO MUCH FOR THE HAPPY ENDING, HUH?
YEAH...

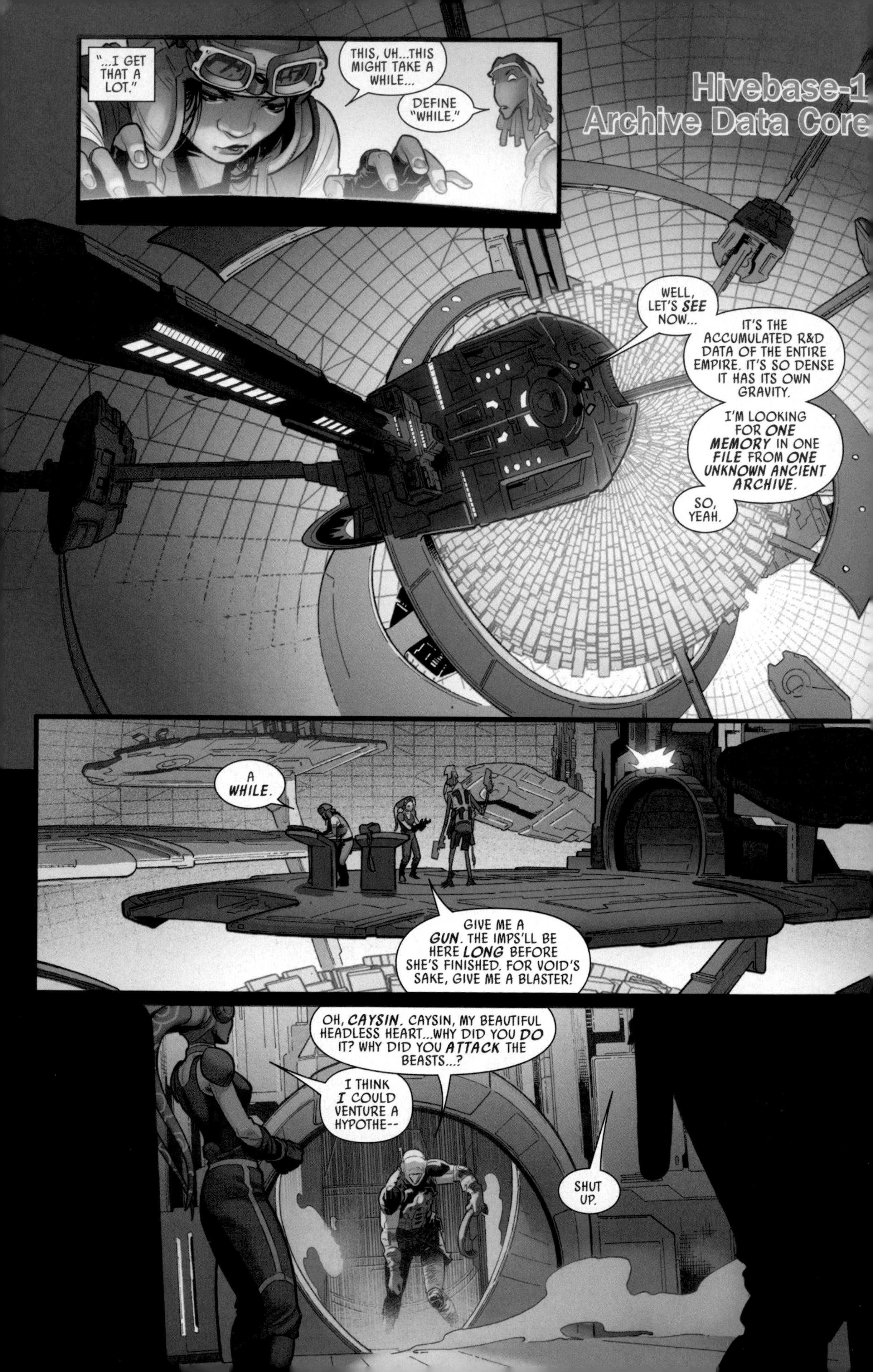
"...I GET THAT A LOT."
THIS, UH...THIS MIGHT TAKE A WHILE...
DEFINE "WHILE."
Hivebase-1 Archive Data Core
WELL, LET'S SEE NOW...
IT'S THE ACCUMULATED R&D DATA OF THE ENTIRE EMPIRE. IT'S SO DENSE IT HAS ITS OWN GRAVITY.
I'M LOOKING FOR ONE MEMORY IN ONE FILE FROM ONE UNKNOWN ANCIENT ARCHIVE.
SO, YEAH.
A WHILE.
GIVE ME A GUN. THE IMPS'LL BE HERE LONG BEFORE SHE'S FINISHED. FOR VOID'S SAKE, GIVE ME A BLASTER!
OH, CAYSIN. CAYSIN, MY BEAUTIFUL HEADLESS HEART...WHY DID YOU DO IT? WHY DID YOU ATTACK THE BEASTS...?
I THINK I COULD VENTURE A HYPOTHE--
SHUT UP.

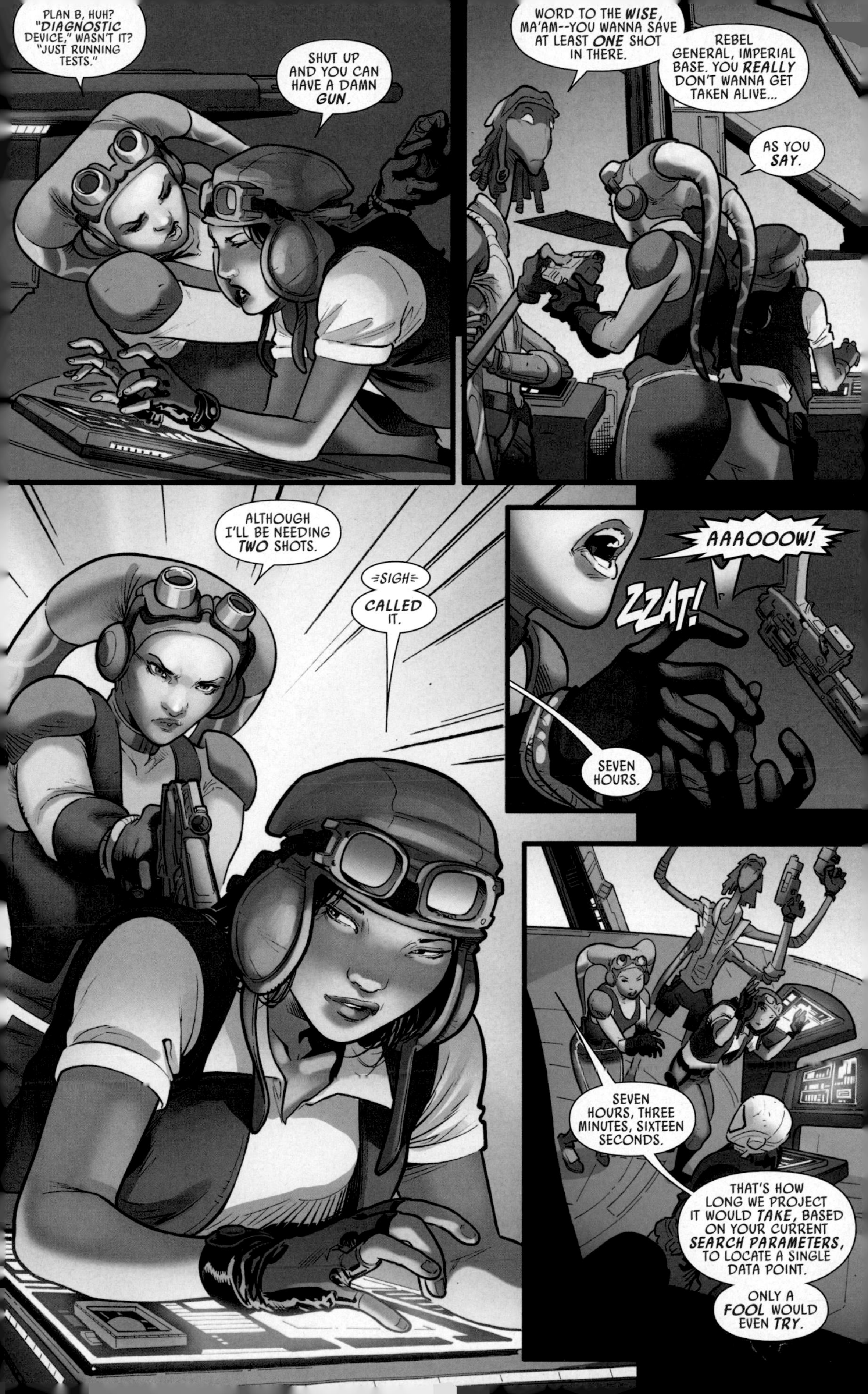
PLAN B, HUH? "DIAGNOSTIC DEVICE," WASN'T IT? "JUST RUNNING TESTS."
SHUT UP AND YOU CAN HAVE A DAMN GUN.
WORD TO THE WISE, MA'AM--YOU WANNA SAVE AT LEAST ONE SHOT IN THERE.
REBEL GENERAL, IMPERIAL BASE. YOU REALLY DON'T WANNA GET TAKEN ALIVE...
AS YOU SAY.
ALTHOUGH I'LL BE NEEDING TWO SHOTS.
=SIGH=
CALLED IT.
AAAOOOW!
ZZAT!
SEVEN HOURS.
SEVEN HOURS, THREE MINUTES, SIXTEEN SECONDS.
THAT'S HOW LONG WE PROJECT IT WOULD TAKE, BASED ON YOUR CURRENT SEARCH PARAMETERS, TO LOCATE A SINGLE DATA POINT.
ONLY A FOOL WOULD EVEN TRY.

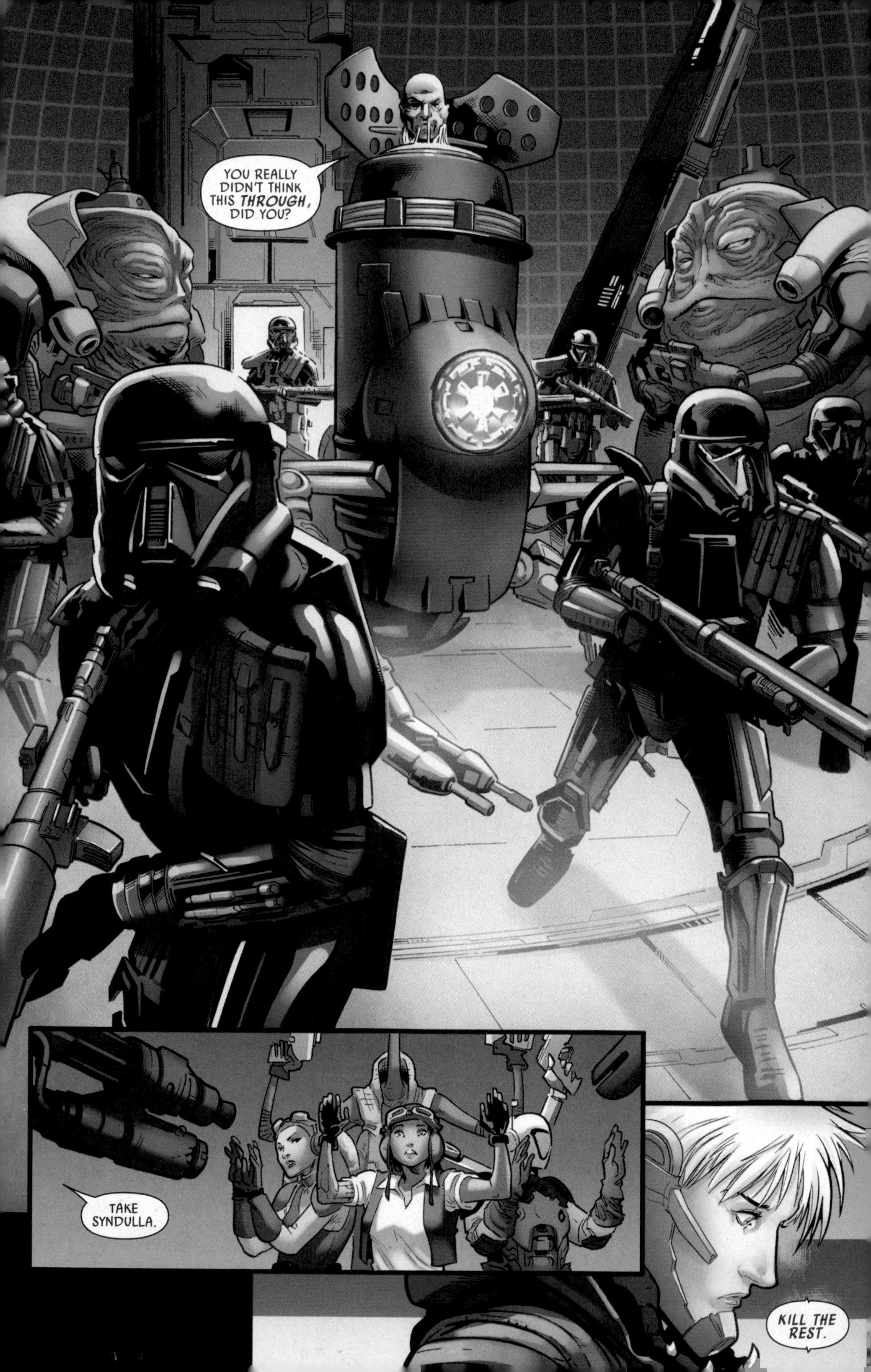
YOU REALLY DIDN'T THINK THIS *THROUGH*, DID YOU?
TAKE SYNDULLA.
KILL THE REST.

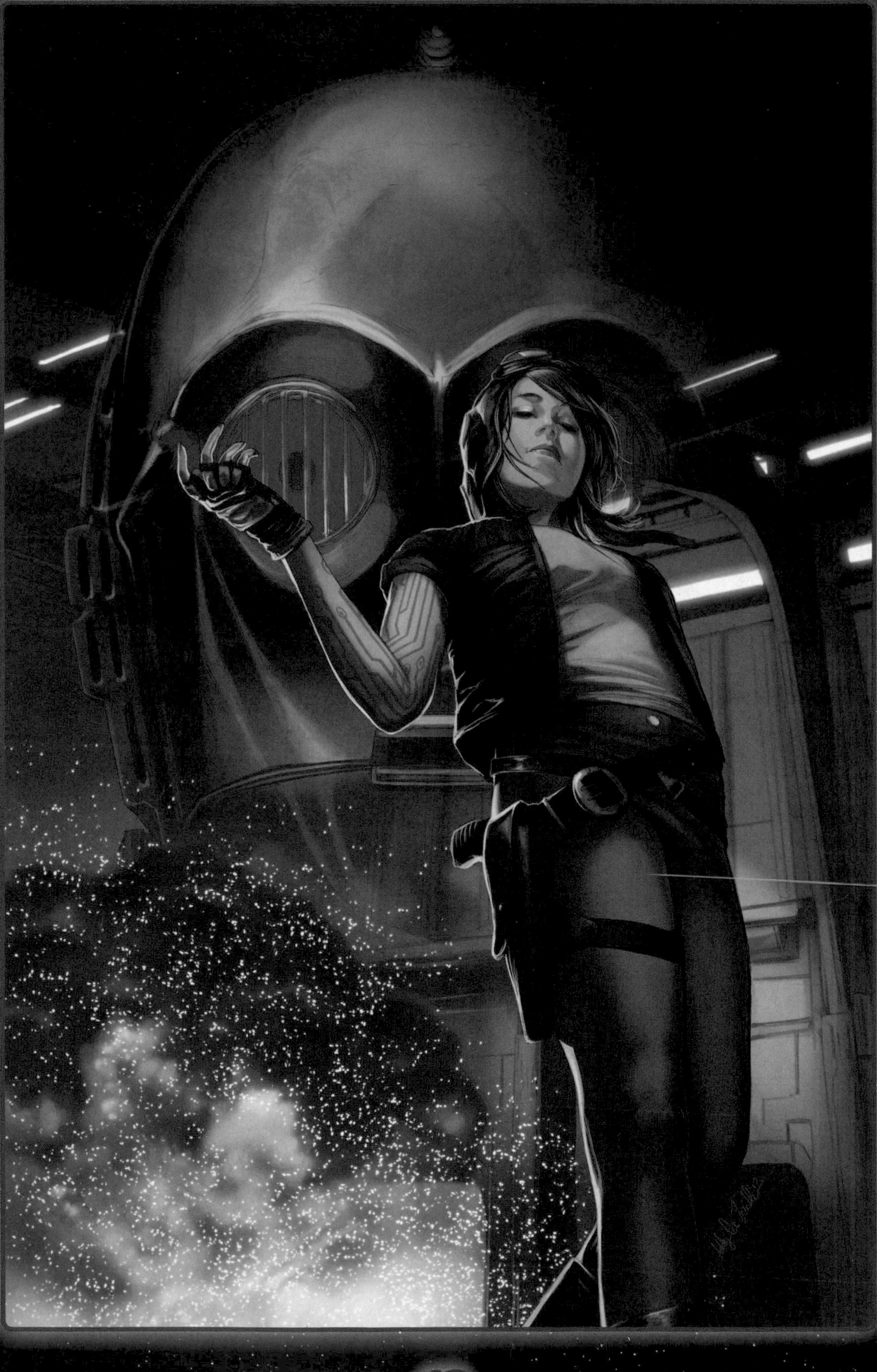

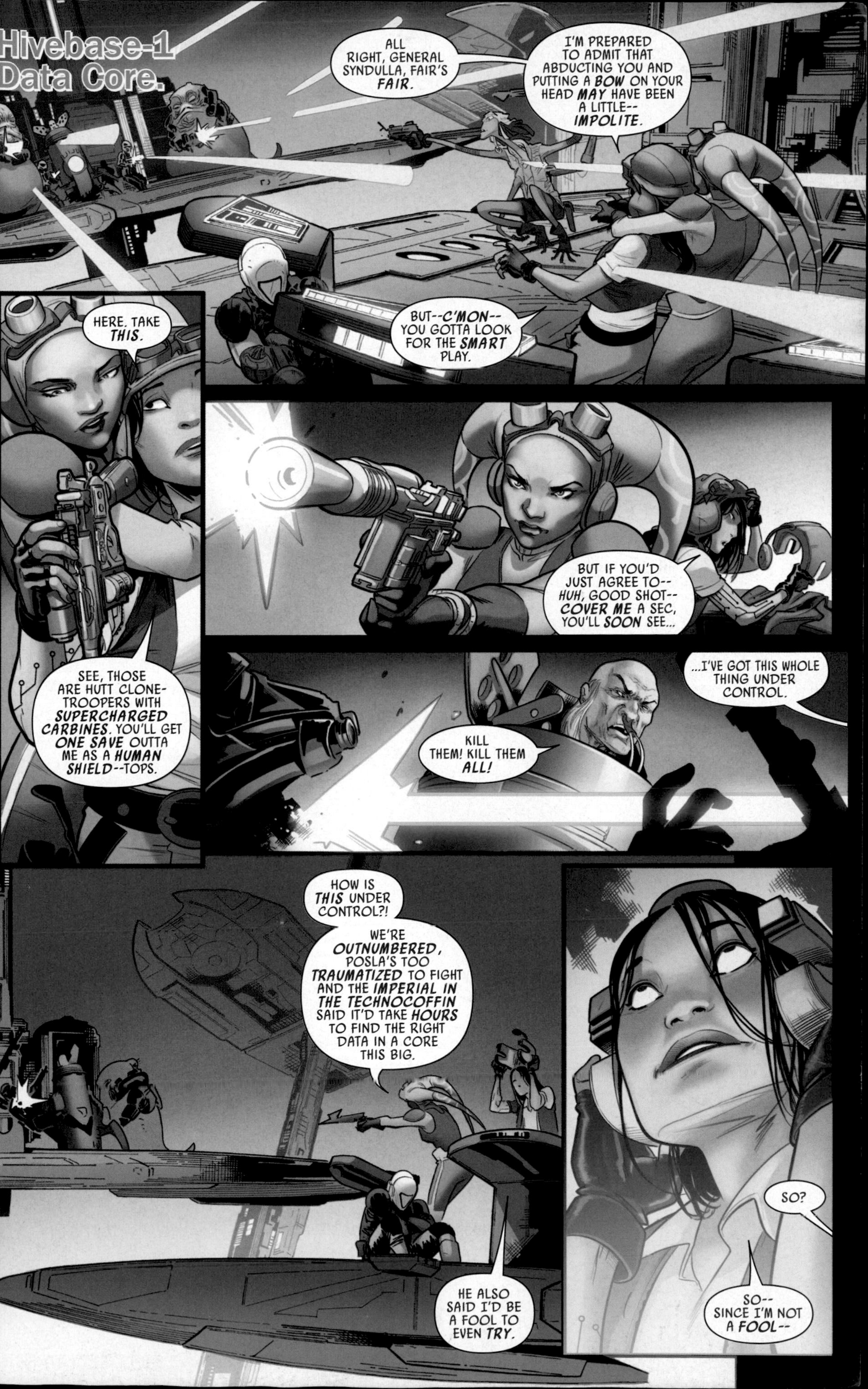
Hivebase-1
Data Core.
ALL RIGHT, GENERAL SYNDULLA, FAIR'S FAIR.
I'M PREPARED TO ADMIT THAT ABDUCTING YOU AND PUTTING A BOW ON YOUR HEAD MAY HAVE BEEN A LITTLE-- IMPOLITE.
BUT--C'MON-- YOU GOTTA LOOK FOR THE SMART PLAY.
HERE. TAKE THIS.
SEE, THOSE ARE HUTT CLONE-TROOPERS WITH SUPERCHARGED CARBINES. YOU'LL GET ONE SAVE OUTTA ME AS A HUMAN SHIELD--TOPS.
BUT IF YOU'D JUST AGREE TO-- HUH, GOOD SHOT-- COVER ME A SEC, YOU'LL SOON SEE...
...I'VE GOT THIS WHOLE THING UNDER CONTROL.
KILL THEM! KILL THEM ALL!
HOW IS THIS UNDER CONTROL?!
WE'RE OUTNUMBERED, POSLA'S TOO TRAUMATIZED TO FIGHT AND THE IMPERIAL IN THE TECHNOCOFFIN SAID IT'D TAKE HOURS TO FIND THE RIGHT DATA IN A CORE THIS BIG.
HE ALSO SAID I'D BE A FOOL TO EVEN TRY.
SO?
SO-- SINCE I'M NOT A FOOL--

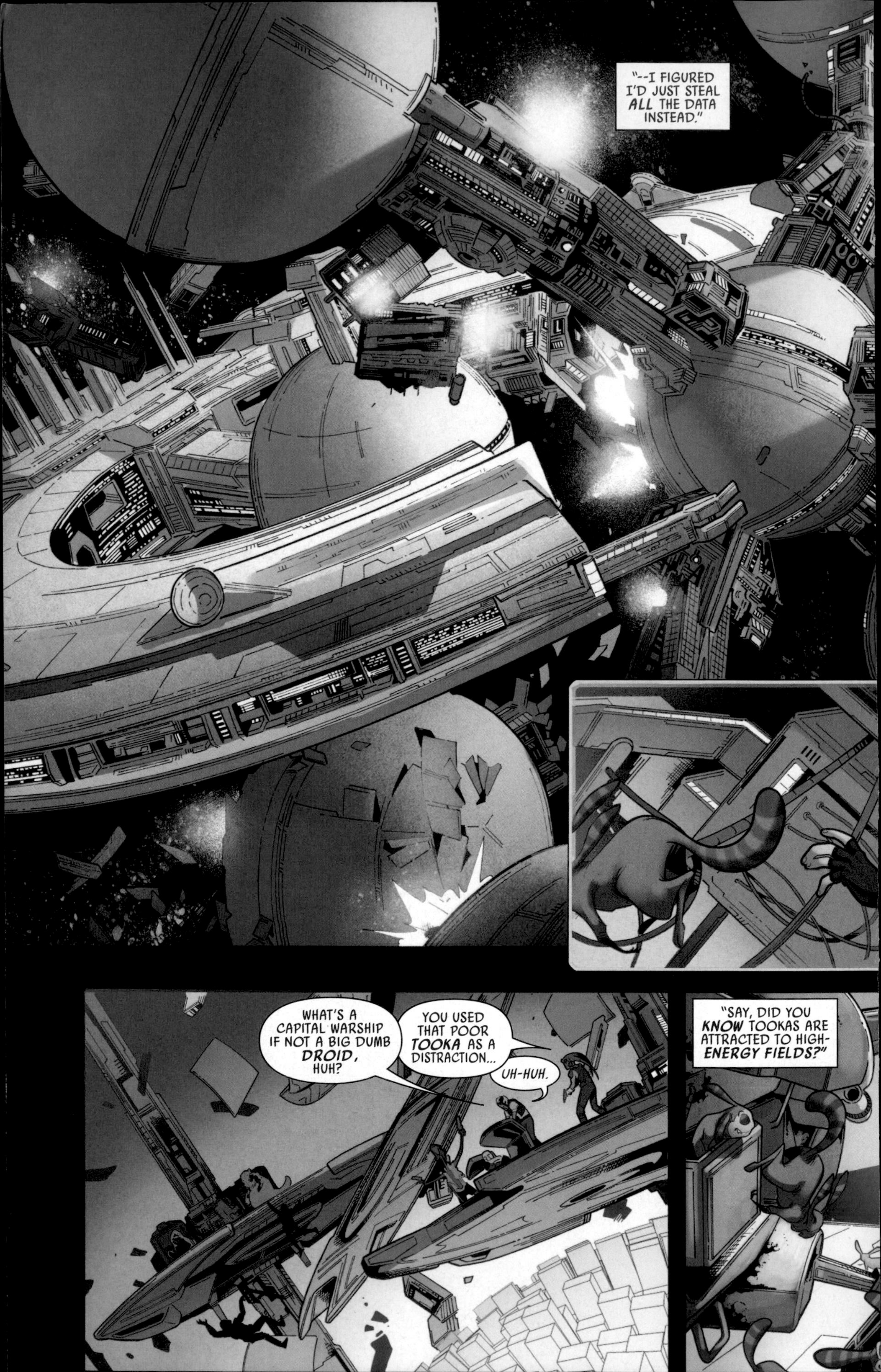
"--I FIGURED I'D JUST STEAL ALL THE DATA INSTEAD."
WHAT'S A CAPITAL WARSHIP IF NOT A BIG DUMB DROID, HUH?
YOU USED THAT POOR TOOKA AS A DISTRACTION...
UH-HUH.
"SAY, DID YOU KNOW TOOKAS ARE ATTRACTED TO HIGH-ENERGY FIELDS?"

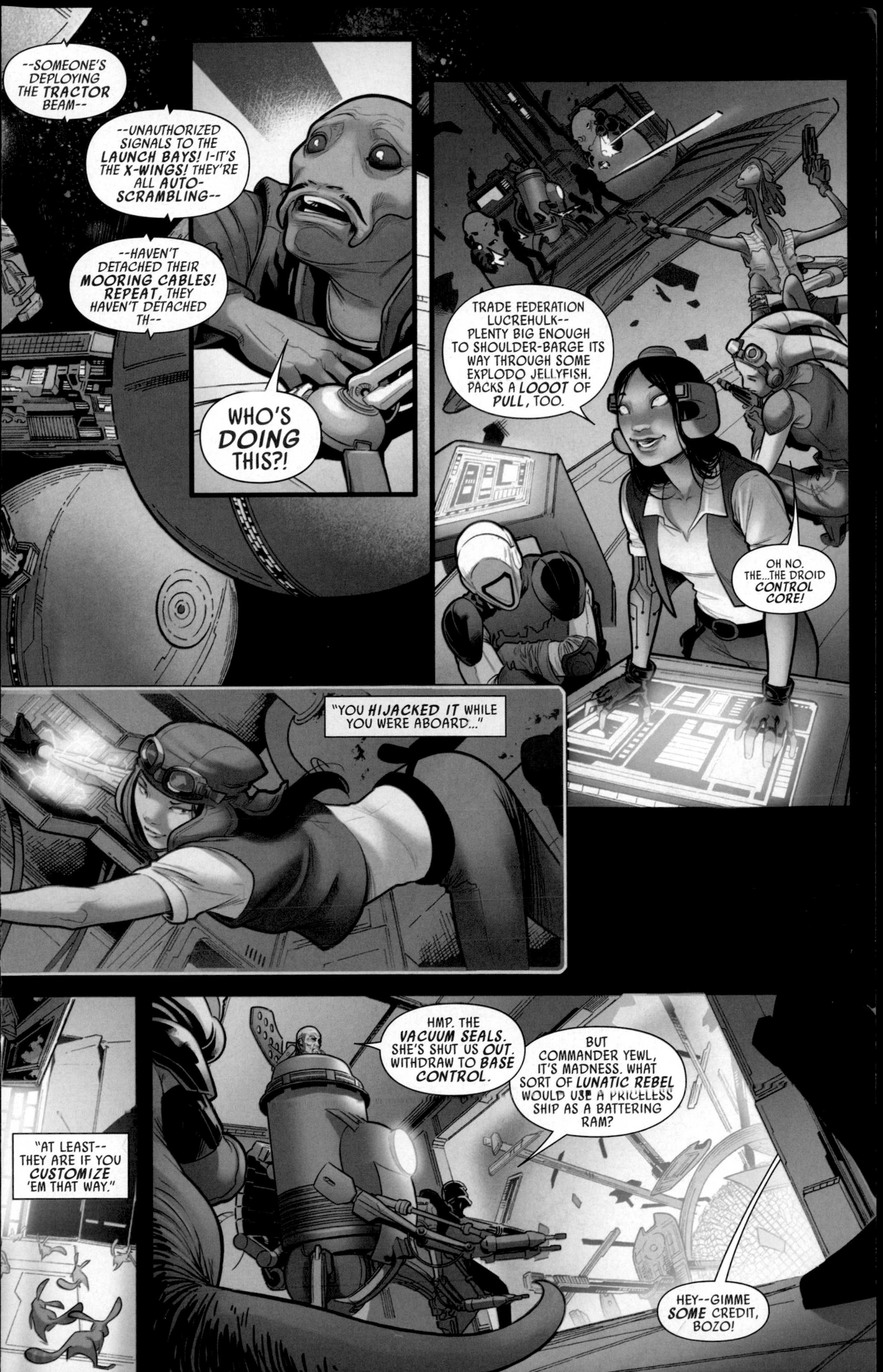
--SOMEONE'S DEPLOYING THE TRACTOR BEAM--
--UNAUTHORIZED SIGNALS TO THE LAUNCH BAYS! I-IT'S THE X-WINGS! THEY'RE ALL AUTO-SCRAMBLING--
--HAVEN'T DETACHED THEIR MOORING CABLES! REPEAT, THEY HAVEN'T DETACHED TH--
WHO'S DOING THIS?!
TRADE FEDERATION LUCREHULK--PLENTY BIG ENOUGH TO SHOULDER-BARGE ITS WAY THROUGH SOME EXPLODO JELLYFISH. PACKS A LOOOT OF PULL, TOO.
OH NO. THE...THE DROID CONTROL CORE!
"YOU HIJACKED IT WHILE YOU WERE ABOARD..."
"AT LEAST--THEY ARE IF YOU CUSTOMIZE 'EM THAT WAY."
HMP. THE VACUUM SEALS. SHE'S SHUT US OUT. WITHDRAW TO BASE CONTROL.
BUT COMMANDER YEWL, IT'S MADNESS. WHAT SORT OF LUNATIC REBEL WOULD USE A PRICELESS SHIP AS A BATTERING RAM?
HEY--GIMME SOME CREDIT, BOZO!

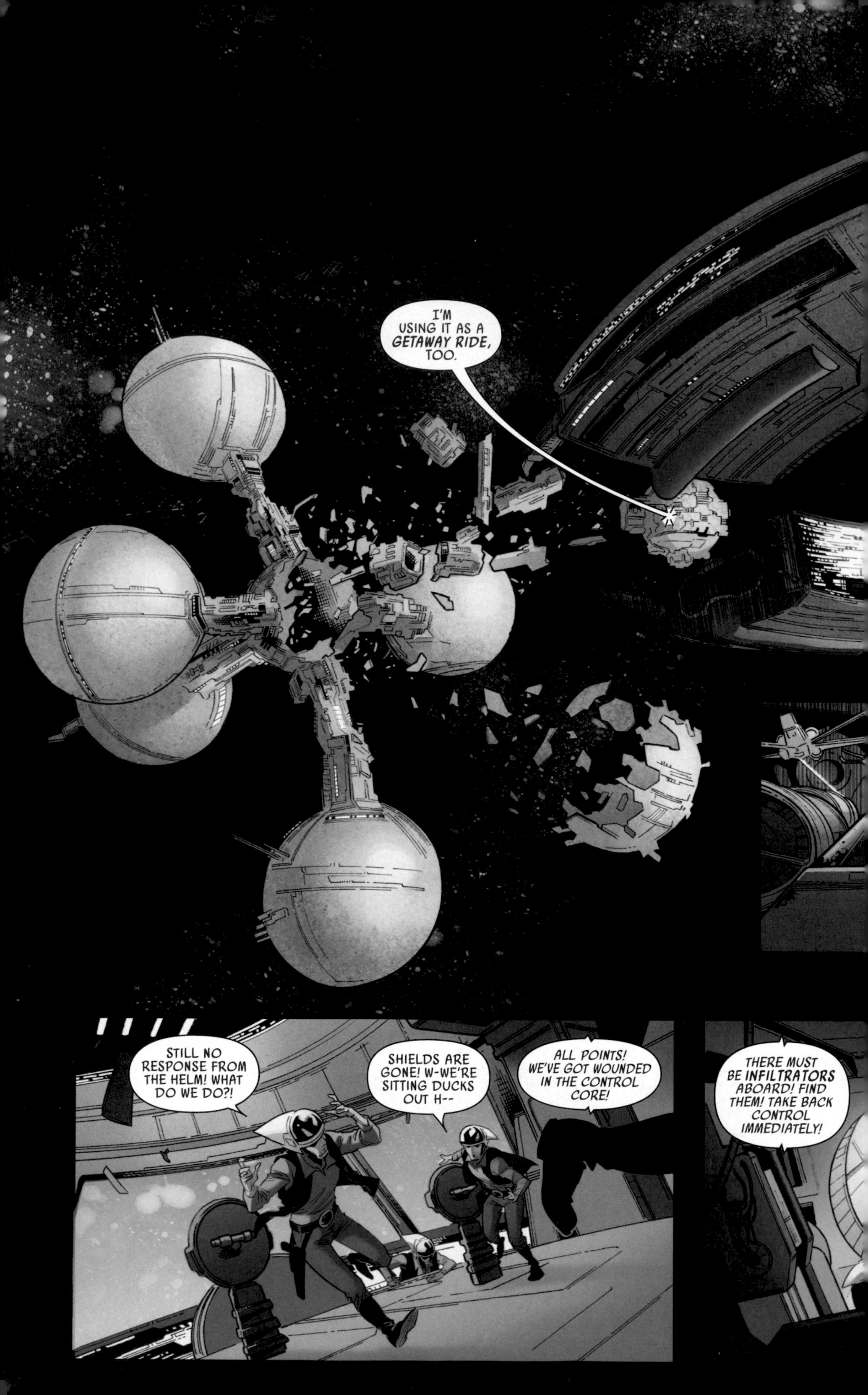
I'M USING IT AS A GETAWAY RIDE, TOO.
STILL NO RESPONSE FROM THE HELM! WHAT DO WE DO?!
SHIELDS ARE GONE! W-WE'RE SITTING DUCKS OUT H--
ALL POINTS! WE'VE GOT WOUNDED IN THE CONTROL CORE!
THERE MUST BE INFILTRATORS ABOARD! FIND THEM! TAKE BACK CONTROL IMMEDIATELY!

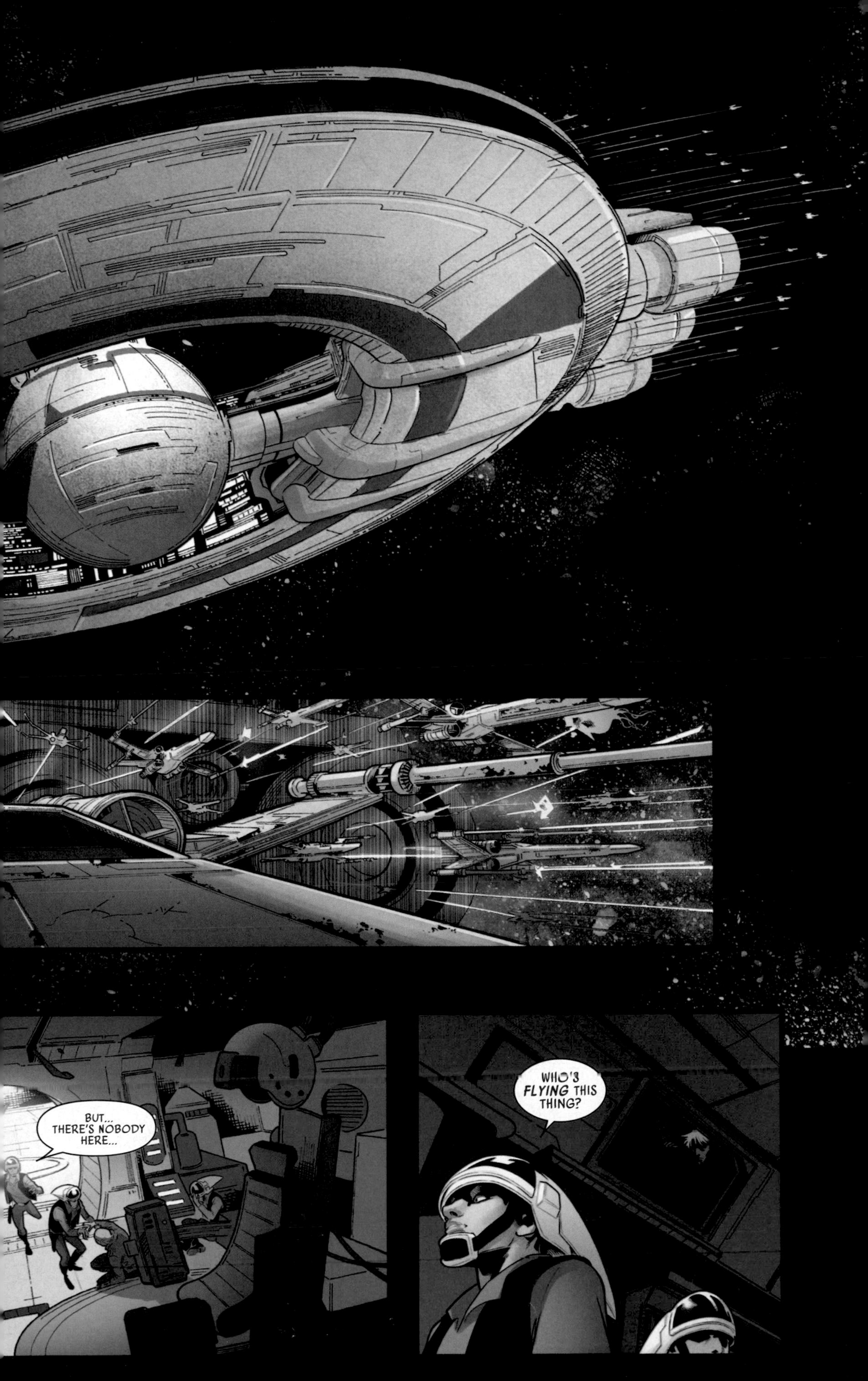
BUT... THERE'S NOBODY HERE...
WHO'S *FLYING* THIS THING?

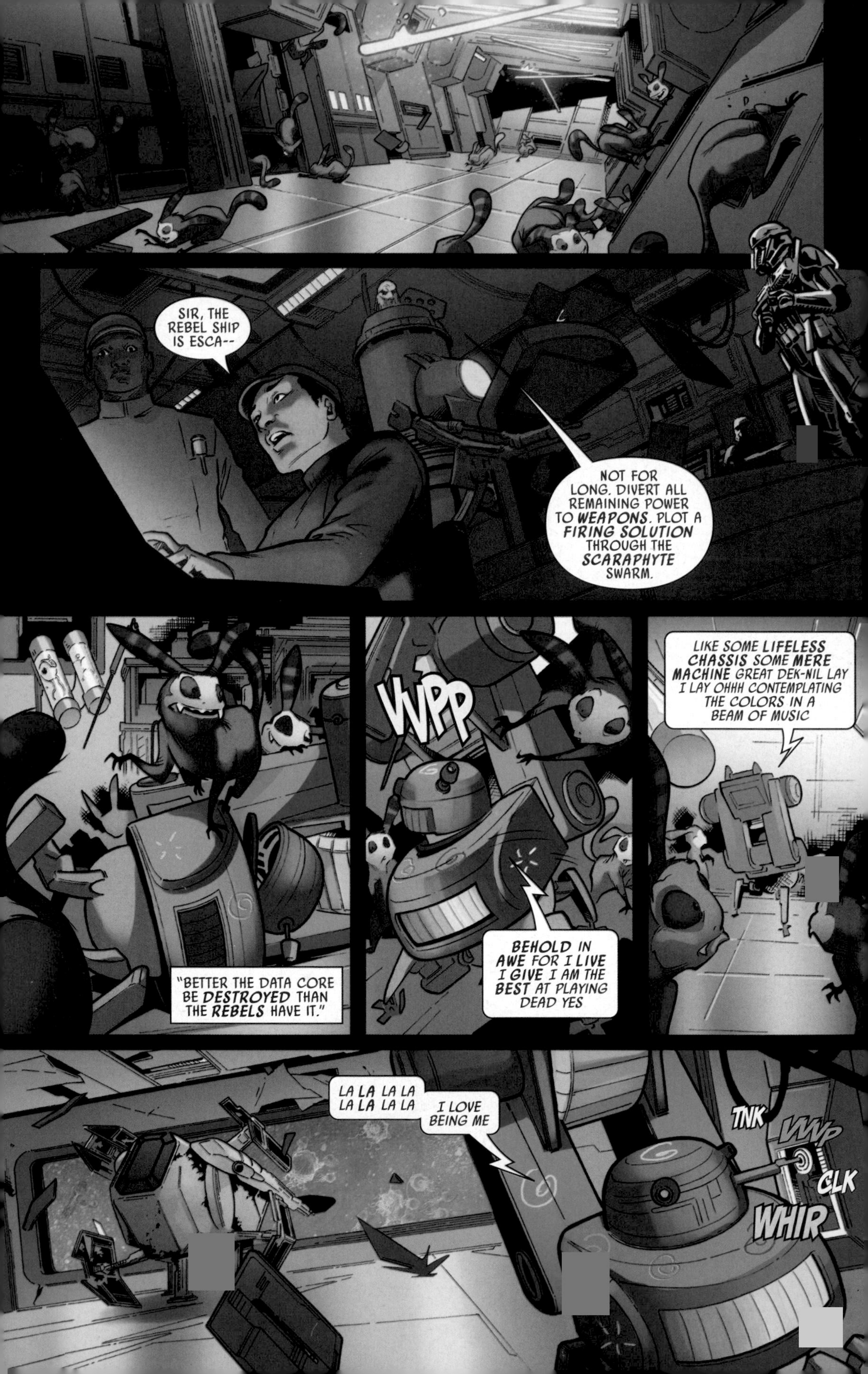
SIR, THE REBEL SHIP IS ESCA--
NOT FOR LONG. DIVERT ALL REMAINING POWER TO WEAPONS. PLOT A FIRING SOLUTION THROUGH THE SCARAPHYTE SWARM.
"BETTER THE DATA CORE BE DESTROYED THAN THE REBELS HAVE IT."
VVPP
BEHOLD IN AWE FOR I LIVE I GIVE I AM THE BEST AT PLAYING DEAD YES
LIKE SOME LIFELESS CHASSIS SOME MERE MACHINE GREAT DEK-NIL LAY I LAY OHHH CONTEMPLATING THE COLORS IN A BEAM OF MUSIC
LA LA LA LA LA LA LA LA
I LOVE BEING ME
TNK
VVVP
CLK
WHIR

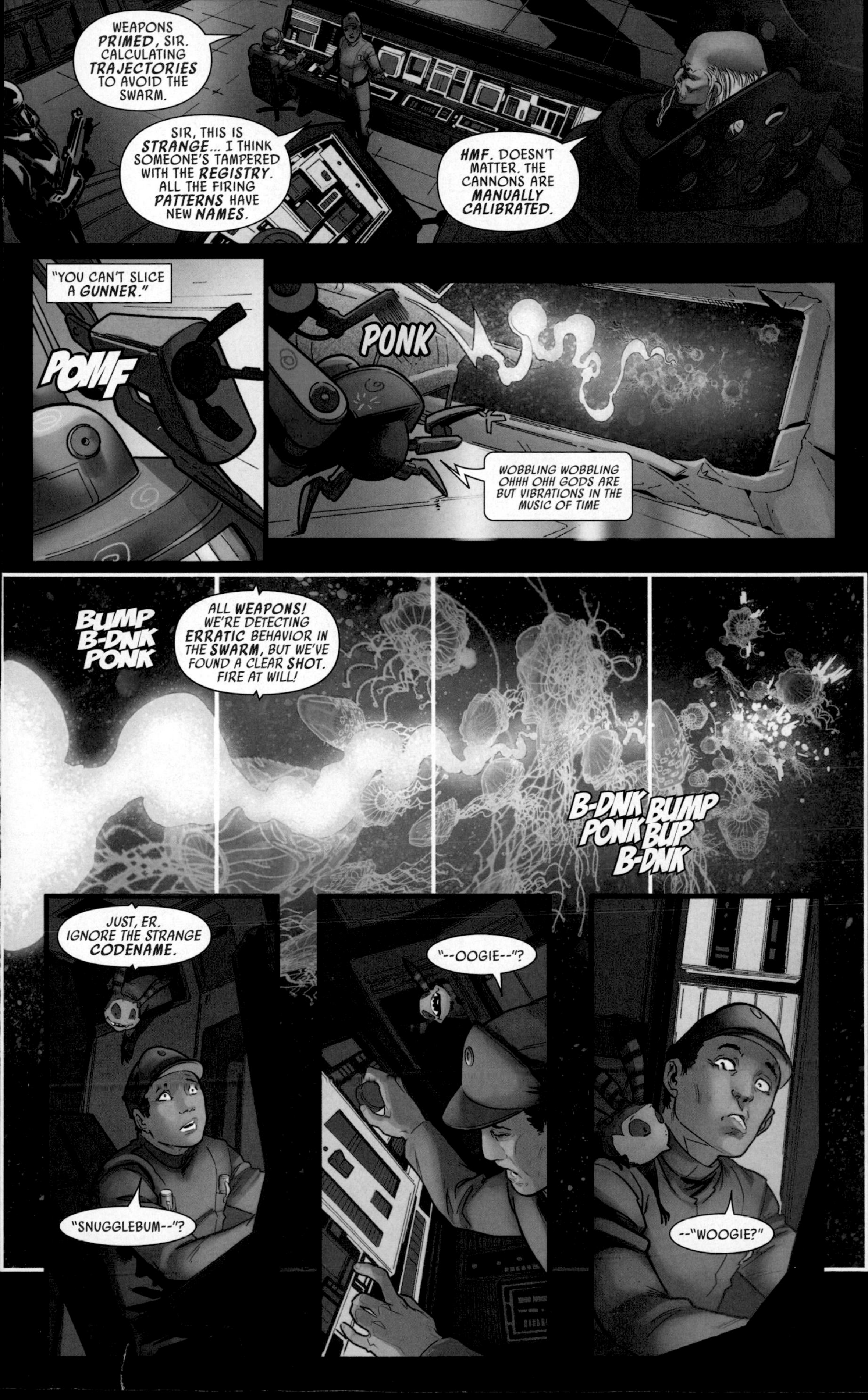
WEAPONS PRIMED, SIR. CALCULATING TRAJECTORIES TO AVOID THE SWARM.
SIR, THIS IS STRANGE... I THINK SOMEONE'S TAMPERED WITH THE REGISTRY. ALL THE FIRING PATTERNS HAVE NEW NAMES.
HMF. DOESN'T MATTER. THE CANNONS ARE MANUALLY CALIBRATED.
"YOU CAN'T SLICE A GUNNER."
POMF
PONK
WOBBLING WOBBLING OHHH OHH GODS ARE BUT VIBRATIONS IN THE MUSIC OF TIME
BUMP B-DNK PONK
ALL WEAPONS! WE'RE DETECTING ERRATIC BEHAVIOR IN THE SWARM, BUT WE'VE FOUND A CLEAR SHOT. FIRE AT WILL!
B-DNK BUMP PONK BUP B-DNK
JUST, ER. IGNORE THE STRANGE CODENAME.
"SNUGGLEBUM--"?
"--OOGIE--"?
--"WOOGIE?"

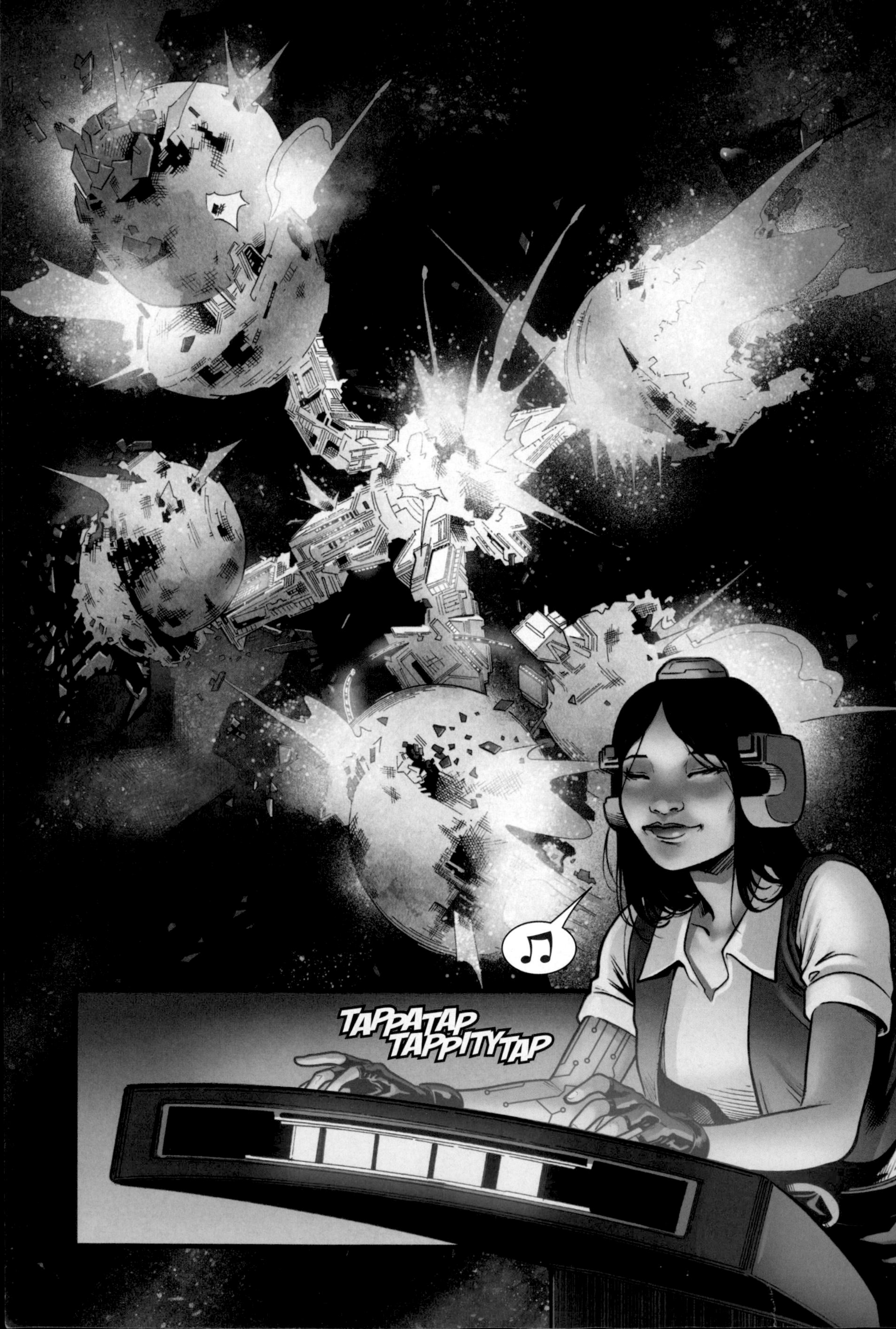
♫
TAPPATAP TAPPITYTAP

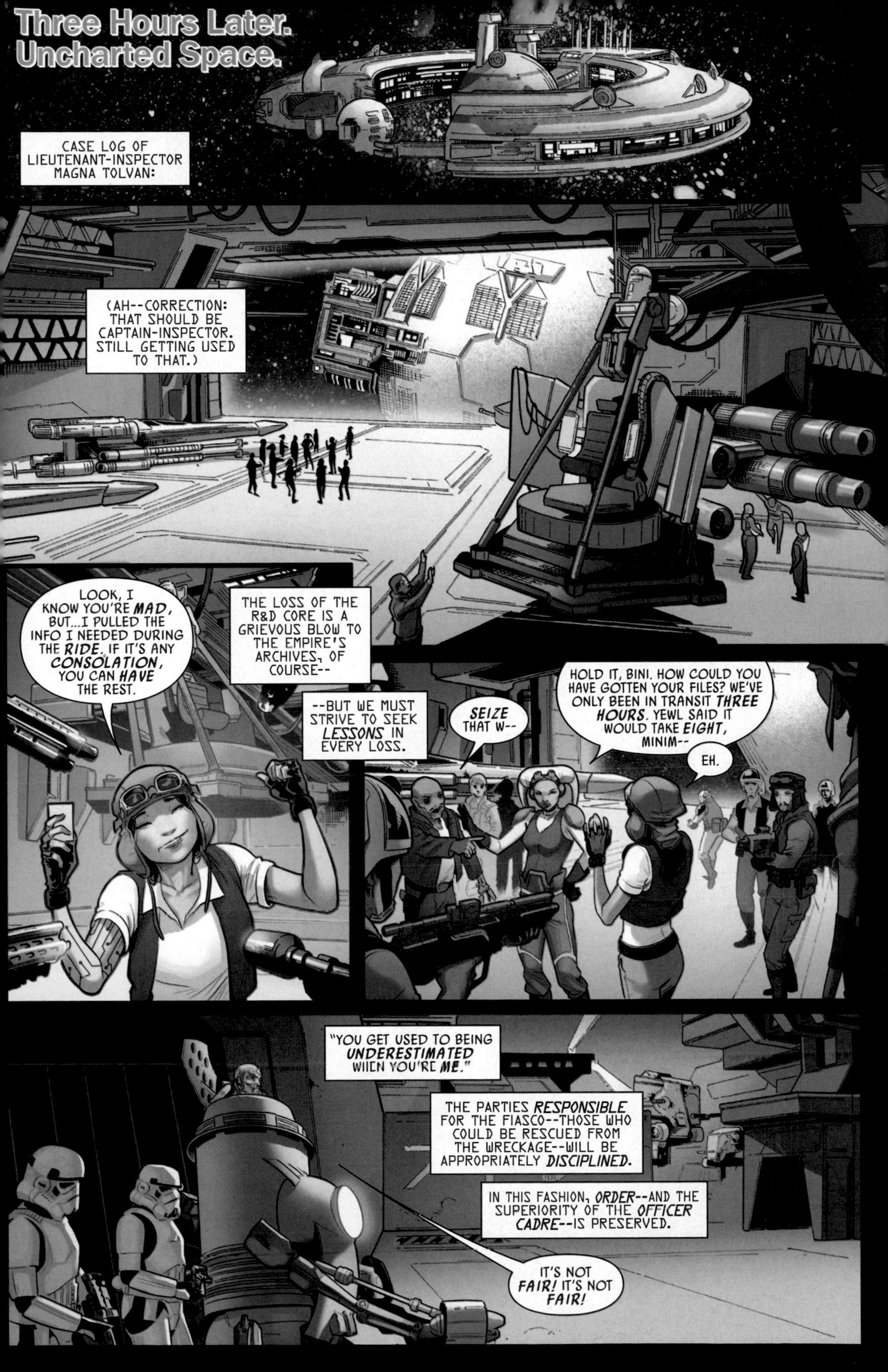
Three Hours Later.
Uncharted Space.
CASE LOG OF LIEUTENANT-INSPECTOR MAGNA TOLVAN:
(AH--CORRECTION: THAT SHOULD BE CAPTAIN-INSPECTOR. STILL GETTING USED TO THAT.)
LOOK, I KNOW YOU'RE MAD, BUT...I PULLED THE INFO I NEEDED DURING THE RIDE. IF IT'S ANY CONSOLATION, YOU CAN HAVE THE REST.
THE LOSS OF THE R&D CORE IS A GRIEVOUS BLOW TO THE EMPIRE'S ARCHIVES, OF COURSE--
--BUT WE MUST STRIVE TO SEEK LESSONS IN EVERY LOSS.
SEIZE THAT W--
HOLD IT, BINI. HOW COULD YOU HAVE GOTTEN YOUR FILES? WE'VE ONLY BEEN IN TRANSIT THREE HOURS. YEWL SAID IT WOULD TAKE EIGHT, MINIM--
EH.
"YOU GET USED TO BEING UNDERESTIMATED WHEN YOU'RE ME."
THE PARTIES RESPONSIBLE FOR THE FIASCO--THOSE WHO COULD BE RESCUED FROM THE WRECKAGE--WILL BE APPROPRIATELY DISCIPLINED.
IN THIS FASHION, ORDER--AND THE SUPERIORITY OF THE OFFICER CADRE--IS PRESERVED.
IT'S NOT FAIR! IT'S NOT FAIR!

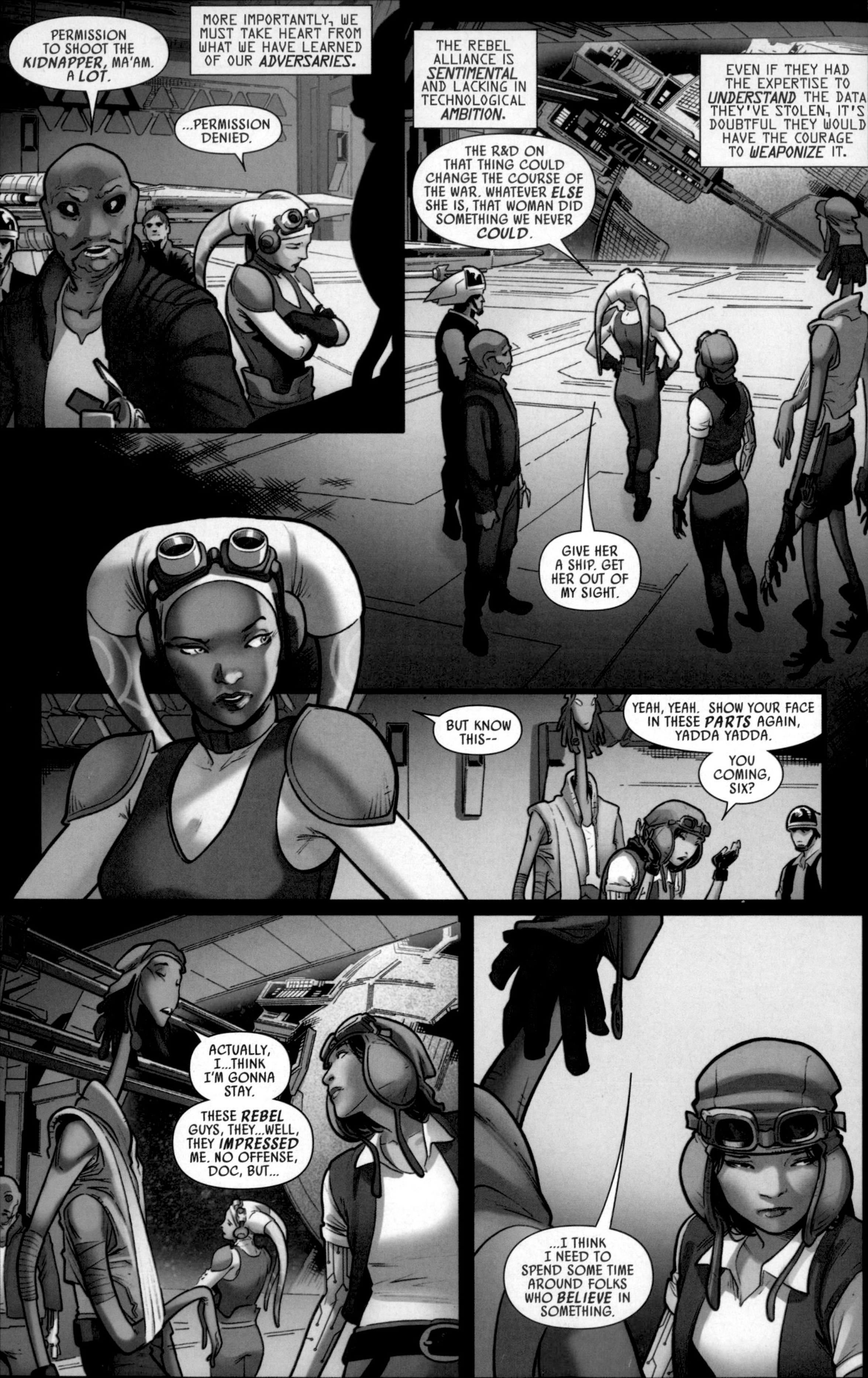
PERMISSION TO SHOOT THE KIDNAPPER, MA'AM. A LOT.
MORE IMPORTANTLY, WE MUST TAKE HEART FROM WHAT WE HAVE LEARNED OF OUR ADVERSARIES.
...PERMISSION DENIED.
THE REBEL ALLIANCE IS SENTIMENTAL AND LACKING IN TECHNOLOGICAL AMBITION.
EVEN IF THEY HAD THE EXPERTISE TO UNDERSTAND THE DATA THEY'VE STOLEN, IT'S DOUBTFUL THEY WOULD HAVE THE COURAGE TO WEAPONIZE IT.
THE R&D ON THAT THING COULD CHANGE THE COURSE OF THE WAR. WHATEVER ELSE SHE IS, THAT WOMAN DID SOMETHING WE NEVER COULD.
GIVE HER A SHIP. GET HER OUT OF MY SIGHT.
BUT KNOW THIS--
YEAH, YEAH. SHOW YOUR FACE IN THESE PARTS AGAIN, YADDA YADDA.
YOU COMING, SIX?
ACTUALLY, I...THINK I'M GONNA STAY.
THESE REBEL GUYS, THEY...WELL, THEY IMPRESSED ME. NO OFFENSE, DOC, BUT...
...I THINK I NEED TO SPEND SOME TIME AROUND FOLKS WHO BELIEVE IN SOMETHING.

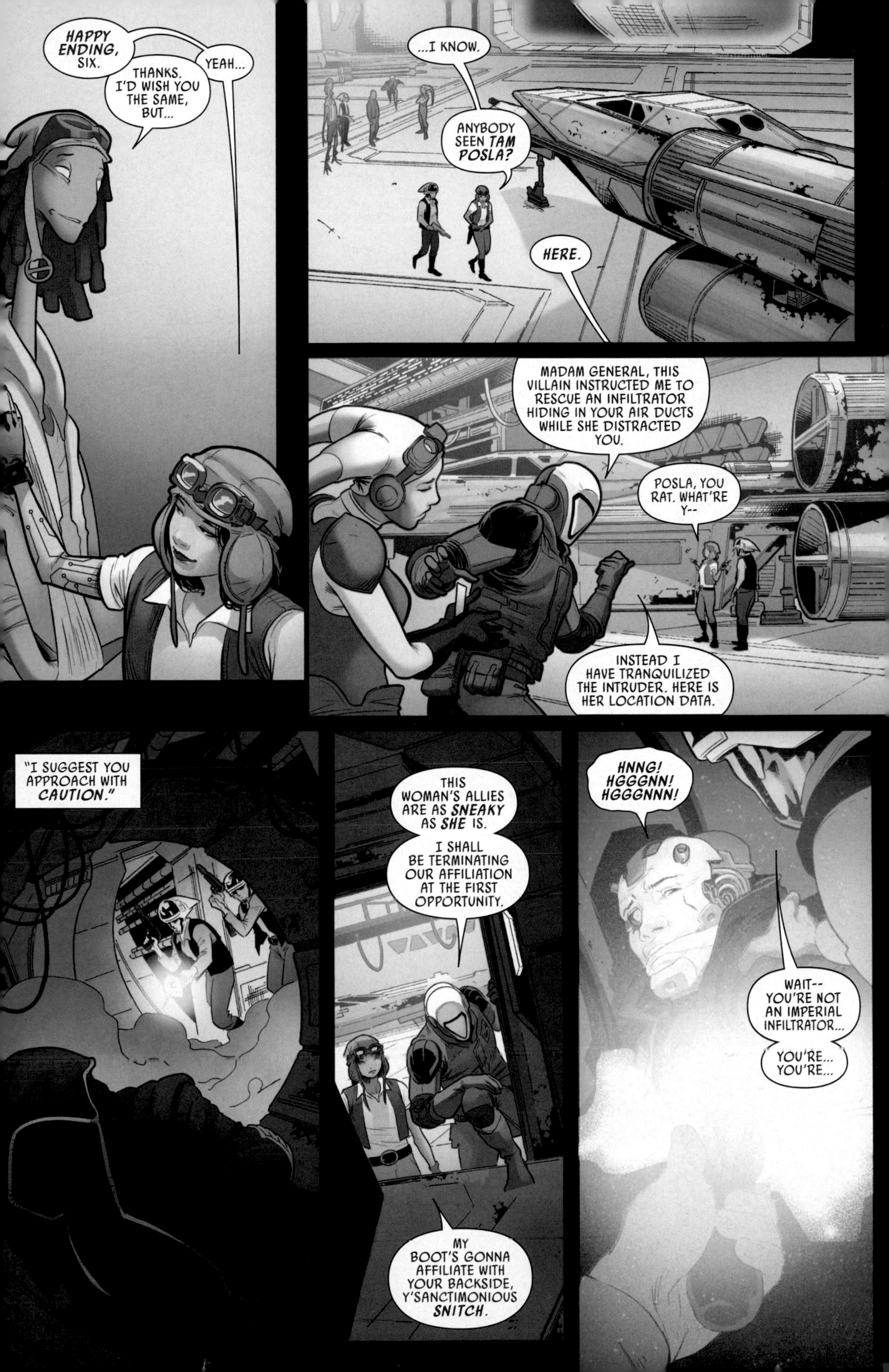
HAPPY ENDING, SIX.
THANKS. I'D WISH YOU THE SAME, BUT...
YEAH...
...I KNOW.
ANYBODY SEEN TAM POSLA?
HERE.
MADAM GENERAL, THIS VILLAIN INSTRUCTED ME TO RESCUE AN INFILTRATOR HIDING IN YOUR AIR DUCTS WHILE SHE DISTRACTED YOU.
POSLA, YOU RAT. WHAT'RE Y--
INSTEAD I HAVE TRANQUILIZED THE INTRUDER. HERE IS HER LOCATION DATA.
"I SUGGEST YOU APPROACH WITH CAUTION."
THIS WOMAN'S ALLIES ARE AS SNEAKY AS SHE IS.
I SHALL BE TERMINATING OUR AFFILIATION AT THE FIRST OPPORTUNITY.
MY BOOT'S GONNA AFFILIATE WITH YOUR BACKSIDE, Y'SANCTIMONIOUS SNITCH.
HNNG! HGGGNN! HGGGNNN!
WAIT-- YOU'RE NOT AN IMPERIAL INFILTRATOR...
YOU'RE... YOU'RE...

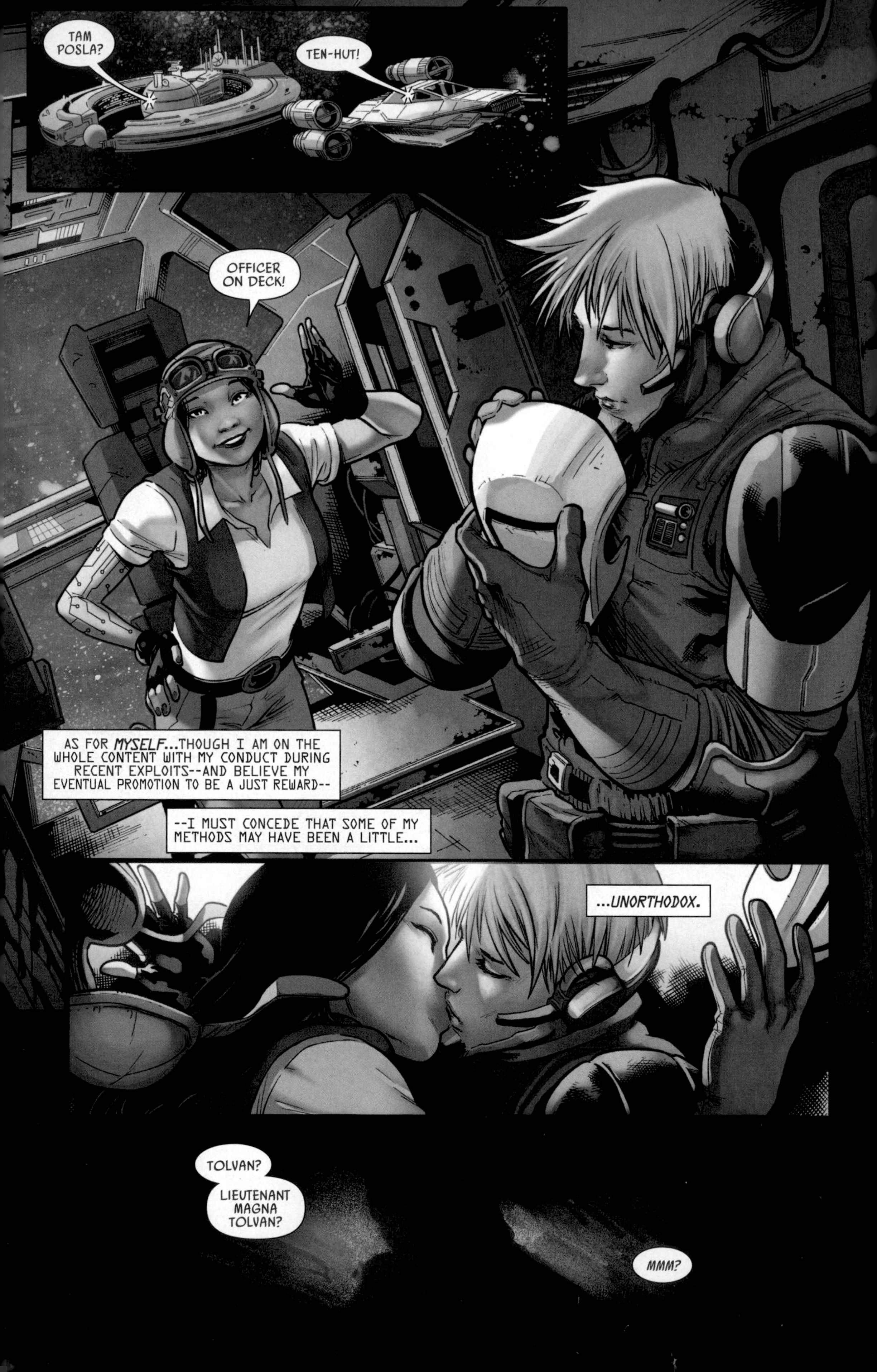
TAM POSLA?
TEN-HUT!
OFFICER ON DECK!
AS FOR *MYSELF*...THOUGH I AM ON THE WHOLE CONTENT WITH MY CONDUCT DURING RECENT EXPLOITS--AND BELIEVE MY EVENTUAL PROMOTION TO BE A JUST REWARD--
--I MUST CONCEDE THAT SOME OF MY METHODS MAY HAVE BEEN A LITTLE...
...UNORTHODOX.
TOLVAN?
LIEUTENANT MAGNA TOLVAN?
MMM?

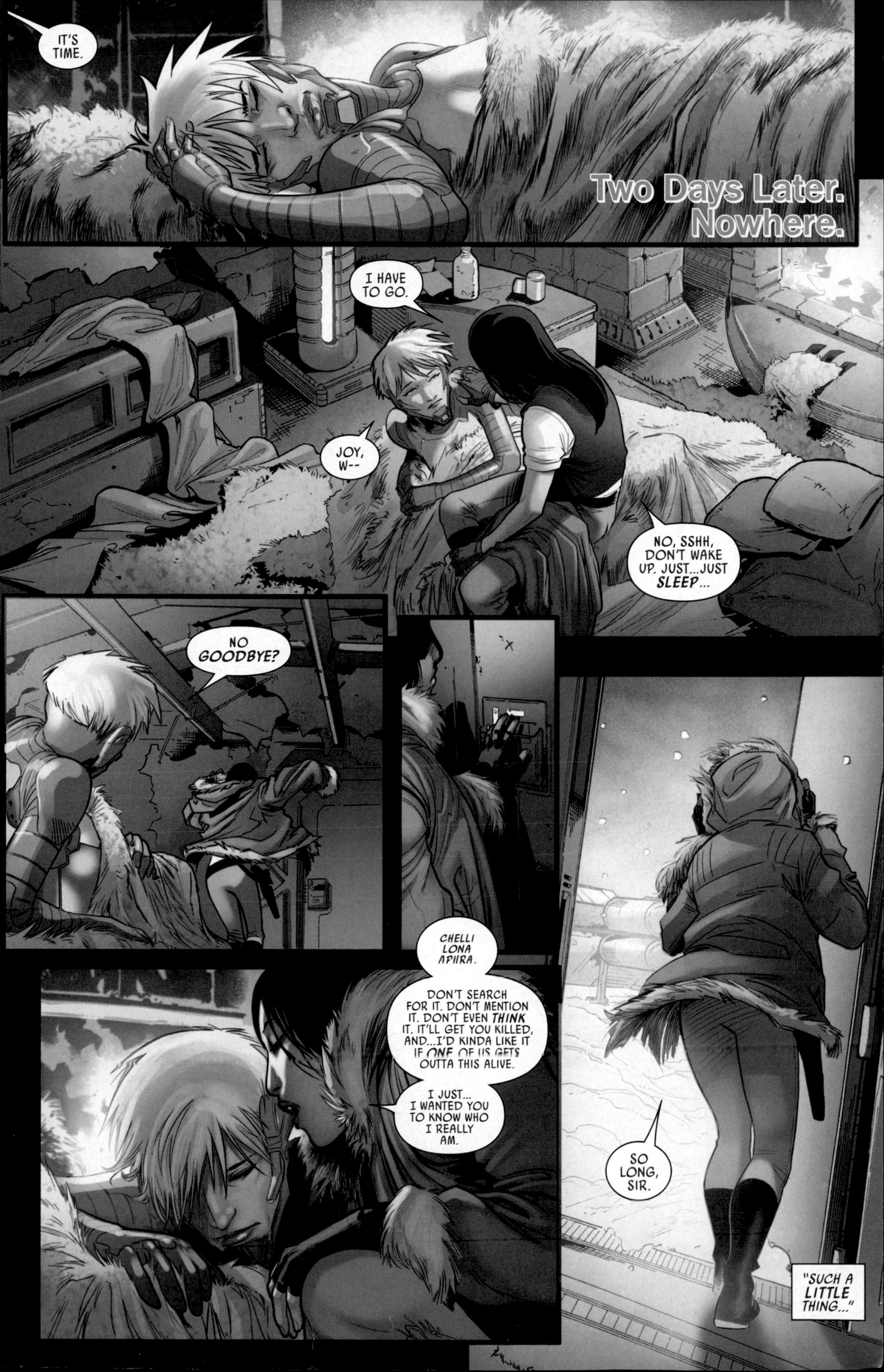
IT'S TIME.
Two Days Later. Nowhere.
I HAVE TO GO.
JOY, W--
NO, SSHH, DON'T WAKE UP. JUST...JUST SLEEP...
NO GOODBYE?
CHELLI LONA APIIRA.
DON'T SEARCH FOR IT. DON'T MENTION IT. DON'T EVEN THINK IT. IT'LL GET YOU KILLED, AND...I'D KINDA LIKE IT IF ONE OF US GETS OUTTA THIS ALIVE.
I JUST... I WANTED YOU TO KNOW WHO I REALLY AM.
SO LONG, SIR.
"SUCH A LITTLE THING..."

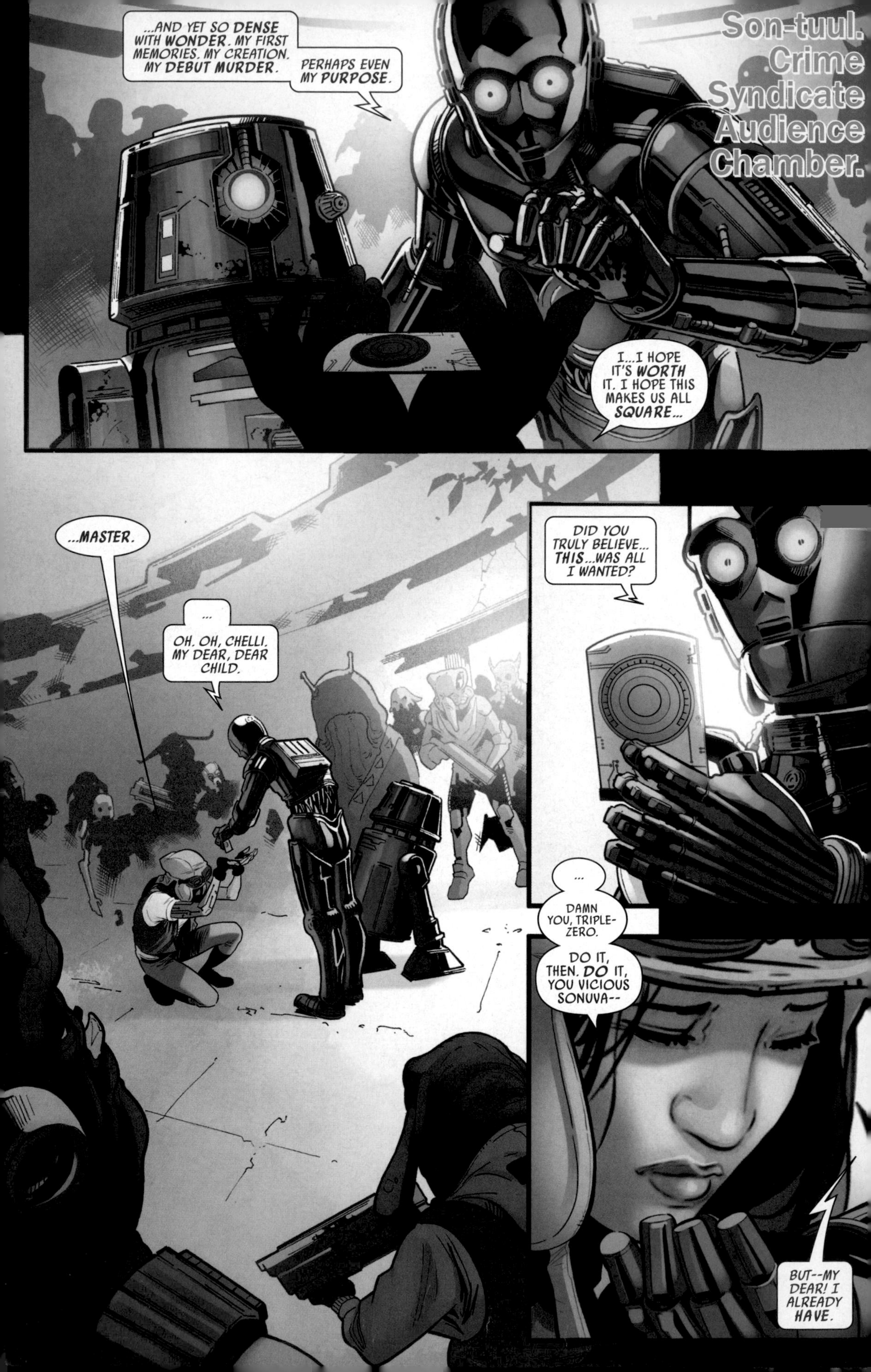

Son-tuul. Crime Syndicate Audience Chamber.
...AND YET SO DENSE WITH WONDER. MY FIRST MEMORIES. MY CREATION. MY DEBUT MURDER.
PERHAPS EVEN MY PURPOSE.
I...I HOPE IT'S WORTH IT. I HOPE THIS MAKES US ALL SQUARE...
...MASTER.
...
OH. OH, CHELLI. MY DEAR, DEAR CHILD.
DID YOU TRULY BELIEVE... THIS...WAS ALL I WANTED?
...
DAMN YOU, TRIPLE-ZERO.
DO IT, THEN. DO IT, YOU VICIOUS SONUVA--
BUT--MY DEAR! I ALREADY HAVE.

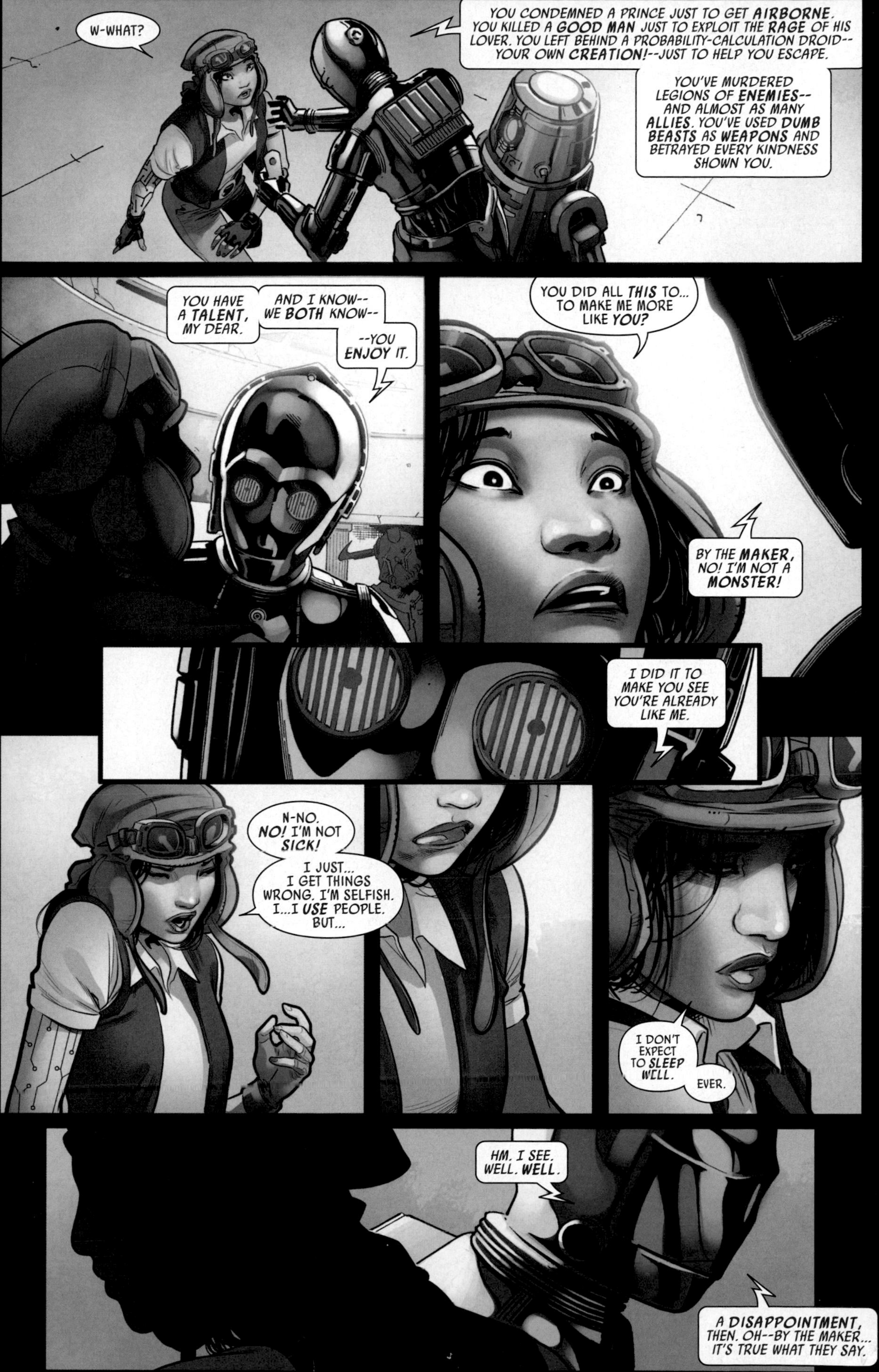
W-WHAT?
YOU CONDEMNED A PRINCE JUST TO GET AIRBORNE. YOU KILLED A GOOD MAN JUST TO EXPLOIT THE RAGE OF HIS LOVER. YOU LEFT BEHIND A PROBABILITY-CALCULATION DROID--YOUR OWN CREATION!--JUST TO HELP YOU ESCAPE.
YOU'VE MURDERED LEGIONS OF ENEMIES--AND ALMOST AS MANY ALLIES. YOU'VE USED DUMB BEASTS AS WEAPONS AND BETRAYED EVERY KINDNESS SHOWN YOU.
YOU HAVE A TALENT, MY DEAR.
AND I KNOW--WE BOTH KNOW--
--YOU ENJOY IT.
YOU DID ALL THIS TO... TO MAKE ME MORE LIKE YOU?
BY THE MAKER, NO! I'M NOT A MONSTER!
I DID IT TO MAKE YOU SEE YOU'RE ALREADY LIKE ME.
N-NO. NO! I'M NOT SICK!
I JUST... I GET THINGS WRONG. I'M SELFISH. I...I USE PEOPLE. BUT...
I DON'T EXPECT TO SLEEP WELL.
EVER.
HM. I SEE. WELL. WELL.
A DISAPPOINTMENT, THEN. OH--BY THE MAKER... IT'S TRUE WHAT THEY SAY.

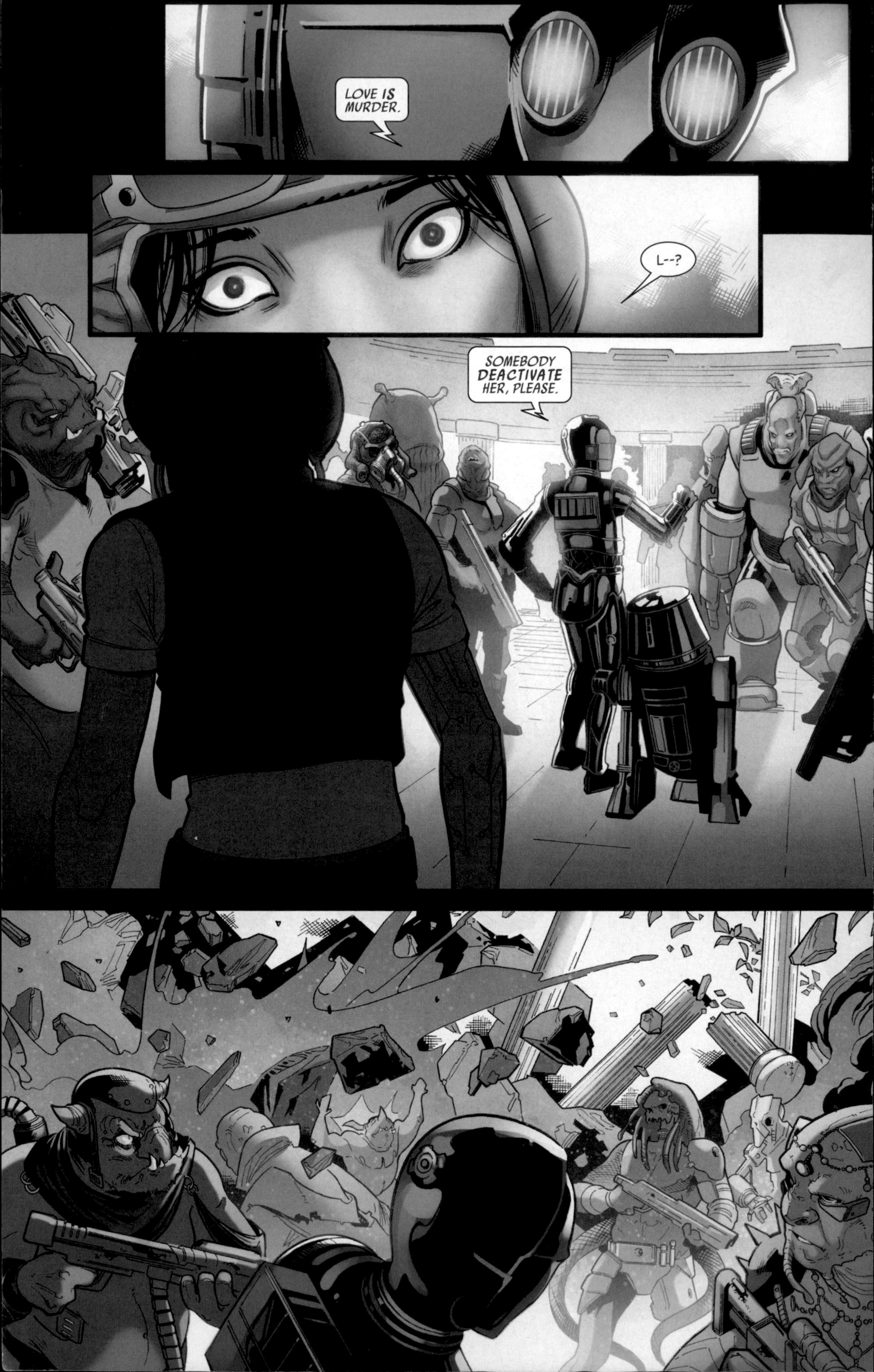
LOVE IS MURDER.
L--?
SOMEBODY DEACTIVATE HER, PLEASE.

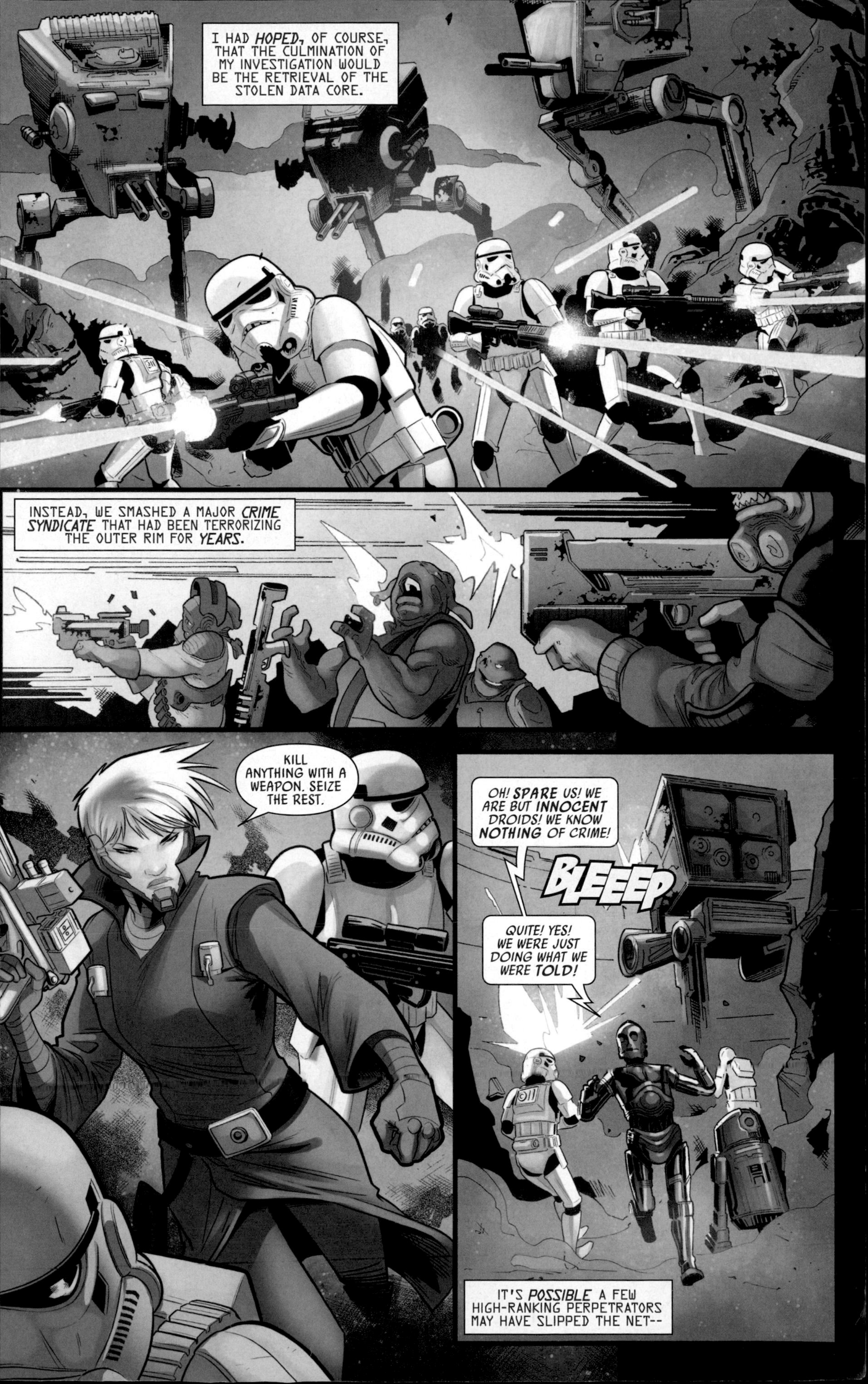
I HAD HOPED, OF COURSE, THAT THE CULMINATION OF MY INVESTIGATION WOULD BE THE RETRIEVAL OF THE STOLEN DATA CORE.
INSTEAD, WE SMASHED A MAJOR CRIME SYNDICATE THAT HAD BEEN TERRORIZING THE OUTER RIM FOR YEARS.
KILL ANYTHING WITH A WEAPON. SEIZE THE REST.
OH! SPARE US! WE ARE BUT INNOCENT DROIDS! WE KNOW NOTHING OF CRIME!
BLEEEP
QUITE! YES! WE WERE JUST DOING WHAT WE WERE TOLD!
IT'S POSSIBLE A FEW HIGH-RANKING PERPETRATORS MAY HAVE SLIPPED THE NET--

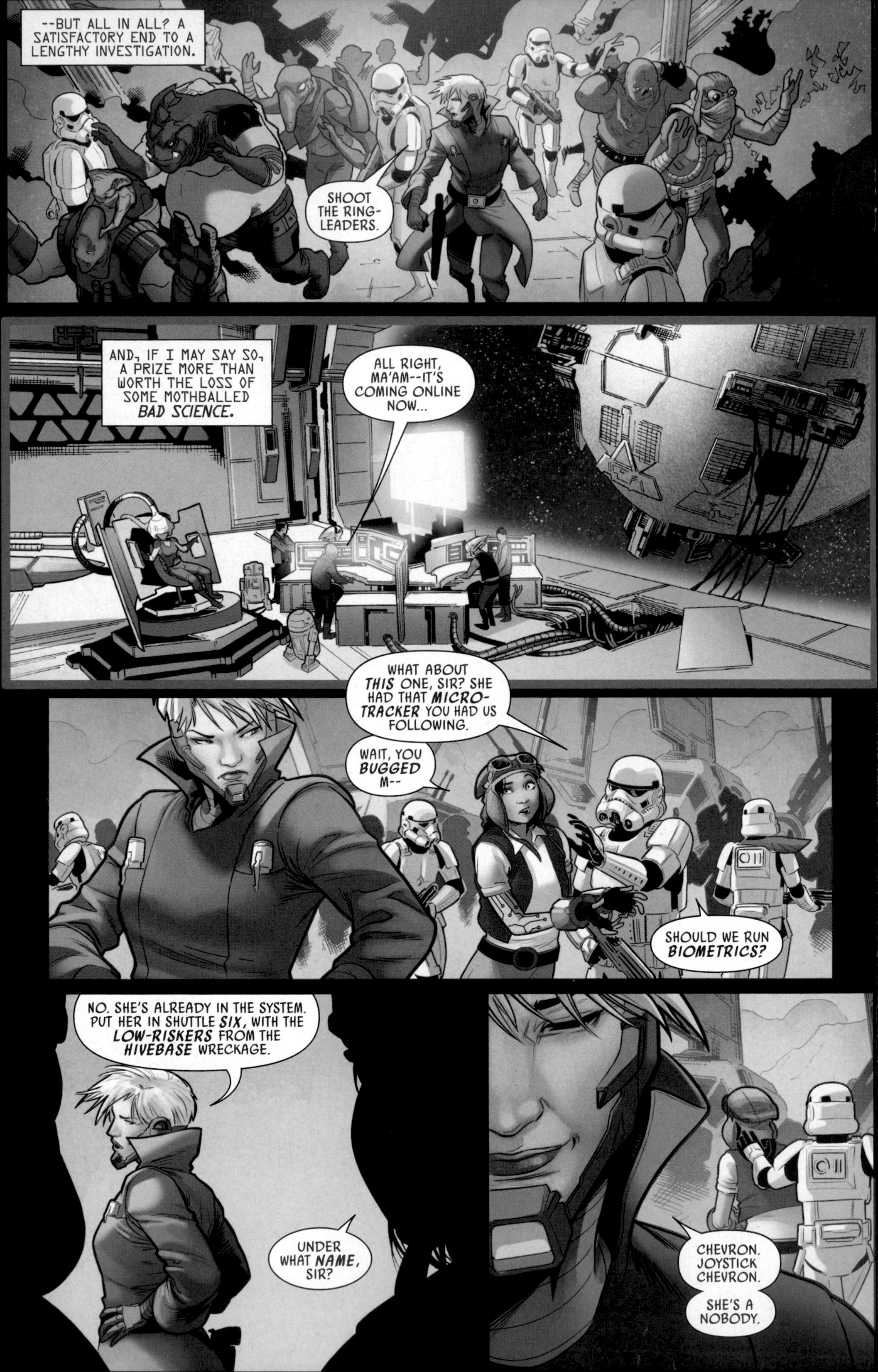
--BUT ALL IN ALL? A SATISFACTORY END TO A LENGTHY INVESTIGATION.
SHOOT THE RING-LEADERS.
AND, IF I MAY SAY SO, A PRIZE MORE THAN WORTH THE LOSS OF SOME MOTHBALLED BAD SCIENCE.
ALL RIGHT, MA'AM--IT'S COMING ONLINE NOW...
WHAT ABOUT THIS ONE, SIR? SHE HAD THAT MICRO-TRACKER YOU HAD US FOLLOWING.
WAIT, YOU BUGGED M--
SHOULD WE RUN BIOMETRICS?
NO. SHE'S ALREADY IN THE SYSTEM. PUT HER IN SHUTTLE SIX, WITH THE LOW-RISKERS FROM THE HIVEBASE WRECKAGE.
UNDER WHAT NAME, SIR?
CHEVRON. JOYSTICK CHEVRON.
SHE'S A NOBODY.

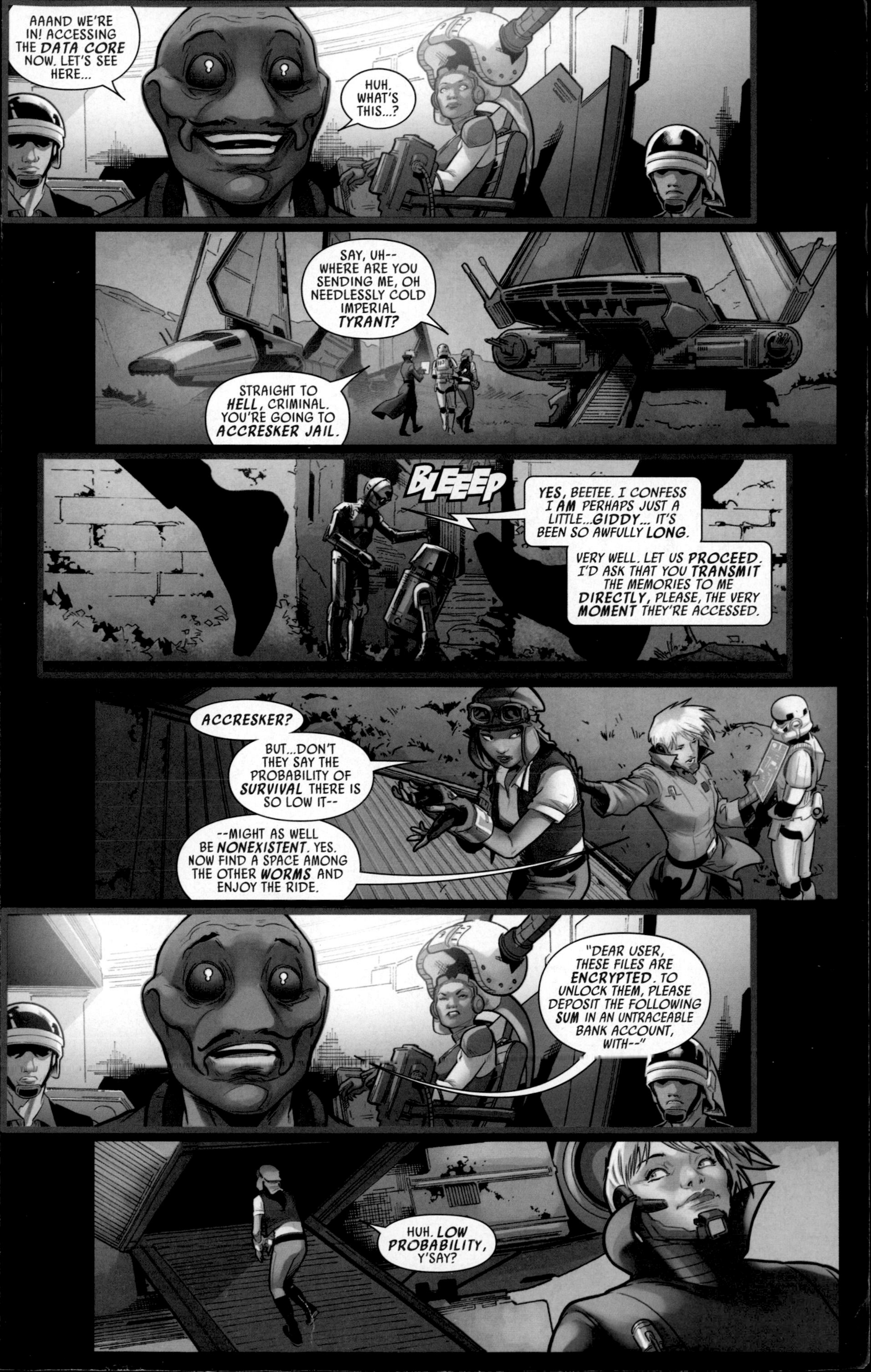

AAAND WE'RE IN! ACCESSING THE DATA CORE NOW. LET'S SEE HERE...
HUH. WHAT'S THIS...?
SAY, UH-- WHERE ARE YOU SENDING ME, OH NEEDLESSLY COLD IMPERIAL TYRANT?
STRAIGHT TO HELL, CRIMINAL. YOU'RE GOING TO ACCRESKER JAIL.
BLEEEP
YES, BEETEE. I CONFESS I AM PERHAPS JUST A LITTLE...GIDDY... IT'S BEEN SO AWFULLY LONG.
VERY WELL. LET US PROCEED. I'D ASK THAT YOU TRANSMIT THE MEMORIES TO ME DIRECTLY, PLEASE, THE VERY MOMENT THEY'RE ACCESSED.
ACCRESKER?
BUT...DON'T THEY SAY THE PROBABILITY OF SURVIVAL THERE IS SO LOW IT--
--MIGHT AS WELL BE NONEXISTENT. YES. NOW FIND A SPACE AMONG THE OTHER WORMS AND ENJOY THE RIDE.
"DEAR USER, THESE FILES ARE ENCRYPTED. TO UNLOCK THEM, PLEASE DEPOSIT THE FOLLOWING SUM IN AN UNTRACEABLE BANK ACCOUNT, WITH--"
HUH. LOW PROBABILITY, Y'SAY?

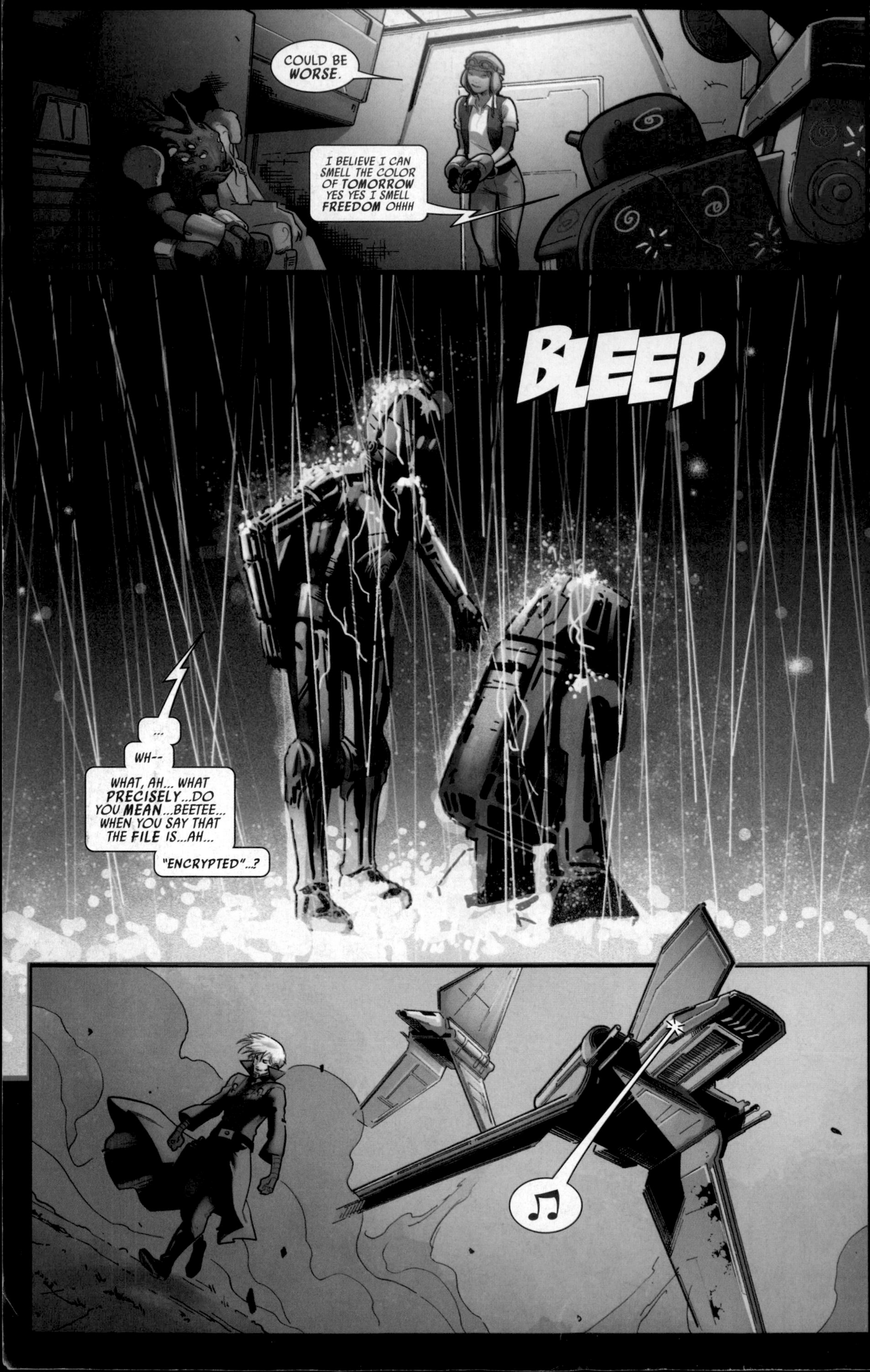
COULD BE WORSE.
I BELIEVE I CAN SMELL THE COLOR OF TOMORROW YES YES I SMELL FREEDOM OHHH
BLEEP
...
WH--
WHAT, AH... WHAT PRECISELY...DO YOU MEAN...BEETEE... WHEN YOU SAY THAT THE FILE IS...AH...
"ENCRYPTED"...?
♫

MARVEL
SOULE
MALEEV
MOUNTS
STAR WARS
LANDO
"...a fast-paced, seat-of-the-pants adventure"
— New York Daily News

MARVEL
DUGGAN
NOTO
STAR WARS
CHEWBACCA
"A fantastic story with amazing art makes this one of Marvel's best Star Wars titles."

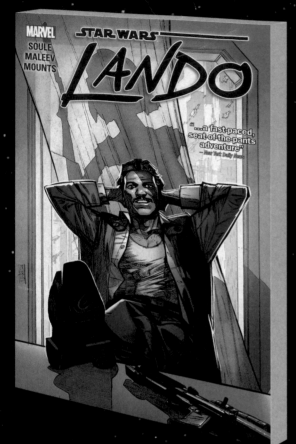

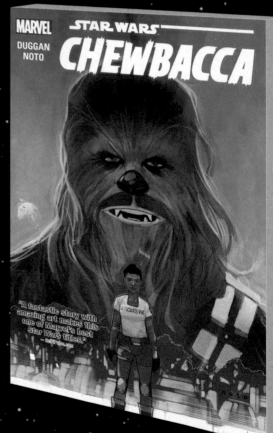

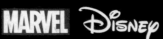

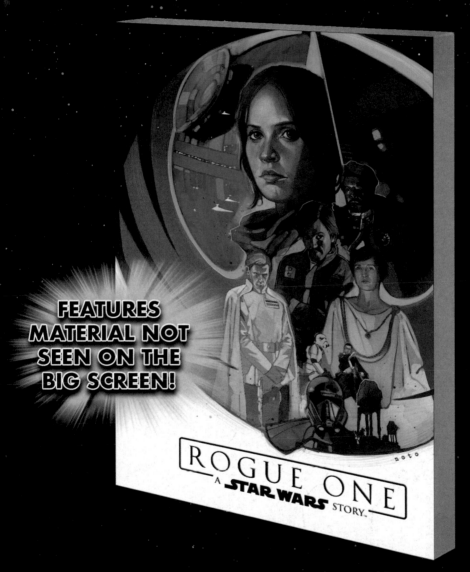

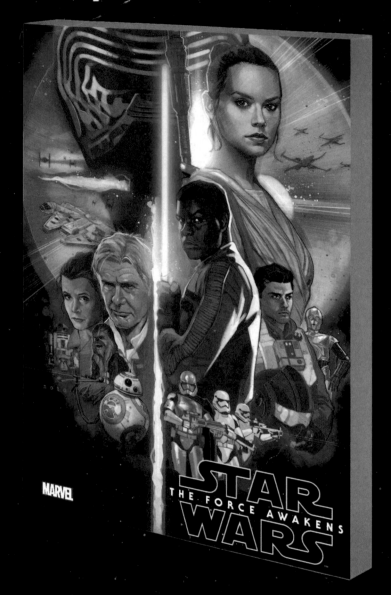

RETURN TO A GALAXY FAR, FAR AWAY!

STAR WARS: THE FORCE AWAKENS ADAPTATION TPB
978-1302902032

ON SALE NOW
WHEREVER BOOKS ARE SOLD

TO FIND A COMIC SHOP NEAR YOU, VISIT COMICSHOPLOCATOR.COM